WHITE ESKIMO

WHITE
ESKIMO

Knud Rasmussen's

Fearless Journey into the

Heart of the Arctic

STEPHEN R. BOWN

A Merloyd Lawrence Book
DA CAPO PRESS
A Member of the Perseus Books Group

Designed by Trish Wilkinson
Set in 11.5 point Adobe Caslon Pro

Library of Congress Cataloging-in-Publication Data

Bown, Stephen R.
    White Eskimo : Knud Rasmussen's fearless journey into the heart of the Arctic / by Stephen R. Bown. — First Da Capo Press edition.
        pages   cm
    "A Merloyd Lawrence book."
    Includes bibliographical references and index.
    ISBN 978-0-306-82282-7 (hardcover) — ISBN 978-0-306-82283-4 (e-book) 1. Rasmussen, Knud, 1879–1933. 2. Explorers—Denmark—Biography. 3. Anthropologists—Denmark—Biography. 4. Racially mixed people—Denmark—Biography. 5. Rasmussen, Knud, 1879–1933—Travel—Arctic regions. 6. Arctic regions—Discovery and exploration—Danish. 7. Greenland—Discovery and exploration—Danish. 8. Inuit—Social life and customs. I. Title.
    G635.R3B68 2015
    917.1904'2092—dc23   2015019154

First Da Capo Press edition 2015

Published simultaneously in Canada by Douglas & McIntyre
Published as a Merloyd Lawrence Book by Da Capo Press
A Member of the Perseus Books Group
www.dacapopress.com

Da Capo Press books are available at special discounts for bulk purchases in the U.S. by corporations, institutions, and other organizations. For more information, please contact the Special Markets Department at the Perseus Books Group, 2300 Chestnut Street, Suite 200, Philadelphia, PA 19103, or call (800) 810-4145, ext. 5000, or e-mail special.markets@perseusbooks.com.

10 9 8 7 6 5 4 3 2 1

Igjugarjuk, who was not beyond flattering a guest, declared that I was the first white man he had ever seen who was also an Eskimo.

—Knud Rasmussen, from Across Arctic America

A NOTE ON TERMINOLOGY

Eskimo, Inuit and *Greenlander: Eskimo* is the historical term for the culturally similar indigenous peoples who inhabit Greenland, northern Canada and Alaska. There are various possibilities for the meaning of *Eskimo,* such as "people who speak a different language," "people who make snowshoes" and "people who eat raw meat." None of these descriptions are universally accepted by linguists or the people themselves.

Although considered by many to be a slur today, *Eskimo* is not inherently a pejorative word and was originally how all Arctic peoples were known. Now, the term *Inuit* is generally preferred by the people of Arctic Canada. In Alaska, the preferred terms are *Eskimo* or *Alaska Native*, and in Greenland the common term is *Greenlander* or, among English speakers, *Inuit*. In academic literature, the word *Inuit* is now prevalent.

In this work, I have opted to use the word *Inuit* except when quoting from historical documents.

In his time, Rasmussen was sometimes called a white Eskimo.

Tribe: In his writings, Rasmussen referred to the various small nomadic and seminomadic groups of Inuit he encountered throughout the Arctic as *tribes*. Today the term is rarely used, the sense sometimes being captured by the words *band* and *community*. For the sake of clarity and continuity, I have opted to retain Rasmussen's use of the word *tribe* to describe these groups of Inuit hunters as they existed a century ago.

CONTENTS

PART FOUR
NORTHERN LIGHTS

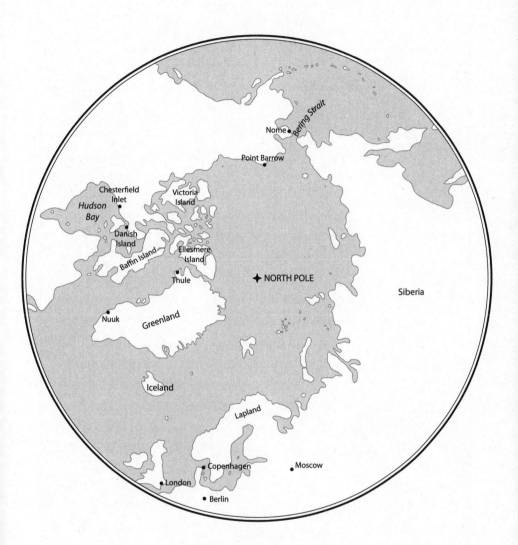

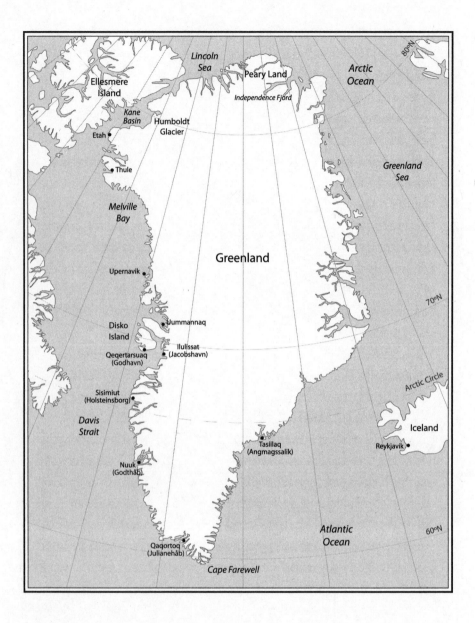

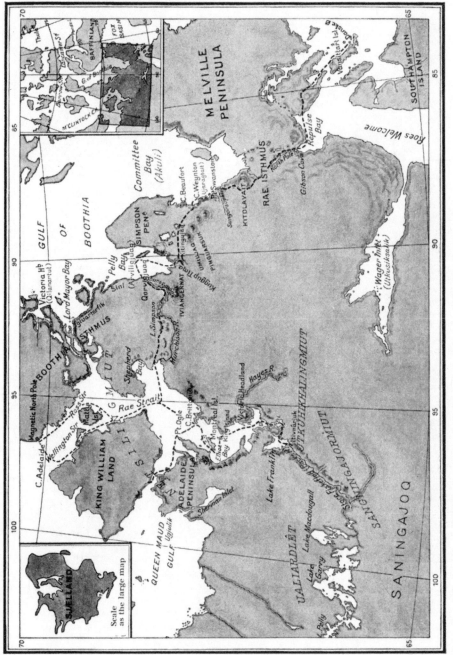

Route of Rasmussen's journey from Danish Island to King William Island.

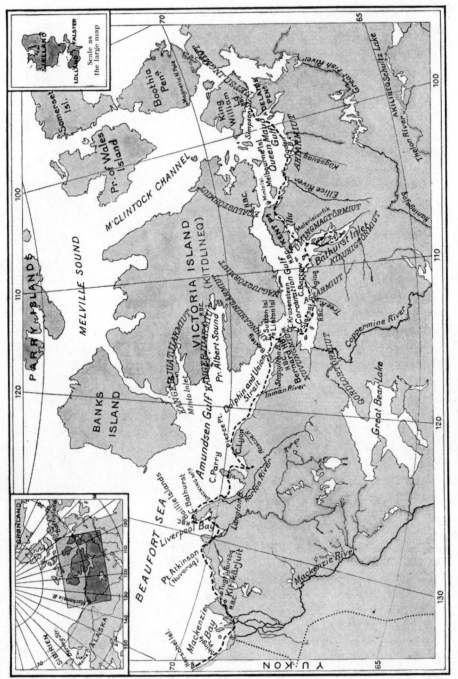

Route of Rasmussen's journey from King William Island to Herschel Island.

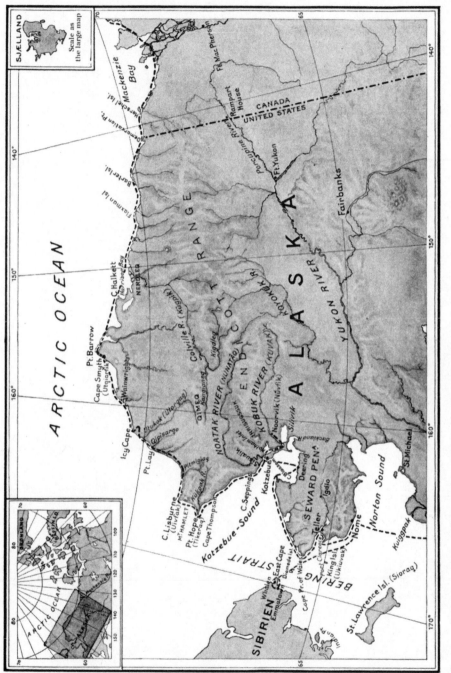

Route of Rasmussen's journey from Herschel Island to East Cape.

PROLOGUE

"I MUST GO AND SEE
THE NEW PEOPLE"

IN THE WINTER of 1921, Knud Rasmussen invited about one hundred of Copenhagen's eminent citizens—politicians, artists, journalists and business leaders—to join him at the city's prestigious Palace Hotel for a special dinner. It was an honor to receive a personal invitation from Rasmussen, a national hero known for his Arctic expeditions and his books about the lives, myths and legends of the Inuit. His guests arrived in formal attire for the event, and the entertaining speeches, good conversation and fine food made for a superbly successful evening. Once the meal was finished, Rasmussen stood up and clinked his glass for attention.

"Now I hope that everyone is well fed, that everyone is happy, and that everyone feels good!" he declared. "Since you've all eaten and drunk well, would you all be able to swear to just such a fact?" Once there was a general murmur of agreement, Rasmussen continued: "Well, there's only one question left . . . who will pay?"

The room fell silent. After the shock had subsided, people began fumbling for their wallets, aware of the presence of the other dignitaries and concerned for their reputations. None wished to appear mean or stingy. "Now that we have wallets at the ready," Rasmussen announced, "Peter [Freuchen] and I have some plans for an expedition that we would have funded."

RASMUSSEN WAS A living legend in an era when polar exploration was the height of fashion and public interest—the era when Roald Amundsen, Ernest Shackleton, Robert Falcon Scott, Robert Peary, Richard Byrd, Vilhjalmur Stefansson and Fridtjof Nansen made headlines, and when dangerous journeys to the remote regions of the planet were part sporting event and part scientific expedition, draped in a cloak of nationalism. But, unique among these adventurers, Rasmussen was as much an explorer of people as of place. During nearly three decades of travel by dogsled throughout the polar world, he visited every Inuit tribe then known to exist. In addition to writing the books describing his own journeys, Rasmussen published dozens of anthologies of Greenlandic and Inuit songs, stories, folk tales, legends and poems—mythology and philosophy—painstakingly collected and translated into Danish and English. These were a priceless contribution to world culture that would otherwise have disappeared.

Rasmussen was enormously popular among the Greenlanders and Inuit, of course, as well as in Denmark and Europe. But he was also a celebrated public figure throughout North America. His books were best-sellers, crowds flocked to his public talks, and his opinions were sought on Arctic matters. His charismatic and forceful personality drew both people and institutions into his orbit, and he collected a diverse entourage when he traveled and appeared in public.

Although Rasmussen never completed his studies at the University of Copenhagen, where he took an interest in theater and journalism, his life's accomplishments were so outstanding that he was awarded honorary doctorates by the University of Copenhagen and the University of St. Andrews in Scotland, along with an armful of other medals, awards, honorary memberships and decorations from countries around the world, including Great Britain, France, Norway, Sweden, Italy, and the United States. The American Geographical Society granted him an honorary fellowship and awarded him its prestigious Daly Medal. The Royal Geographical Society of Great Britain awarded him its gold Founder's Medal. The Canadian government hired him as a consultant on matters relating to the Arctic and its indigenous peoples. In Greenland, he helped the local people establish their Council of Hunters to regulate animal conservation, crime and other issues.

Such was Rasmussen's international stature that his speech at the International Court of Justice in The Hague in 1932 helped secure Greenland for Denmark rather than Norway. Rasmussen enjoyed the institutional respectability that his contemporaries, such as Roald Amundsen, longed for but never achieved. He was even a pioneer in the new world of motion pictures. His first and only film, *The Wedding of Palo*, was hailed in the *New York Times* upon its posthumous premiere as "a labor of love . . . like a tone poem by Sibelius or a nocturne by Grieg. There is much more than the cold, bleak desolations of the North in this film."

Yet somehow Rasmussen was also a bohemian. While honored by academia, he was simultaneously admired for his unconventional views and devil-be-damned courting of danger and adventure. He was as comfortable in bearskin pants on a featureless wind-lashed plain as he was in a formal suit and bow tie attending the opera. He loved hunting walrus but was equally enthusiastic about poetry and the theater. He was born and raised in Greenland, and his playmates as a child were the local Inuit boys. Fluent in Kalaallisut (the Greenland dialect of the Inuit language) and Danish, he was accepted among traditional hunters and shamans in the Arctic as well as among artists, scientists and politicians in Denmark. He was content to inhabit these disparate and seemingly incompatible worlds. "Nobody did really know Knud Rasmussen if they had only seen him in a civilized country," claimed the anthropologist Kaj Birket-Smith. "He ought to be seen among Eskimos."

Part Inuit on his mother's side and with a Danish father, Rasmussen could shoot a gun and harness a team of sled dogs by the time he was eight. Tireless and patient, he would earn the trust of northerners over days, weeks and months of shared experiences—daily living, hunting, building houses, dogsledding and exploring—before slowly turning to his quest, the collection of stories, poems and religious beliefs. "No matter whether it was Greenlanders or Eskimos in Canada and Alaska, he came to them as one of themselves," wrote Birket-Smith. "They unfolded their soul to the greatness and warmth of his being, and in return he received their simple tales of life and its struggles with the mysterious powers, their wild legends and fine poetry, with the open and understanding mind that can only be explained in one way: in his heart they touched strings that vibrated in harmony with them." Birket-Smith also wrote that Rasmussen "knew everyone up there, and was king, friend, and comrade at once. The people loved him; one who has arrived at Thule in the company of Knud Rasmussen will never forget the jubilation and devotion that greeted him."

Shaggy-haired and handsome, with the exotic looks of his Inuit ancestry, Rasmussen was always eager for a celebration, whether to sing, dance or tell stories. His eyes were crinkled from frequent smiles and laughter. He loved music, having at one time briefly pursued a career as an opera singer. On many of his polar journeys he brought a portable phonograph strapped to his dogsled. To enliven the dark nights, he astonished his nomadic hosts with the strains of Mozart or such favorites as "Alexander's Ragtime Band." Rasmussen hunted with the men, flattered and danced with the women, and feasted with them all. Women both in Ultima Thule, in the farthest reaches of Arctic Greenland, and in sophisticated Copenhagen vied for his attention. His Danish wife was the talented pianist Dagmar Andersen, with whom he had two daughters and a son, yet he also had Inuit mistresses during the many years he spent living in the Arctic, an arrangement that caused some friction with Dagmar. His editor and co-writer, Tom Kristensen, recalled that when they worked together on the manuscript for *Across Arctic America*, ensconced in a remote farm in the Danish countryside, they were frequently interrupted by groupies and female fans. "I could not keep the girls away, they fell like manna in the desert of Knud's masculine charm. When I kept guard at one door, they slipped in through the other." Inuit seamstresses would compete to make him footwear as gifts, and "his manner of taking them was so gracious that the ladies were never more proud than when they saw him wearing a pair of their boots." Freuchen jokingly called Rasmussen the Elsa Maxwell of the Arctic, after the famous American hostess and gossip columnist.

Although barely five feet five inches tall, Rasmussen dominated a room with his charm and presence. His enthusiasm was infectious and his social intelligence and intuition guided him seemingly unerringly, whether in a lecture hall in Copenhagen or a snow house in the Arctic. Rasmussen had many followers but few close friends, although he was generally admired by his fellow explorers. Many of his comrades attest to his unparalleled ability to subdue others, to get them to do his bidding by bringing them into his world, making them believe that his dream was their dream. Although domineering and occasionally manipulative, he inspired loyalty. One travel companion, Therkel Mathiassen, recounted that "His energy and enthusiasm for the business at hand communicated themselves to the whole expedition, with the result that the work went on brightly and briskly, no matter how tough it was. Personal squabbles and pettishness melted away in his presence; he had an astonishing gift for knocking different kinds of people into one whole with a single purpose: the success of the expedition . . . one little word of acknowledgment from him was thanks enough for all the toil and moil." Rasmussen also routinely acknowledged the contributions of others, no matter how minor. When he completed his epic three-year, 20,000-mile dogsled expedition through the Northwest Passage, he even remarked: "I am overwhelmed by a warm feeling of gratitude to all our patient and uncomplaining dogs."

Rasmussen claimed to be happiest when enduring the hardships of polar travel, when he was "hungry and shrunk from lack of meat, [and] we espied distant settlements with the smell of unknown people." The prospect of hazardous travel and hardship was more appealing to him than enduring boredom and inactivity. He and his small team of explorers repeatedly dogsledded through boulder-strewn chasms bounded by rock cliffs, across featureless expanses of pebbly, snow-dusted plains and along rocky jagged coastlines. Plagued by ferocious storms, they traversed ice fields broken by deadly crevasses, waded freezing streams and clambered down ice walls. Only two people ever died on the trail with Rasmussen—a remarkable feat, considering that his expeditions went into unknown and uncharted terrain, that they had only a vague understanding of the dangerous geography they would be traversing, and that they lived off the land, hunting for the majority of their food. Even Roald Amundsen, renowned for his caution and survival record, lost three men during his expeditions, whereas Robert Falcon Scott and four of his men died returning from the South Pole. Rasmussen maintained a jovial demeanor in the face of starvation and suffering. "When one has decided on the hazards of a journey," he pronounced, "one must take everything that occurs like a man—that is, with a broad grin."

Rasmussen was a superb writer, chronicling his adventures and the people he met with lyrical aplomb. His stories don't convey the reality of a dirty, tiring and frustrating slog—as surely much of the time on the trail must have been—but instead conjure a dreamlike bubble in which daily life mimics a tale from ancient mythology. It was "a beautiful and exciting time," he wrote of the departure on one of his expeditions, "with races from morning till night. One sledge after another shoots across the ice like a swift bird flying out into the darkness . . . and ahead beckon the skull-capped peaks and slit glacier tongues." Another time, he marveled at the strangeness of eating canned pineapple in the Arctic: "Here on the skull of the world, we eat a tin of Mauna Loa pineapple, the only one we possess, tinned at Hawaii . . . And as we see before us the dark-eyed, garlanded girls who picked the fruits, it is as if we cut through all horizons and conquer the world . . . So we cook musk ox meat from Nares Land, drink coffee from Java, after the tea from the Congo, and smoke tobacco from Brazil!"

On the return journey from one of his forays over the massive Greenland Ice Cap, Rasmussen urged his starving team on with descriptions of food read aloud at night from a housekeeping magazine he had brought along for that specific purpose. While they huddled in their huts, gnawing on bands of tough walrus hide that had once been their sled runners, sipping weak tea and trying to ignore their empty stomachs, Rasmussen would proclaim to his companions, "Scrambled eggs and bacon! That's what we're dining on tonight." Peter Freuchen, his fellow explorer on many expeditions, returned with, "Right you are! With pancakes!" Rarely did he lose his sense of humor. We "try to stimulate each other by poking fun at the miserable appearance many of us present," Rasmussen wrote. "There is nothing for it but sucking nourishment from one's humour during these days."

An endearing humanity prevented Rasmussen from becoming overly heroic and mythologized. He brought scissors to trim his hair even on the longest polar expeditions and washed his face every day with freezing water, even at great discomfort. Although he mostly avoided smoking in Denmark, on expeditions he was, according to Freuchen, "tremendously addicted." He was always losing his pipe and running short of tobacco, which would make him grumpy and irritable. "Every time we would leave our home I would ask, 'Have you got enough tobacco along?' and he always answered that he did, and he always would run out." Freuchen learned to bring along extra tobacco and to keep it hidden for a couple of evenings of "complaining and grumbling" before producing it to "great joy."

On one journey, Rasmussen developed sciatica in his left leg. The usually tireless leader, capable of herculean feats of endurance, could no longer walk. Reduced to lying on a dogsled, he suffered excruciating pain as the sled thumped over the ice-hummocked terrain, so he chomped on a dirty piece of seal hide to stop himself from crying out. When the sled rolled over one particularly uneven patch of snow, he slipped off to the ground and nearly fainted. Eyes closed and face white with pain, he muttered, "This is unpleasant." He soon recovered, however, and bounded alongside the sled dogs with his usual energy.

On another occasion reported by Freuchen, Rasmussen was out in his kayak hunting walrus, one of his favorite pastimes. He thrust his harpoon into the body of one rising beast, but as it dove, the tether became entangled around his arm and dragged him from his kayak into the frigid water. His companions, stunned and helpless, scanned the water's surface until Rasmussen burst up a distance away gasping for breath before being pulled beneath the surface again. When he finally emerged spluttering from the water, he claimed that he had merely hung onto the flotation bladder to tire the desperate animal and that he was in no danger.

Freuchen said, "You'd better go home for a change of clothes."

Rasmussen eyed him. "Don't you see this is our chance for a big killing?"

A little later Freuchen asked his wet and rapidly freezing friend if he didn't want his clothes wrung out.

"Why?" Knud asked.

"Because you're wet as hell!" Freuchen replied.

"By God. I forgot that!" Rasmussen said.

Peter Freuchen wrote in a biography of his friend: "The life of one's youth is rich, and it provides experiences and impressions; and in my youth I lived in the same house as Knud Rasmussen, I went on sled journeys with him, and I sat next to him in kayaks. Together we fought ice and current . . . For many years I travelled around in these regions with [him] and I knew him as did no one else. Nothing draws men closer than to hunger together, to see death in each other's eyes. Lying together in snow huts during snowstorms of many days' duration, waiting for better weather, and seeking to drown out hunger by each telling the other everything he knows—then you pour out your life, and old memories emerge in your mind."

As close to Knud Rasmussen as anyone could ever be, Freuchen may have understood what drove his friend, the childhood dream that made Rasmussen risk danger, ice and death. "Even before I knew what travelling meant," Rasmussen wrote, "I determined that one day I would go and find these people, whom my fancy pictured different from all others. I must go and see 'the New People' as the old story-teller called them."

Part One

NEW SUN

1

ON GREENLAND'S
STONY SHORES

Then, all meat seemed juicy and tender,
and no game too swift for a hunter.
When I was young,
every day was as a beginning
of some new thing,
and every evening ended
with the glow of the next day's dawn.

—Collected and translated near Hudson Bay
by Knud Rasmussen, *The Report of the*
Fifth Thule Expedition, 1921–1924

THE WORLD KNUD Johan Victor Rasmussen was born into
on June 7, 1879, was the vast, sparsely populated coast of
central western Greenland. Rasmussen's boyhood home was the
parsonage of the town of Jakobshavn, now known as Ilulissat.
Inhabited by only a few hundred people, Jakobshavn was then
the largest settlement in northern Greenland. It offered an unparalleled training ground, both culturally and geographically, for
a future Arctic explorer. Bounded by the frigid waters of Disko

Bay to the west and the unexplored Greenland ice sheet to the east, it was a land of growling ice and fog in the low hills. Disko Bay is one of the world's main sources of icebergs, which calve from the mighty glaciers of the Greenland ice sheet and congregate in their aquamarine brilliance before drifting off south.

There were no roads through the endless snow plains beyond the town. Rugged and unconquered, it was a place of few social constraints, but it demanded ceaseless toil to survive. Travel between the isolated settlements that dotted the coastline was by sailboat in the brief summer and by dogsled the rest of the year. The haunting specter of starvation and death by exposure was a constant and real threat. Not a forgiving land or an easy one to survive in, it was nevertheless a land of raw vitality, with endless possibilities for the curious and restless to explore.

Greenland, the largest island in the world at about 836,300 square miles, is bounded by the Atlantic Ocean to the southeast, the Greenland Sea to the east, the Arctic Ocean to the north and Baffin Bay to the west. About 80 percent of the land is covered by an enormous inland ice sheet up to two miles thick, and the island's average temperatures are similar to those in Arctic North America. In January, the range is between −4° and −22° Fahrenheit (−20° and −30° Celsius) in the north, warming to a little above freezing in the short, brilliant summer. In the south, winter temperatures range between 25° and −4° Fahrenheit (−4° and −20° Celsius) and rise to 45° Fahrenheit (7° Celsius) in summer. The island has been inhabited intermittently for thousands of years by people migrating east from Ellesmere Island and the Canadian Arctic Archipelago. Norse voyagers arrived from Iceland in the west in the tenth century, during the great Scandinavian expansion, and settled along the southwest coast during a warm period that lasted until the fifteenth century. The Greenland Norse were a European farming and livestock culture made famous by the sagas of Erik the Red and Leif the Lucky.

Erik, an independent-spirited and violent man, had been exiled from Iceland for murder during a feud with other landholders. He set off for the west with his extended family and slaves in a fleet of longships, discovering a new land he called Greenland for its verdant fjords, and to attract additional settlers with a promising name. They established two main settlements that attained a combined population of nearly 5,000 at their high point. During most of this time, the communities were indirectly ruled by European kingdoms, first Norway and then Denmark.

In the thirteenth century, as the Arctic climate cooled, the ancestors of the modern Inuit arrived in northern Greenland from Ellesmere Island and traveled south. These people of the "Thule culture" had the distinctive cultural innovations of dogsleds for travel and harpoons for hunting marine mammals such as seal, walrus and whale. Conflict between the Norse and the Inuit—during which one group struggled to cope with the colder climate while the other was particularly adapted to it—contributed to the abandonment of Norse settlements and the eventual extinction of the Greenland Norse. The Inuit were still living throughout the southern coastal regions when a "second wave" of Scandinavians—whalers and sealers—arrived in the 1720s, along with missionaries searching for the long-lost Norse colonists, to bring word of the Protestant Reformation. Denmark, which had never forgotten that it once held dominion over southern Greenland, reasserted its sovereignty in the eighteenth century despite the absence of Scandinavians there. Soon, missionaries and merchants established an administration over what emerged as the hybrid culture of Greenlanders—people of mixed Danish and Inuit ancestry and culture. Even at the time of Rasmussen's birth, there was only a handful of Danish-born officials in the country, and only three Danish families in Ilulissat.

Rasmussen's father, Christian Vilhelm Rasmussen, was a Danish missionary originally from the Zeeland village of Vråby. After studying at the seminary in Copenhagen, Christian immigrated to Greenland in 1873. A practical as well as an intellectual man, he was not a fire-and-brimstone pastor but more of a humanist, and he viewed his job as that of an advocate rather than a crusher of local language and customs. He immersed himself in the local culture and encouraged his children to do so as well. Fluent in the Greenland dialect of Eskimo-Kalaallisut, Christian was the author of a Greenlandic-Danish dictionary and later taught the Greenlandic language at the University of Copenhagen.

During his twenty-eight years in Greenland, Christian Rasmussen was well known for his herculean dogsled expeditions to the farthest regions of his sprawling parsonage, a district about five hundred miles long that included the entire northern half of Danish-colonized Greenland. At one time he administered five parishes simultaneously. Most winters he spent in constant travel—from Christianshåb (Qasigiannguit) over to Godhavn (Qeqertarsuaq) on Disko Island or north to Uummannaq, even all the way north to Upernavik, marrying couples, baptizing children, and presiding over funerals. His job required great stamina and physical endurance. He had to be strong, frugal and committed in order to do his work, and he often took young Knud with him.

Whereas Christian was from Denmark and had become familiar with the Greenlandic culture and language after arriving in Greenland, Knud's mother, Sophie Louise Fleischer, learned to speak Danish only while being schooled in Copenhagen in her youth. Her family had lived in Greenland for over a century, and she was one-fourth Inuit. Sophie's father, Knud Fleischer, was a respected and prosperous colony manager and had never left Greenland. Her mother, a half-Inuit orphan named Regine Paulussen, was rescued by Fleischer when she was near starvation during a famine in Christianshåb. In 1875, soon after Sophie returned from school in Copenhagen, she met and married the local priest, Pastor Christian Rasmussen.

While Christian exposed Knud to a restless life of challenging and exhausting travel, Sophie inspired him with her pride in her Greenlandic heritage. She was greatly respected in the community for her generosity and her dedication to children. Once, when an Inuit infant's mother died, rather than see the baby perish, Sophie breast-fed the girl alongside her own daughter. The door to the kitchen at the rectory was always open, especially in lean times when meat was scarce. She dispensed rye bread and coffee, and her countless other small kindnesses endeared her to the people. Peter Freuchen recalled a long conversation with Rasmussen about his mother. "Knud's mother had recently died, and he talked for hours about her faith in him and in the good that exists in the world. A mother who had never demanded, who had always given. We sat and froze in a hut, but there a son delivered a eulogy to his mother."

Both Danish and Greenlandic cultures were equally represented in Rasmussen's family, and Greenlandic was most commonly spoken at home. His uncles and aunts were both Danish and Inuit, and included several who had never left Greenland. He and his siblings wrote and spoke fluent Danish and spoke Greenlandic like natives; Rasmussen once claimed that he spoke Greenlandic better than he did Danish and that he dreamed in Greenlandic. Although he was often reported to be half Inuit— with his raven hair, dark complexion, small size, strength and skill in the outdoors, and animated hand movements when speaking— he was really only about one-eighth Inuit. One of Rasmussen's travel companions, Kaj Birket-Smith, wrote that "his feeling of kinship with the Eskimos had even to some extent left its traces in his appearance, although . . . his features were more like those of an American Indian than of an Eskimo."

Although Rasmussen didn't have much Inuit ancestry, he absorbed a great deal of the culture. His maternal grandmother, Regine, lived with his family when he was growing up, and he heard her stories of the Inuit past. The Danish artist Andreas Riis Carstensen traveled through Disko Bay when Rasmussen was ten and recalled the boy in his memoirs: "The priest's son spoke the Eskimo language to perfection and was a bright boy, who helped with the unloading of the boat and the pitching of tents and everything else."

In Ilulissat, Rasmussen had an upbringing that prepared him like no other for the life of an Arctic explorer. In traditional cultures, one of the advantages given to children is that the games they play and the toys they use develop the skills they will rely on as adults. The toys merely get larger and the games more serious as they grow. The skills Rasmussen acquired as a child—his facility in spoken and written languages, his hunting ability, his familiarity with travel by dogsled, his early exposure to Greenlandic and Norse myths and legends—all combined to create a unique personality ideally suited not only to geographical but also to cultural Arctic exploration. "From the very nature of things," Rasmussen recalled, "I was endowed with attributes for Polar work which outlanders have to acquire through painful experience." His later journeys "were like happy continuances of the experiences of my childhood and youth. . . . the most strenuous sledge-trips became pleasant routine for me."

Kununguaq ("Little Knud") spent many of his days outdoors with his Greenlander playmates, including his two younger siblings—his sister, Vilhelmine Regine, known as Me; and his brother, Christian Ludwig—and usually assumed the role of leader. One of their most popular pastimes was pretending to be explorers on expeditions. Rasmussen also loved the freedom of dogsledding in open terrain and driving a dogsled. He went hunting with the other boys when he was ten and was given his own sled puppies to raise. The only adventure he was denied was having his own kayak. Inuit boys had their own kayaks by the time they were six, but Knud's father felt this was too dangerous, and Rasmussen later complained that he wasn't much good in a kayak because of his lack of early training.

Young Knud was also somewhat dreamy and easily distracted from chores or studies. He would stare out the window in the morning, pondering the icebergs drifting lazily in the bay. If a kayak paddled by he would imagine its adventures, past or future, inventing stories as it slipped past. He preferred fishing for polar cod to doing his math or grammar homework, and he would recite his Danish language lesson only while lying on his stomach over a chair.

IN 1888, A then-unknown Norwegian adventurer named Fridtjof Nansen led five comrades on a daring trek across the vast and unexplored Greenland Ice Cap, traversing the desolate island from an uninhabited spot on the east coast to the settlements of the west. Nansen chose this route after careful deliberation: the only way to safety was to push forward rather than to retreat. The final destination was to be somewhere in Disko Bay. There was much excitement in Ilulissat, and a reward was offered to the first person to spot the arrival of the victorious explorers. No one knew what lay in Greenland's vast interior. Rasmussen, then nine years old, and his friend Jørgen Brønlund talked endlessly about the epic journey and (to them) enormous reward. One summer evening, as the light lingered late into the night, the two boys set off from the coast, heading inland across the low hills in their search for the adventurers. Spurred by their youthful fantasies, they trudged on until, after climbing yet one more slow-rising hill, they were able to see far to the east. There was no sign of Nansen. When the boys realized that they could see farther than they could walk, they reluctantly turned around and dragged themselves home—much to the relief of their parents.

Nansen did eventually reach the west coast after a grueling and treacherous forty-nine-day slog, but at the much more southerly destination of Godthåb (now Nuuk), where he and his companions spent the next seven months of winter before being picked up by a ship in the spring. He wrote that "it was not without sorrow that we left this place and these people, among whom we had enjoyed ourselves so well." Word of Nansen and his troop caused a sensation among the Greenland boys even though they never met him, and they took up skiing so that they could play at being explorers. Although wood was scarce in Greenland, the youngsters were not discouraged. They made their skis from barrel staves and soon became proficient skiers.

Other popular games for boys in Ilulissat revolved around hunting. In Rasmussen's time, as it had been for centuries, survival in Greenland depended upon the hunting of wild animals: musk oxen in the north and east; caribou on the patches of plains; seals and other marine animals on the coast; and fish and millions of birds on their seasonal migrations. As the boys grew bigger, their harpoons, bows and spears likewise grew larger. This was also true of their sleds and the dogs needed to pull them. As a boy, Rasmussen enlisted his playmates to be his "sled dogs," and later in life he recalled his experiences with his imaginary dogs. "The first dog I had," he wrote, "was two-legged, because before my father entrusted me to run with real dogs, I had a whole team, which consisted of my Greenland playmates . . . In the morning, when I came out, they flocked around me, and their zeal was great because my good mother always gave me delicious dog food. It was Rye bread and Ship's biscuits or figs and prunes, a diet that these Eskimo boys never had at home! After feeding, they were excited for real belts and harnesses. I had a really long dog whip. But when my first dog was my own playmate, I of course never used a whip, and that is perhaps why I never ever later in my life was really comfortable using a long dog whip. Dogs should not pull out of fear, but out of desire."

On one occasion, Rasmussen tied his "dogs" up and went inside his home to get bread. Upon seeing him, his mother was reminded of his neglected chores and sent him off to complete the tasks. His companions remained outside, tied up for several hours, until he finally remembered to return with bread for his "dog team."

His future companions commented on his facility with his sled dogs, undoubtedly a combination of innate talent and a lifetime of practice. Many Inuit had similar abilities with dogs and dogsledding, but as was the case with a fluency in the Greenlandic language, few who did not cultivate these skills in their youth could ever perfect them. Rasmussen "could always get his dogs to persevere," wrote Freuchen, "to do what they had to do no matter how exhausted they were. When, finally, a dog in Knud's team laid himself down, it was death that had defeated him." Rasmussen could apparently "hypnotize" his dogs by staring in their eyes so that they gave all their strength. According to another one of his future traveling companions, Therkel Mathiassen, he had "a marvellously keen eye for the ability, faults and needs of each one of his dogs . . . He loved his dogs so they loved him, not with the slavish lickspittle affection of civilized dogs, but with the half-wild beast's feeling of 'belonging' in thick and thin."

Rasmussen's boyhood was rich in imaginary play and adventures tied to the traditional pursuits of the Inuit. In the late nineteenth century, Greenland's coastal communities were defined by the seasons, and Rasmussen was temperamentally suited to this slow annual cycle. Ships from Europe and America arrived in Greenland only rarely, perhaps only a few times a year, and always in the height of summer, after the ice had broken up on the bay and before the fall freeze (ships frequently stayed the entire winter frozen in the ice if they arrived late in the season). Powered by wind and subject to its whimsy, these majestic sailing vessels would weave their way through the obstacle course of icebergs, appearing phantomlike from the fog, bringing desperately needed supplies and welcome news from family in Europe. Their arrival was an occasion of great celebration. They brought new foods, parcels and packages from Denmark and were an opportunity to meet new people. There were prizes for the person who spotted the first ship of the season; when the ship sailed in close to the pebbly shore, the local people pushed longboats into the water and rowed out to tow it in, with children vying for places in the boats to be part of the momentous event.

Another exciting time was when hunters were loading up their dogsleds before setting off. The children would join in the general excitement. As the equipment was bundled onto the sleds, the dogs were rounded up and strapped into the harnesses, soon to set off in a great burst of barking and panting.* The children would rush up and leap onto the sled, grasping the runners as the dogs strained to drag the human chain across the snow. Later in life, when Rasmussen and Peter Freuchen were setting off on a foray from Thule Station, Freuchen complained about the pestering Inuit boys jumping on the sleds for a free ride across the snow. Rasmussen quietly admonished him with a smile: "You don't know what a thrill it was for me to hang onto the sleds and run after them far over the harbour . . . We ran and ran, and then we would decide to go back, but we would run still farther, and when we got back we bragged to each other about how far we had gone."

---

*The terms "sledge" and "sled" are often used interchangeably. A sled can refer to a smaller craft used for personal transportation with a smaller dog team, whereas a sledge involves hauling some kind of heavy equipment with a larger dog team. Most of the time, travel in the Arctic involved what technically would be called sledges rather than sleds, but for consistency with historical and contemporary writings the more common term "sled" is used throughout.

One of the most momentous events in the cycle of the seasons in Ilulissat was related to the celebrations when hunters returned with their kill, especially when a whale had been harpooned and the sleds were loaded with *mattak*, chunks of whale blubber attached to the thick skin. In the lean season of spring, after a period of subsisting on the tough shark meat normally reserved for dogs and chewing old hides, *mattak*—"the tenderest delicacy one can imagine"—marked the end of the seasonal hunger. In Greenlandic tradition, meat belongs to the entire community, not merely the hunter who wielded the successful harpoon. In Ilulissat, every hunter was entitled to plunge his knife into the whale and carve out great chunks of meat and blubber. They would be followed by the community's other men and women, and even children. Soon they were all clambering over the carcass "like wild dogs attacking a quarry," Rasmussen recalled. As a boy, he snuck off to participate in these feasts, joining in "the excitement of getting the meat and blubber and *mattak*" and "competing to see who could flense out the biggest piece." He would return hours later smeared in blood and grease with a big grin on his face.

EVERY SETTLEMENT IN Greenland had its distinct legends, songs and beliefs about mysterious occurrences. Rasmussen liked to visit old women in their sod houses and hear their stories. These women were repositories of cultural knowledge from ancient times, and he was intrigued by the bewildering tales they shared with him. They welcomed him because of his family's respected status and generosity as well as his own charm. Rasmussen came and went as he pleased, always bringing a small gift, sometimes a piece of rye bread and at other times an unusual pebble that he had found. These offerings were treasured as gifts from "Little Knud."

He once journeyed with his father to Qeqertaq, in northern Disko Bay, to visit a people "who lived isolated lives and had strange imaginations," whose fantasies were nourished by "the dismal rumbling of the enormous icebergs that steadily fell out of the glaciers and the winter darkness." Here an old woman told him tales of phantoms, of people who wandered far from the settlements and into the mountains, and who were possessed by an evil spirit and could not return. Apparently, they were fired at if they came too close to dwellings. The woman related the eerie tale of an unlucky man whose wife and children were killed by a tumbling iceberg that had crushed the boat they were traveling in. Consumed by grief, the man had run off into the mountains. Ten days later he was found dead, partway through a frightening metamorphosis. His face was covered in black hairs, and one of his feet was withered and looked like a caribou hoof. Another brooding tale concerned happenings in a nearby ravine, where witches, orphaned children, and old and sick people who could no longer take care of themselves were exiled. The tale brought to Knud's mind his grandmother, who was an orphan. He ran home through the dark, burst into the house and proclaimed that he would never allow his mother and father to be tossed into the ravine.

The tales of the Inuit elders nurtured Rasmussen's interest in Greenlandic legends, culture and history and inspired his future adventures and travels. His interest in exploring the expanses of wilderness that hemmed in Greenland's tiny settlements grew as he got older, and he became fixated on a little-known group of Inuit in the extreme north who had been isolated from southern Greenland by the inland ice cap for over a century. "When I was a child I used to hear an old Greenlandic woman tell how, far away North at the end of the world, there lived a people who dressed in bearskins and ate raw flesh. Their country was always shut in by ice, and the daylight never reached over the tops of their high fjords."

The old storytellers tried to quell Rasmussen's curiosity by frightening him with tales of how these distant people lived in a land of gloomy darkness—they were wild heathens, killers and tormentors, not to be trusted. These fantasies, based on fear or the understandable desire to protect Rasmussen, did not have the desired effect. Even as a child, he vowed that as soon as his pups grew big enough he would sled north to discover these people for himself. The elders chuckled at the boy's outrageous claims, and of course Knud didn't get there at the age of twelve as he had envisioned. But he never gave up on this ambitious goal, even during all the years he spent away from Greenland. He was an explorer of people rather than geography: what interested him about the remote and unexplored regions of Greenland was not the possibility of a new trade route, of accessing valuable resources, or of attaining a symbolic geographical objective such as the North Pole. It was the possibility of meeting new and unusual people and sharing in their ideas that fascinated him.

From his mother, Rasmussen inherited a cultural and genetic link to the native people of Greenland, to their customs, language and beliefs, and personality traits that were vital to his success as an explorer. From his father, he inherited something quite different. Besides the strong cultural affiliation with their Danish heritage, father and son also shared a characteristic easily overlooked for its less-than-romantic connotations: a logical and systematic approach to organizing information. Rasmussen's father was a seeker of efficiencies and a planner able to establish and work toward a larger goal, such as the Greenlandic dictionary he spent many years compiling. He would take a large project and turn it into a series of smaller ones. This trait would prove invaluable when Rasmussen later set out on his life's quest to "map" Inuit culture across the polar world.

There was, as well, a vital and distinguishing aspect of Rasmussen's upbringing in Greenland of which he may have been unaware, because it was never discussed: his family's social status. This status was the foundation of his charisma, his confidence and his lofty egalitarianism. It stemmed from his father's position as rector for northern Greenland, making him its spiritual leader, the public face of colonial and linguistic power, an authority appointed from Denmark. The elder Rasmussen presided over births, marriages and deaths, and he dispensed advice. He always helped other families during times of hardship, while he and his family were immune to that hardship.

While eschewing traditional notions of authority and prestige, the Rasmussen family was nevertheless the first among equals. The family home was a two-story rectory, built with expensive imported pine, that dwarfed all the other buildings in the community. It signified authority. The Rasmussen name was known throughout all the communities of western Greenland. Wherever the young boy went, he was recognized and well treated, and always indulged. An endearing child, to be sure, but he was also afforded the respect due to his family's status, standing out as being from a superior social class. It gave him the confidence to speak and do what he pleased, knowing that it would be accepted, that he would be listened to, that his opinions would be given consideration. He could make decisions for other people in the belief that if he led, they would follow.

When Rasmussen was twelve years old, his family's long-anticipated voyage to Denmark became a reality. His father, the only family member with strong memories of Denmark, wanted his children to see his homeland and perhaps have his sons attend the same school as he had, the Herlufsholm boarding school for boys. He requested a leave of absence from his post as rector, and in June 1891, the entire family boarded a ship for Copenhagen. As the young Rasmussen leaned on the railing and the ship headed out to sea, leaving behind the snow-encrusted mountains and icebergs in the bay, he viewed his impending adventure with both excitement and trepidation. His father spoke of the camaraderie of the dormitory and the pride of wearing the school uniform, and he looked forward to sharing the experiences with his son, reliving the stories and triumphs of his own youth. But Knud had never been so far away from home, and the thought of his family returning to Ilulissat without him loomed like a dark cloud.

The first days in Copenhagen must have been a shock. Knud had never been in the company of more than a few dozen people at any time. The city was an alien and bewildering place, one with seemingly endless rows of stone and wooden buildings many stories high, where winding, mazelike cobbled streets were filled with a crowded mass of humanity, horses and dogs. He saw bridges, canals, towering stone churches, tunnels, roads and waterfronts with hundreds of ships—things he had only read about in books or heard his father describe. Here were strange noises, unfamiliar smells and the chaotic spectacle of a European capital city of nearly 300,000 people, spreading out into farms and towns in the surrounding territory. It was also lush, green and warm here, with massive, leafy trees—the complete opposite of anything the boy had ever encountered. Snow in Copenhagen would come later but perhaps for only three months of the year, and it did not last long when it fell, often turning to rain in the relatively mild climate. The people spoke only Danish and wore garments of wool and cotton rather than animal skins and furs. They also ate strange foods. Rather than featuring the flesh of wild game, Rasmussen's dinner plate now offered peculiar sauces, spices and strange vegetables.

Within a few days of their arrival, father and son rode the train from Copenhagen to Herlufsholm School, about two hours away. To young Rasmussen, the locomotive was a giant beast, belching smoke and steam as it clacked and roared along steel rails at a speed he had never imagined. When they arrived at the school, Knud settled down for the entrance examination—admission was not assured, not even for the children of alumni. But the boy had never been much interested in academics. He had gotten by, and he had usually succeeded at everything he tried.

He failed the entrance examination, owing particularly to his weakness in mathematics. It was his first defeat, not being accepted at the chosen school. The slow journey back to Copenhagen with his silent father was a memory that lingered with Rasmussen his whole life. He told Freuchen the story when they were trapped in a storm in Greenland years later. "You mustn't feel bad about this, Little Knud," his father had told him. "After all, there are many other schools, and it might well be that you wouldn't have liked it here at all! It is not you who should feel bad about it. You'll certainly do all right for yourself. It was my failure; it was I who didn't measure up. I obviously have not taught you as well as I should have."

But not all was lost. Soon a new boarding school, the Nørrebro Grammar School, was found in Copenhagen. Knud's first days there were a rude introduction to a world of large groups and noise and rules, of loneliness and cultural alienation. Instead of reveling in his former freedom and usual outdoor adventure, the young Greenlander was encouraged to become sedentary and rule bound. Instead of pursuing his own inclination, he had to do what he was told. Gone was his former life, when he had been at least a partial master of his fate.

When the pastor's leave ended, the Rasmussen family returned to Greenland without Knud. They sailed on June 7, 1893, the boy's fourteenth birthday. He would not be able to visit them, even on extended holidays; Greenland was too remote. He was left in the care of a wine merchant, Mr. Jorgensen, a family friend who lived near the school. Jorgensen and his wife had several children, and Knud was accepted and felt comfortable with the family. But his experience at school was less than pleasant.

Knud's outdoor skills and ranking in the social hierarchy of Greenland had no standing at a boarding school in Copenhagen.

Knud's lack of facility in mathematics came to haunt him. He later told Freuchen that it was "physical torture" to attend school on those mornings when he had a mathematics class, making his loneliness all the more acute. Sensing Rasmussen's weakness, the mathematics teacher would call him to the front of the class, make him demonstrate his faulty equations and then ridicule his failure. The man was, according to Freuchen, "one of those teachers, occasionally to be found, who takes pleasure out of playing the great man in front of a classroom of boys, who, because of their youth and their positions as pupils, have neither the power nor the right to retaliate." Not surprisingly, Rasmussen retained an irrational hatred of mathematics throughout his life.

Mail delivery between Greenland and Denmark was infrequent. It took six months for letters to travel between Ilulissat and Copenhagen, and they arrived only during the sailing season, when Disko Bay was free of ice. Nevertheless, when they arrived, Rasmussen received a large quantity of letters from his parents, his sister, Me, and his aunt, and he wrote long diary entries that he mailed home. The letters he received dwelt on stories of daily life in Ilulissat and reminded him of his life there. Me promised to let Rasmussen's Greenlander friends know about his new life, too. Her letters, peppered with references to specific prayers, reveal that the Rasmussens were a pious family. Knud's own letters are likewise strong on religious references and prayers for his family—although the references seem tagged on as an afterthought, more for his family's benefit than his own.

Rasmussen eventually distinguished himself at grade school by emphasizing his Greenlandic heritage. It was something to hold onto as a cultural anchor while he was awash in the new, strange world of rules, schedules and social conventions. His family's absence made him identify more strongly with Greenland, and he

accentuated his exotic heritage by speaking in Greenlandic, singing Greenlandic songs and telling stories of the Inuit and their
habits and customs. This approach received an enthusiastic response in Denmark and solidified his identity as a Greenlander.
Whereas he stood out in Greenland for his colonial status, in
Denmark he was noted for his Greenlandic status. Each circum-
stance labeled him as an outsider. And, as he was also handsome
and charismatic, his alien characteristics made him "special"
rather than merely different.

Two years later, the Rasmussen family left Ilulissat for good
when Pastor Rasmussen, now in his fifties, was no longer up to
the strenuous travel required to visit far-flung Greenlandic settlements. In 1895, when Knud was sixteen, his father became
the vicar of Lynge, a town on the outskirts of Copenhagen, and
an associate professor of Greenlandic at the University of Copenhagen. Rasmussen's father was studious and respectable, but
also gregarious, known for daily tea and crumpets and croquet
games, whereas his mother was quiet and shy. The family home
once again became a haven where parents, siblings and friends
gathered. Nevertheless, Knud did not join his family in their new
home, but took new lodgings near his school.

A poor student, Rasmussen remained distracted from his
studies by things that interested him more, especially social outings and relationships with girls, which earned him a reputation
for leaving a string of broken hearts. He cultivated an eccentric
image in class and had a barely veiled contempt for his arrogant
teachers. He knew, as did they, that he was not the student type,
not content to sit and do what he was told, to accept what was
said, and to deliver what others wanted. One of his teachers
mockingly asked him if he had a wealthy father—the implication
being that his father must be rich to keep paying for Rasmussen's
education when he was such a poor student. He barely scraped

by in receiving his diploma in 1899, when he was nearly twenty years old.

Nevertheless, while his studies received scant attention, Rasmussen was the king of social gatherings, the sun around whom others orbited. He was charming, smooth, interesting, different. Even as a teenager, he had an intuitive social sense. Whenever he visited his extended family or the homes of friends, he was loved by their children. And his father seems to have understood that Knud's social skills might more than compensate for his academic failings. At a gathering on the lawn of the family home in Lynge to celebrate Knud's graduation, Christian advised his son not to dwell on the past but always to look to the future—advice that came to define Rasmussen's character and his approach to life.

THE TEMPTATIONS
OF COPENHAGEN

The moon shimmered in the ice crystals, and the trembling
arc of northern lights played over the edge of the wood . . .
When I saw my sled disappear into the forest, I suddenly had
a strange feeling that I at once was set centuries back in time
and development. I was alone with the Lapps and I was now
trying to live their lives.

—Knud Rasmussen, *Lapland*

I N THE FALL of 1899, Knud Rasmussen was enrolled in the
University of Copenhagen as a student of philosophy and languages. But instead of diligently pursuing his studies, he devoted
himself to partying and all-night discussions with a bohemian
crowd of artists, actors and writers. When his younger brother,
Christian, began planning for university, the expense was too
much for their parents. The elder Rasmussen called his two sons
to his study for a meeting and informed them that he could not
afford to send them both to school. Rasmussen's father suggested
the younger son should instead pursue a career in trade school,
where the tuition was lower.

According to Freuchen's recounting of Knud's story, Knud spoke up. "No, Father. Christian is more gifted than I, and Christian is much better fitted for a disciplined study career. Let him choose a profession, for I'll be able to take care of myself." It was youthful boasting, but it may have been spurred by Knud's knowledge of his unsuitability for academic life. He withdrew from the university, perhaps with a sigh of relief that the burden of pleasing his parents with academic achievement was ending. The responsibility was now off his shoulders, and he was free to pursue his less straightforward inclinations. He wanted to become an actor.

The theater seemed a natural vocation for someone who was already a talented performer in social situations and comfortable with being the center of attention. But Rasmussen would have to hone his skills and warm up to the idea of being on stage in a more formal venue. He was introduced to the idea through his friendship with Adam and Johannes Poulsen, sons of the famous Danish stage actor Emil Poulsen. Many years later, Rasmussen admitted that he always felt guilty about one aspect of his friendship with the two youths: they were vegetarians, and for a while he pretended to be vegetarian as well. His Greenlandic upbringing on prodigious quantities of meat, however, was too strong to shake. When he had a craving and a little spare money, he would sneak out to a cheap steakhouse and order a slab of beef smothered in onions and butter, leaving the potatoes untouched on the plate. His brief experiment with vegetarianism ended with a change in interest: it was opera that now captured his attention.

Blessed with a naturally powerful voice and with much practice in singing Greenlandic songs at parties, Rasmussen somehow convinced the noted singer and teacher Laurits Tørsleff to take him on as a student. Tørsleff had many paying students, but with Rasmussen he agreed to forgo his usual fee. Instead, they decided that Tørsleff would earn 1 percent of Rasmussen's future income as an opera singer. Either Rasmussen charmed his way into this sweetheart deal or he had actual talent—perhaps a bit of both. But once again, he grew tired with the practice and his slow progress, and he decided to speed things up a little. Presenting his credentials as a student of Tørsleff, he persuaded the celebrated opera star Vilhelm Herold to attend a recital at a fine hotel. Somehow he was able to book a room without payment, and with his illustrious guest in attendance, he sang and performed. "This is not exactly a world-shaking baritone," Herold sniffed, "but you do have material that can be developed." Rasmussen had hoped to make a greater impression. His old school friend Johannes Poulsen wrote a letter urging him not to be disappointed: "As you have a good ear you won't find it difficult to learn the different parts." Rasmussen, however, wasn't prepared to put in the years of training needed to perfect his voice. Thus ended his career in the opera.

Rasmussen had developed a pattern of moving on to new things when he realized they would not be the vehicle for his dreams and ambitions, or when progress didn't occur quickly enough to keep him engaged. Sometimes he withdrew from people as well; both men and women noted that he could become distant or not fully engaged with them after a time, and when they expected more, perhaps a romantic relationship, this disengagement resulted in hurt feelings. But Rasmussen had so many ideas and ambitions, and knew so many people, that he regularly rushed off to the next opportunity as soon as it presented itself. He became a member of several informal social clubs where he mingled with artists, writers, journalists, social revolutionaries and other members of the intelligentsia. These iconoclastic thinkers had a disdain for business and societal convention: they were unusual, and Rasmussen was intrigued. He fit right in, with his outstanding ability in discussion and argument, and he was aided by his unusual heritage and exotic appearance.

In 1900, he decided that he would try his hand at writing, a skill for which he had already shown some talent. He would combine this latest career choice with travel, something else that his restless soul craved—new places, new experiences, new people. His decision to become a writer conveniently coincided with a Student Society trip to Iceland and other northern islands. The purpose of the expedition, funded by the Danish Tourist Association, was to foster closer relations between Denmark and Iceland. Rasmussen, through his father's contacts and with his own enthusiasm, secured a position as a freelance correspondent of the *Kristeligt Dagblad* (*Christian Daily*), which covered his expenses for the trip.

The ship *Botnia* sailed from Copenhagen on June 18 for a four-week voyage. For the first time since he had arrived in Copenhagen as a boy, Rasmussen would be revisiting northern waters. The ship's passengers included dozens of enthusiastic students on their first adventure to see something of the world. The expedition's leader was the outspoken young journalist and social critic Ludvig Mylius-Erichsen, with whom Rasmussen enjoyed a particular rapport. "Presently I am stretched out on the bottom of one of the ship-side dinghies, resting with some rope-ends as a pillow. And my impressions are those of the large, white clouds sailing in full flight over my head," Rasmussen wrote, delighted with his current situation.

Rasmussen wrote many articles during the voyage, honing his evocative style with whimsical musings on the one hand and astute geopolitical observations on the other. He wrote that in his opinion, Iceland needed a bank to truly prosper, observing that Great Britain had recently rented an Icelandic waterfall from the state and was establishing a hydroelectric enterprise. His eyes were opened to the possibility that Greenland would fall under foreign influence if it wasn't managed properly.

When the *Botnia* arrived in Reykjavik, it moored for many days and the students were able to stay ashore long enough to be hosted by local families. There Rasmussen met Euphemia, daughter of Indriði Einarsson, the country's most celebrated playwright. He charmed her, and they apparently fell in love. Writing to Rasmussen after he had returned to Copenhagen, Euphemia claimed: "There is something so intoxicating about you, even if you are a teetotaller and not particularly fond of being intoxicated." Perhaps wise to the impetuous and charming Greenlander, she declined to profess her undying love.

On the voyage, Rasmussen was particularly vocal about the merits of Greenland, though he hadn't seen it for many years. Expedition leader Mylius-Erichsen became frustrated because Rasmussen continually spoke to anyone who would listen about the beauty of Greenland, and then tried to convince Mylius-Erichsen to change the *Botnia*'s course and steer farther west. He claimed they were so close to Greenland that they could follow in the path of Erik the Red. Mylius-Erichsen finally had to tell Rasmussen to stop agitating for a trip to Greenland. He knew very well that Greenland was near and that it had historical ties to Iceland, but he didn't have the authorization for such an unplanned detour, nor did he have the finances. However, Mylius-Erichsen had apparently been considering the risky scheme, until the commander of a Danish navy ship advised against it: there was a high likelihood of encountering ice, and the *Botnia* was not reinforced to survive collisions with ice.

Nevertheless, Rasmussen remained determined to find some way to return to his homeland. Before the *Botnia* reached Copenhagen on the return trip, he had convinced Mylius-Erichsen that an expedition to Greenland should be their next project— although they had no idea how such a venture would be planned or financed.

Romantic relationships with women had been part of Rasmussen's world since his teenage years. He was particularly sought after during his youth. His friend Erik Rindom wrote, "I know of no young man . . . who has met his match in this area. He was able to win them all so to speak. Not only was virtually any young woman in love with him, but I have very rarely met with young men who could resist his charm." Peter Freuchen, who met him when Rasmussen was in his late twenties, wrote that "rarely has any more charming young man stepped on the streets. His sharp facial features, his black hair, his . . . gentle and wonderfully sharp look, took in the girls in an indiscriminate fashion, and won older and younger for him." Emil Nolde, a Danish-born German painter who met Rasmussen in 1901 and who eventually married one of Rasmussen's girlfriends, wrote that Rasmussen "was a man full of primordial force and a strange charm." He had so many girlfriends during these years that he was bound to get into trouble eventually.

In the summer of 1898, when he was nineteen years old, Rasmussen had begun a tentative and sporadic relationship with his cousin Vilhelmine Clausen, who was two years older than he and a friend of his sister, Me. Vilhelmine's letters to him reveal the ups and downs of a young woman irritated and hurt by the vacillating and unfaithful actions of her charming paramour. Rasmussen often romanticized about living in the present without looking to the future, but on those occasions when he failed to meet her as they'd agreed, he would offer flimsy excuses in a letter. At one time she referred to him as a "ruthless, vacillating ragged doll boy"; at another, she wrote, "I think so indescribably much of you, and I can no longer bear to live in the uncertainty of whether you also reciprocate my feelings."

For Rasmussen, it all seemed good fun, and he had other women friends during this time. Vilhelmine broke off their relationship in February 1899 with great dignity, waxing poetic about letting him fly free. But he wrote back to say how much he loved her, and they met again. "You were great," he claimed. "I was only great in fickleness and capriciousness." He won her back just before leaving for Iceland.

Their letters reveal a long and tortured relationship, in which Vilhelmine is subject to his erratic and fickle moods and desires. For the young man, experimenting and testing the limits of his power, it was clear that he was either unwilling or unable to acknowledge that he bore some responsibility for others. To a certain extent his behavior could be dismissed as part of the typical drama of youthful love, but on at least one other occasion, his games had more serious consequences. In November 1900, a brief affair in Copenhagen with a young woman named Anna Olivia, a butcher's daughter who was four years older than he, had a more lasting outcome.

WHEN RASMUSSEN RETURNED from Iceland and his voyage in the North Atlantic, his articles were well received and he seemed to have a future as a freelance journalist. Then another opportunity presented itself. He read about a new sporting event to be called the Nordic Games, modeled on the Olympic Games, that would be held in Stockholm, Sweden, in a few months. The first Nordic Games, scheduled for February 1901, would feature northern sports such as skiing, skating, ice sailing, bandy (similar to ice hockey), steeplechase (terrain riding) and even automobile racing on ice. Rasmussen was immediately enthusiastic, seeing the Nordic Games as a way to continue his travels and get out of Copenhagen, which was boring him even though he had been home for only a few months. He wrote a letter to the Swedish headquarters of the Nordic Games:

> I was born and brought up in Greenland where the grand natural conditions gave me great love of all outdoor activities, but my enthusiasm was strongest when on a clear winter day I would be allowed to hunt on dogsled beyond the endless horizon: it was like going straight into eternity, I thought, and by my love of this healthy sport as well as in my youthful enthusiasm I gradually acquired the ability to manage dogs for sleds so that I could challenge, and even emerge victorious, over any Greenlander I came upon. I am Greenlander enough that my blood gets hot at the thought of again obtaining that flying speed, but conditions here in Denmark never allow such a thing: we lack both dogs and snow.

After the lengthy preamble he at last came to the point of his letter: "It hit me the other day after the announcement on the large sports event to be held in Stockholm in February that here was the long-overdue opportunity for me to go dogsledding." He invited the organizers to introduce dogsled races as part of the Nordic Games and contacted the Copenhagen Zoo to inquire about the number and availability of their sled dogs. His enthusiasm was so infectious that the zoo's director made the unprecedented offer of several Greenland dogs so that Rasmussen could give a dog-driving demonstration at the Nordic Games. Alas, these efforts bore no fruit: despite the enthusiasm of Rasmussen and the director, the organizers felt dogsledding would be inappropriate.

In the fall of 1900, Rasmussen left the *Christian Daily* and signed on as a freelancer with the *Illustrated News,* specifically for the chance to travel to Stockholm and cover the Nordic

Games. He had to make a living somehow; he couldn't just chase women and party with intellectuals, as pleasant a life as that undoubtedly was. He traveled to Stockholm and diligently wrote stories about the Nordic Games competitions and celebrations. His articles were well received but did not pay very much, and he had to use his own money to pay for some of the illustrations that accompanied the text. He was also having a difficult time meeting his living expenses. He wandered around Stockholm with a similarly impoverished fellow journalist searching for the cheapest restaurants while awaiting the additional funds he had requested from the *Illustrated News*. When the *Illustrated News* package arrived, he tore it open, only to find the enclosed sum insufficient to cover the cost of the illustrations he had purchased, let alone large enough to enable him to live in Stockholm. With a defiant flourish, Rasmussen ignored his desperate situation, placed the funds in a return envelope and sent it back to the *Illustrated News*. The enclosed note proclaimed, "From such a poverty-stricken publication I neither can nor will accept any payment."

Afterward, he spent the day strolling around the Swedish capital, no doubt pondering his fate and his next move, as well as the source of his next meal. He knew that a banquet was being held for members of the foreign press that very evening. It was a formal affair, with many courses, wine, speeches and the mingling of important journalists, politicians and cultural figures. Naturally, he wasn't invited. And equally naturally, this did not deter him from arriving at the doors expecting to be admitted. As he approached, the doorman stepped up and asked for his invitation—Rasmussen didn't look like he belonged, dressed as he was in a workaday suit rather than the tie and coattails of the other guests. He affected a frown and proclaimed, "I am a foreign journalist." When the shabbiness of his dress was pointed out, he loudly protested how insulted he felt and how offended other

Danish journalists would be—after all, they were in Stockholm solely to publicize the Nordic Games, and there would be a scandal when it became known that he had been denied access to the dinner merely because he was traveling light. Hearing the commotion, several Swedish journalists came over and ushered him past the gatekeepers.

Rasmussen was now in his element: a large social gathering of educated and intelligent people in a festive mood. Seated at his side at the magnificent dining table was a distinguished older gentleman with whom Rasmussen quickly established a rapport by telling amusing tales and asking insightful questions. When Rasmussen heard that the gentleman was the head of the Swedish National Railway, he told him of his desire to one day visit Lapland by rail—if only he could afford the journey. He suspected that he might feel some kinship with the Lapps, or Sami, the indigenous people of northern Norway, Sweden and Finland as well as Russia's Kola Peninsula. Perhaps they would remind him of Greenlanders and his homeland. Later on during the dinner—and this was not entirely a surprise to the charming young writer—the railway magnate invited him to make the trip as a guest of the Swedish National Railway.

Later in the evening, Rasmussen became bored with the string of speeches. At a pause in the agenda, he bounded up to the front of the room to make his own, unscheduled, speech. It was initially met with polite reserve and some indignation—after all, who was this young underdressed upstart? By the end of his rousing speech, however, Rasmussen had won over the entire room with a lively toast to sport and to life. One of the men he impressed was the famous Swedish artist and writer Albert Engström, who took an instant liking to Rasmussen and agreed to pay his hotel bill if he would write an article for Engström's magazine, *Strix*.

Briefly freed from financial pressures, Rasmussen used the opportunity to begin planning his trip to Lapland. He negotiated an advance from the magazine *Berlingske Tidende* for a series of articles based on his travels. He then set off to the far north, to the outer edge of Scandinavia on the coast of the Arctic Ocean. This was way beyond where the railroad penetrated, past the large, dense forests and into the plains of stunted trees where travel was possible only by skis or horse- or reindeer-drawn sleighs. Over the months of his journey, he was stuck in blizzards, crammed into small sleeping huts ripe with the smell of unwashed bodies and the sounds of snoring. He ate reindeer meat roasted over an open fire and reveled in the hardships of the trail and the people who lived on the edge of civilization.

During his travels to Lapland, Rasmussen met many Swedes, Finns and Norwegians, as well as Sami. Although Danish, Norwegian and Swedish are similar written languages, the only spoken language Rasmussen had in common with all the people he met was English, which was used by quite a few northerners as a sort of lingua franca. The Sami reminded him of his beloved Greenlanders and made a deep impression on him. One man in particular features in Rasmussen's account of the early part of his journey: Silok, a young man on his way to seek work at an ore quarry that Rasmussen would also be visiting. Striking up a friendship, they discovered they were both avid skiers and decided on a short expedition. Rasmussen described their shared joy of launching themselves off ridges and curving down the pristine slopes, making tracks around each other and winding through the fresh snow of a sparse pine forest. Silok was an exuberant skier who also reveled in the wilderness and the sheer joy of exploring. "When he stood and looked down over the steepest slope, and raised his head and arms," Rasmussen wrote, "he looked like a bird who sailed with the wind. Across the plains, he flew until he collapsed in the snow and laughed uncontrollably with joy at the excellent lead."

Reaching the bottom of a hill, Silok stopped, cocked his ear and asked Rasmussen if he heard anything. "No," Rasmussen replied. They listened again and heard what at first seemed like thunder but was actually the sound of dynamite and machinery. The two youths skied over the hill, and their adventure ended. Before them lay a profusion of rail lines and welding machinery, incandescent lamps and trucks. Loud explosions shook the air. In an instant the skiers were taken from one world to another, from a wilderness offering fun and adventure to a harsh industrial reality. A few days later, Rasmussen, walking the streets of the nearby town, found Silok collapsed in a snowbank, in a drunken stupor, with vomit staining his coat. Apparently the young Sami had spent his wages on liquor, which though illegal was readily available.

Rasmussen's interpretation of his experience in Lapland took a broad view; in his estimation, life should embrace personal freedom and aspects of the natural world as well as its unexplained phenomena. He drew a comparison between the mythical past, where magic reigned and strange supernatural occurrences were common, and the clear and rational present, where machines blasted mountains and tore down forests. "There is war now in Lapland, and the combatants are two cultures. And the new must prevail, because it carries with it the future. But any victory causes death. The Lapps will be conquered in their own land and depart with the quiet resignation of the condemned, leaving the new people forging ahead with railways and dynamite. And they will die just as quietly and unobtrusively as they have always lived up there."

Rasmussen's stories of his time with the Sami are entertaining and lively, but they can also be viewed as a subtle defense of the lives and culture of a quiet and simple people, against a history of exploitation and contempt. Rasmussen instinctively felt a kinship with the Sami, a feeling apparently absent in many of the Scandinavian travelers he met. Perhaps he perceived something of the Greenlander in them, as he claimed, or perhaps it was his inborn sense for sniffing out injustice. Whatever the case, Rasmussen detailed the historical abuses of the Sami by the southerners, including Christian missionaries calling their shamans devils and working to destroy their religion. He also discussed the condescension and prejudice that he witnessed throughout the region. Rasmussen had a great respect for the Sami way of life, for their resigned attitude toward the vagaries of fate, toward the way fortune could turn from good to bad and back again, for their pleasure in the smallest of kindnesses. He described their folklore, religion and contemporary practices as well as their songs, stories and poetry. He portrayed the venerable culture of reindeer herding, as well as their present situation: how some Sami were settling down, intermarrying with southerners and farming or raising cattle, while others were continuing with a nomadic lifestyle, following the reindeer herds. In recounting his trip, he tried to give a rounded portrait of the Sami culture, blended with his own travelogue as he toured their land. It was a novel and intriguing literary style, an approach he would perfect in later years.

Although he did not formalize his thoughts then, Rasmussen began thinking broadly and critically about the world and its people. He lamented the passing of the old ways as traditional culture gave way to the juggernaut of modernity, as tradition and myth were replaced by the soullessness of the market economy. As he toured northern Scandinavia, Rasmussen developed the themes that would prevail throughout his many future literary works. In the end, he was convinced that to achieve understanding and acceptance, people needed to overlook the Sami's apparent material poverty and see their rich inner life. It was the first expression of an idea that would so powerfully inform his own life—that social culture, not its architecture or mode of locomotion or diet or clothing, was the true mark of a society's soul. "There was once a time here on earth," Rasmussen wrote, "when there was less wisdom and more happiness. Men were more simple and more reasonable than now, and we are told that they lived life for life's sake." Here he expressed a philosophy that would accompany him all his life, a vision that led him to his great interest in the mythical world of the Arctic's native peoples.

If the Sami reminded Rasmussen of the Inuit of his native Greenland, then surely the battle between the modern, industrial world and the ancient, mythological and natural world would be coming to Greenland as well. Rasmussen saw the destruction and the loss of ancient culture; most important, he saw a great loss of freedom in the new world order, in the progression from traditional societies to market societies, and perhaps a crushing of the spirit. The Sami's former freedom, just like the freedom of the Greenlanders, came with a price: the hardship of living on the harsh fringes of the world. But what would happen when there was nowhere left to escape, when even the fringes were overtaken by civilization?

BALANCING OUT HIS philosophical musings about culture, technological change and the meaning of life, Rasmussen had some more earthy adventures as he rode the rails around Lapland. Once, he shared a railcar with a crowd of railway laborers who broke out their potent bootleg "dynamite" liquor and began swigging. When Rasmussen declined to accept an offered bottle, the laborers became enraged, goading him until he took a big gulp of the fiery liquid. Not accustomed to alcohol, he became so intoxicated that he passed out, later waking up on a railway platform. Luckily, the laborers had put him off at his destination. On another occasion, he was traveling from northern Sweden to the Norwegian city of Narvik by reindeer sled. Although his Sami companion was experienced at managing the notoriously unpredictable animals, one of the larger reindeer went berserk, turned around and charged the sled, and attacked the passengers—apparently a not-uncommon occurrence. Rasmussen and his friend quickly turned the sled over and crawled underneath it while the bad-tempered beast vented its frustration by stomping its hooves and bashing the sled's runners with its antlers until its tantrum subsided. The crisis over, the travelers continued on their way.

From the northernmost coast of Norway, Rasmussen took a steamer south to Tromsø, the northern Norwegian city in which a young Roald Amundsen was testing and refitting his newly purchased ship *Gjøa*, before launching it toward the Northwest Passage and embarking on a meteoric career as a polar explorer. Rasmussen had no real intention of staying any longer in Tromsø than the time it took his steamer to dock and refit for the southward journey. But apparently he was distracted, not for the first time, by a girl. Having gotten lost while wandering the outskirts of the city, he noticed the young woman approaching and crossed the street to talk to her. At first she was afraid because of his ragged appearance, but after he reassured her that he intended no harm, they became friends and she brought him down to the harbor. Rasmussen decided it would be more fun to remain with her in Tromsø than to board his ship. When the ship sailed, he was partying with his newfound friend in the town of Charlottenborg, near the mountains.

Rasmussen eventually returned from his travels in Lapland, but not to Copenhagen. He rented cheap accommodation in Stockholm and began writing articles for magazines. It was here, conveniently far from Copenhagen and his family, that he received word that he was to be a father. The child had been conceived with Anna Olivia, the butcher's daughter, the previous November, before Rasmussen left Copenhagen to cover the Nordic Games in Stockholm.

The child, Oda Amalie, was born in the Copenhagen Birth Foundation, a discreet refuge where women could go for the later months of their pregnancies. She was given up for adoption, which was arranged by a local pastor on July 12, 1901. The parents remained anonymous, but the financial responsibility was probably borne by Rasmussen's father because Knud was still in Sweden and had no money. There is no doubt that the now twenty-two-year-old Rasmussen knew of the child's birth, yet he remained in Stockholm throughout the fall of 1901, writing to his parents, apologizing and admitting his failure and irresponsibility, but only alluding vaguely to the reason: "I have been so unhappy that it has been quite impossible to write and think . . . I have failed terribly, now I have penance to do the rest of my life." He announced to his family that the best thing for him would be to keep traveling, and in fact a few months later he was planning his first expedition to Greenland with Ludvig Mylius-Erichsen. "Think of me, and do not forget that I am your unhappy son Knud." It is not clear how many people were aware of his predicament. When Peter Freuchen wrote his biography of Rasmussen in the 1930s, he did not mention his friend's secret child, either because Rasmussen, out of embarrassment or shame, never mentioned her during their long seasons of isolated travel, or because of an unwritten pact to keep the child a secret.

At some point while Rasmussen was ensconced in Stockholm, removed from the turbulent domestic events in Copenhagen, he decided to turn the events and ideas stemming from his experiences in Lapland into a book. He wanted not only to tell the tales of his travels but also to further explore his opinions of the Sami people and the clash of cultures. He had little money, so he lived cheaply in a garret, diligently plugging away at the manuscript day and night. Freuchen told the perhaps apocryphal story of how Rasmussen remained awake and alert throughout the night while toiling over his manuscript. Seeing an advertisement in a magazine proclaiming that "Sleep is Milk," Rasmussen decided that "maybe that is so, but then maybe milk is also sleep!" When he needed to stay up he would go to a store, buy a bottle of skim milk and drink it, and then work all night. After many months of work, he had produced a neatly typed manuscript and sent it to a prominent publisher in Copenhagen. A letter arrived soon after: the company would be pleased to publish his manuscript on Lapland, if he would agree to cover part of the expense. After all, who would buy a book on the Sami, however well written?

Rasmussen, who had by now returned to Copenhagen and was living in another ratty garret, still had no money. When he approached his father to see if he would help with the publication, his father refused to pay, claiming that the work was too good for such poor treatment, and urged his son to be patient. Rasmussen was already working with Mylius-Erichsen on their upcoming Greenland expedition, which would surely last several years, so his father reasoned the book could wait: Rasmussen wouldn't be in Denmark to see it in print anyway. He moved into his parents' home in Lynge as the final preparations for the trip were being made.

With the problem of Knud's unwanted child only months in the past, the elder Rasmussen was enthusiastic about his son's Greenland plan. He had given up hope that Knud would take an interest in theology, study to become a priest, and return to Greenland as he himself had done. Perhaps he reasoned that removing the young man from the temptations of Copenhagen could only be a benefit. Moreover, in Greenland the vicar still had connections who might keep an eye on his son.

3

THE DANISH
LITERARY EXPEDITION

It was midday, and a ray of red sunlight penetrated the haze,
like the reflection of a fire very far away; on the south-west
wing the colours were sharp and yellow, the sky overcast and
rent with gashes of blue. The dark blue precipices at the edge of
the glacier itself stood out like walls against the soft, red blush
at the summit; but the ice on the sea, out beyond the glacier,
gleamed pale green in the daylight. This was the Polar day in
all its splendour.

It is good sometimes to feel the power of Nature. You bend
in silence and accept the beauty, without words.

—Knud Rasmussen,
The People of the Polar North

A FTER THE LUTHERAN missionary Hans Egede visited
Greenland in 1721 and set in motion the Danish colonization, or re-colonization, of the island, Denmark had kept the land
mostly isolated. Foreign ships were discouraged from sailing there
except in emergencies, and even Danish citizens were forbidden
to visit without government approval. As a result, Greenland was

remote from both Europe and America in a way not conceivable today. Because only Danish government officials and missionaries were allowed to visit the remote colony, Rasmussen couldn't return, though he had been born there. Even if he could find a ship willing to take him to Greenland, it would be, if not technically illegal, at least in defiance of Danish government regulations.

This isolationist policy stemmed from the Danish government's paternalistic desire to allow native Greenlanders to avoid commercial exploitation so that they could adapt more slowly to outside cultural influences. As a result, by the early twentieth century, no travelers or journalists had visited the colony to report on local conditions.

Ludvig Mylius-Erichsen, who had been Rasmussen's companion on his voyage to Iceland, was determined to change that. An outspoken journalist, poet, and law student, Mylius-Erichsen, then about thirty years old and on the staff of the prominent newspaper *Politiken*, had discussed with government officials the possibility of visiting Greenland. He had been planning the expedition since being inspired by his discussions with Rasmussen during their voyage to Iceland. Mylius-Erichsen wanted to tour the southern "civilized" regions of Greenland in order to compare them with the distant northern communities that Rasmussen had always dreamed of visiting. He called his expedition the Danish Literary Expedition because he hoped to find things to write about when he toured the island. Perhaps he would uncover corruption or government incompetence, which would make for good magazine and newspaper articles and fit nicely with his antiestablishment disposition.

As he didn't speak Greenlandic, Mylius-Erichsen was excited that the charismatic Rasmussen, who could serve as a guide and cultural interpreter, was eager to join the Danish Literary Expedition. They would need other expedition members, so Rasmussen convinced a painter, Count Harald Moltke, to join them.

Moltke, then thirty years old, was experienced in northern travel, if not northern culture. He had made several trips to Lapland and Iceland, and even a brief trip to southern Greenland, where he had worked as an artist for a geological expedition. In the coming months, Mylius-Erichsen recruited a fourth expedition member, the twenty-five-year-old Danish physician Dr. Alfred Bertelsen.

Financing the voyage was another issue. Mylius-Erichsen worked tirelessly to secure a grant from the Carlsberg Foundation, a charitable foundation that had been established by the brewer and philanthropist J.C. Jacobsen in 1876. The Carlsberg Foundation was the world's first foundation funded by private industry to support the arts and sciences, particularly in the north. Later, the Carlsberg Foundation was to cover costs for Rasmussen's various other Greenlandic undertakings. Rasmussen, meanwhile, made a brief trip to Kristiania (now Oslo) in the spring of 1902 to speak to the now-famous Norwegian explorer and statesman Fridtjof Nansen to secure his support in breaking down any barriers the Danish government might erect to block the expedition. Happily for Rasmussen, not only was Nansen in favor of the endeavor, he was also quite taken with the young Greenlander's enthusiasm and prospects. He suggested that Rasmussen would make an excellent ethnographer, adding: "Of course, your work does not end with a description of West Greenland and the Smith Sound Eskimos—you must go on to Cumberland and Alaska, and you have benefits like no other researcher before you." Around the same time, the young Norwegian Roald Amundsen, who was also planning his first major adventure— sailing through the Northwest Passage—was seeking Nansen's advice and support as well. These early meetings reflected changing attitudes in Denmark: the notion that isolation was the best policy for the Inuit was eroding. Thus, despite some initial resistance from Danish officials, after Mylius-Erichsen's second application, and bolstered by Nansen's endorsement, there was no more opposition to the expedition from Denmark's director of Greenlandic affairs.

Throughout the winter and spring of 1902, Mylius-Erichsen and Rasmussen calculated and purchased the necessary provisions, then tested and collected various types of equipment and clothing. As the only one who had any experience living in Greenland and was familiar with the traditional methods of travel and hunting, Rasmussen knew that nothing they could buy in Copenhagen in the way of clothing, dogsleds, harnesses and tools would be anywhere near as useful as what they could obtain in Greenland. He wrote notes to his relatives in Greenland informing them of his arrival and mentioning that he might need supplies.

Finally, in late May, the day for the Danish Literary Expedition's departure arrived. Owing to Mylius-Erichsen's connections in the press and the fact that this was the first civilian expedition to visit Greenland, the event caused great fanfare. The ship made a two-week voyage to Greenland, first arriving at the colonial outpost of Godthåb (now Nuuk) in southwest Greenland, and then sailed north to Rasmussen's old home, Ilulissat, where the adventurers planned to overwinter, acquiring additional equipment and dogs before setting off for the north in the following spring. Mylius-Erichsen hired one of Rasmussen's old Greenlander friends, Jørgen Brønlund, to act as an interpreter and worker. Brønlund, who had received a year's leave from his position as a catechist and teacher, was eager to join the expedition with his old boyhood friend. Rasmussen was not only pleased to have his friend join the expedition, he was also relieved: he hated acting as a translator, conveying and explaining other people's thoughts and ideas into a different language. He lacked the patience for this, as he had too many of his own ideas to convey. He was too much of a conversationalist to be satisfied with merely communicating the conversations of others.

In Ilulissat, Rasmussen was warmly welcomed by those who remembered him from his childhood. The Danish Literary Expedition members stayed in Rasmussen's old home at the invitation of the new pastor, Gustav Osterman. Rasmussen's connections in the local community ensured that they soon acquired dogs and sleds, and now they began to learn how to drive them— Mylius-Erichsen and Moltke had never done it. As training for the coming season, Mylius-Erichsen, a demanding and somewhat impractical leader, wanted to launch an excursion across Disko Island and back to test the expedition's equipment and gain experience. Moltke didn't want to go and was content to remain in Ilulissat, sketching and drawing. Undaunted, the other three members set out to cross the island. This first venture proved to be a disaster: Mylius-Erichsen was a poor dog driver and never seemed to get the knack of it; he was also at a disadvantage in not understanding the Greenlandic language or culture. When angry, Mylius-Erichsen roared, annoying everyone near him. Brønlund, too, was impatient and irritable.

Their tents were blown down by the terrific mountain winds, and several dogs ran away after gnawing through their leather harnesses. The weather was foul and they remained stuck in the mountains; the food ran low and they began eating the dogs' rations of frozen fish and seal, eventually killing some of the remaining dogs for food before the storm broke. Finally they straggled into Qeqertaq, where Rasmussen had family—Uncle Carl and Aunt Augustine lived there. Seeing the trekkers' desperate condition, Carl outfitted them with new clothing and gave Rasmussen twelve dogs for the rest of the journey. A few days later they reached Uummannaq, farther north on the coast, where another of Rasmussen's uncles, Jens Fleischer, lived. They spent several days relaxing there while Rasmussen visited local storytellers and collected legends about the land and its people.

The fiasco exposed difficulties in the relationship between Rasmussen and Mylius-Erichsen, who regularly quarreled with each other. Both men had literary ambitions, and Mylius-Erichsen feared that Rasmussen's work about Greenlanders' imagination and thoughts would compete with his plan to write a history of Greenland. Although the two writers were working on two very different projects that would never really compete, the tension between them remained. Mylius-Erichsen, the official leader of the expedition so far as Denmark was concerned, was also annoyed that wherever they went, Rasmussen was treated as the natural leader, on account of his family ties, fluency in the language and dog-driving skills. The unfortunate Moltke needed several months to mediate the quarrel between the two men. Nevertheless, by March 1903, they were sufficiently reconciled to make the final acquisitions of dogs and equipment for the journey north.

As the five men dogsledded north to Upernavik ("the Springtime Place") in the spring of 1903, they passed through numerous tiny communities and seminomadic settlements. Rasmussen, the first to arrive, was regularly greeted by villagers clapping him on the back and congratulating him, ignoring the others. He was also given gifts of frozen fish for his dogs, which he shared with the other members of the expedition. While the others went about their various pursuits in the communities, including Dr. Bertelsen's cursory medical examinations of the villagers and treating of their minor ailments, Rasmussen was so delighted to be back in Greenland that he spent most of his time chatting and gossiping with the local people, telling stories and listening to others' tales, happy to be surrounded by the Greenlandic language again.

On reaching Upernavik, the northernmost community in "Danish" Greenland with a government outpost, the visitors were welcomed as usual. There Rasmussen organized a series of celebrations and parties, including a dance in which the participants donned a succession of costumes during the evening. The villagers advised the travelers to stay through the winter and to catch a boat back to Denmark the next summer; their planned journey north was too long and hazardous to contemplate. From Upernavik it was almost four hundred miles north and west, paralleling the frozen shores of Melville Bay to Cape York and the northernmost human settlement in the world. Rasmussen recalled their warnings: "Whoever wished to go there, must travel with the South wind, right up to the Lord of the wild northern gales."

Not to be swayed, at the end of April all the members of the expedition but one set off for the north. Dr. Bertelsen, the lone holdout, declined to venture north of "Danish" Greenland. Perhaps he had tired of the quarreling between Rasmussen and Mylius-Erichsen. He remained in Upernavik and then headed south to continue his medical research and treatments in remote Greenland communities.* Rasmussen found a replacement for Dr. Bertelsen: Gabriel Olsen, whom everyone called Gaba, was the nephew of a local Danish trader. Yet the northbound party remained small, now with six members: Rasmussen, Mylius-Erichsen, Moltke, Brønlund, Gaba and the Inuk hunter Elias. No other Greenlanders could be tempted to make the journey because so many terrible things had been heard about the pagan northerners. For all of them, it was a venture into the unknown.

The people of Upernavik all knew they had kinsmen living north of Melville Bay beyond the ice barrier. A Greenlander elder

---

*Dr. Bertelsen remained in Greenland for many years, until 1927.

told Rasmussen a story he remembered from his childhood. The man's story, detailing a close encounter from the foggy past, began: "Once upon a time there was a man who lived farther north than any of the settlements. He hunted bears every spring on a dog-sledge."

On one of his journeys, the man noticed unfamiliar sled tracks that led farther north. He decided to follow them to find out more, and the next spring, during his annual bear hunt, he set off earlier in the season than usual. He drove his dogs north for three days and came upon a collection of stone-and-snow huts that had a strange design, one using narwhal tusks for the roof beams and support posts. Fresh sled tracks led away from the huts, and he never saw any of the people. Returning south, he went on with his life until the next spring, when he again headed north on his annual bear hunt. He loaded his sled with wood, a rare and valuable commodity. Still he encountered no people, just the evidence of their tracks mysteriously disappearing to the north. He was afraid to venture farther north than he had come, so he buried the wood in the snow near their houses as a gift and departed.

On his third expedition, the man "raised the best team of dogs that he had ever had, and earlier than was his custom he drove north after bears and the strange people. When at last he reached the village it was just as it had been the other years: the inhabitants had gone, but in the snow, where he had left his wood, they had hidden a large bundle of walrus tusks, and inside, in the entrance passage, lay a magnificent bitch and her puppies. These were the return gifts of the strangers. He put them on his sledge and drove back home; but the people who lived north of all other men he never found." Nor had any other Greenlander, apparently, and nor did routine trade ever develop between the two regions. So it was into this unknown that, in the spring of 1903, three Danes and three Greenlanders—with sixty-seven dogs hauling

six sleds packed with provisions and gifts—ventured north to ful-
fill Rasmussen's childhood dream.

SIXTY-SEVEN SLED dogs consume a lot of meat. During the
winter a single dog at rest can consume 4,500 calories per day,
and on an active day, up to an astonishing 10,000 calories. In addition to carrying the usual camp equipment and travel clothing,
the sleds were loaded with vast quantities of frozen seal and fish.
Even so, it was impossible to carry sufficient food for men and
dogs on an excursion they estimated would take many weeks.
In order to fill that many stomachs for weeks of hard travel, the
travelers knew they would have to rely on hunting, which added
a degree of uncertainty to the expedition. After hauling all day,
the dogs became hungry and often dangerously feral. They would
snarl at each other and fight if no food was available and would
then devour their leather harnesses and traces. Roald Amundsen
faced similar problems on his race to the South Pole several years
later, in 1911, when his dogs were starving and he and his men
huddled in their tents for fear of being attacked by their dogs.
Only Rasmussen, Elias and Brønlund were experienced dog drivers and hunters, so the success of the expedition was disproportionately heaped on their shoulders.

As they traveled around the rim of the ice-encrusted Melville
Bay, their daily routine was to eat breakfast, pack up, sled and ski
as long as daylight allowed—the days were getting longer with
the coming of summer—and then set up camp as the light waned.
After eating, they would smoke their pipes and write in their journals. Mylius-Erichsen was tasked with taking accurate distance
measurements, and Moltke was assigned to sketch prominent
geographical features and correct the expedition's rudimentary

maps wherever possible. No one knew anything about the terrain or the weather they were likely to encounter as they pushed north. Despite the April sun shining almost constantly, the temperature was a bracing –4° Fahrenheit (–20° Celsius) on the coldest days.

After nearly two weeks of hard travel, Rasmussen and Elias ventured ahead to break trail and hunt. The dogs were well trained in what Rasmussen called "the bear signal." When a hunter found evidence of bear tracks, he repeatedly yelled in a way that to the dogs signified an imminent feast of fresh bear meat. They would go wild with anticipation and surge forward with renewed vigor to catch the nearby bear. Melville Bay was one of the greatest polar bear hunting regions in Greenland because the prevailing west winds blew giant icebergs into the bay from Lancaster Sound and Jones Sound, and these icebergs sometimes had bears on them. On this occasion, the dogs unerringly led the hunters to two polar bears, which Rasmussen and Elias shot and triumphantly brought back to the others. The great beasts were cut up quickly before the meat froze, and meal-sized quantities were portioned out for the dogs and steaks cut for the explorers.

Travel conditions deteriorated even more near the Cape York headland, and the dogsleds now struggled over immense ice blocks and pressure ridges. The dogs were behaving better on a diet of polar bear meat and had stopped eating their harnesses and straps, but the men endured freezing nights in their tents, as they didn't have either the time or the knowledge to construct snow houses. Moltke spent hours outside sketching and drawing, perched on wind-lashed rock promontories and ice hummocks, until exhaustion and cold led to his illness. While the others crawled into their freezing sleeping bags, Moltke sweated and burned with fever, unable to eat or sleep. Also unable to ski, he was placed on a sled and pulled. Rasmussen led the procession, breaking trail for the others.

When the bear meat ran out, the dogs once again became wild with hunger. The expedition had left some provisions behind to lighten its load and now had barely enough food for a single good daily meal for its members. At this point they encountered the remnants of some abandoned snow-and-stone houses, and what looked like fresh tracks leading north. "The first time one sees a house of this description," Rasmussen recorded, "one is struck by how little human beings can have and still be content. It is all so primitive, and has such an odour of paganism and magic. A cave like this, skilfully built with gigantic blocks of stone, makes one think of half supernatural beings. You see them, in your fancy, pulling and tearing at raw flesh, you see the blood dripping from their fingers, and you are seized yourself with a strange excitement at the thought of the extraordinary life that awaits you in their company."

His excitement was not universally shared.

Gaba and Elias were afraid that people lurked nearby, ready to attack. When Mylius-Erichsen crawled into the entrance of one of the houses, he kept a revolver in his hand as a defense against surprise attack by polar bears, Inuit or feral dogs. He described the huts as "all worn, sooty, greasy, disgusting smelling and presumably vermin filled. A creepy cave of wild beasts." But it was worse than that: the huts were empty. There was "no one to greet us inside—not to put even the meanest food before us and say: Eat up! No one to give us water from melted ice and say, Drink!" In one hut, the men discovered a frozen seal, which they cut up with axes and fed to the ravenous dogs. Soon they would quite happily spend many months in similar dwellings.

Exhausted, they collapsed for a rest in the sun after the preliminary exploration. When they awoke, they inspected the sled tracks leading north and noticed that the tracks seemed narrower and the people's footprints smaller, but the dogs' paw prints were larger. Things were different here, at the rim of the world. Rasmussen, Elias and Gaba concluded that the tracks were fresh and that perhaps they could overtake the mysterious travelers. After they had eaten the last of their food and drunk a cup of warm cocoa, Mylius-Erichsen unpacked three Danish flags and tried to stamp them into the still-frozen ground. They were able to gather enough rocks to build a cairn around the base to hold the flags, and he conducted a brief ceremony that would purportedly take possession of the land for Denmark: all the territory they were about to explore would be "enclosed in the Danish kingdom and be a part of our fatherland."

The ceremony complete, four of the men loaded their sleds "and drove off along the glorious rocky coast, into the clear, light night." Because they were exhausted and Moltke remained dangerously ill, the group decided that Rasmussen and Brønlund would continue north, following the elusive tracks, while Mylius-Erichsen and Moltke would follow at a slower pace. Elias and Gaba would remain behind to try to catch seals at blowholes in the ice. By this time Moltke was so ill that the others feared he was dying, and he was strapped in his sleeping bag onto Mylius-Erichsen's sled, where he continued to slip in and out of consciousness.

Rasmussen and Brønlund surged ahead, following the tracks as fast as their exhausted dogs could carry them. "All the provisions we could take were a few biscuits and a box of butter," Rasmussen wrote. "Still, we had our rifles to fall back upon." Soon the two men came upon even more recent sled tracks and a cairn of stones mounded over a freshly caught seal: people were nearby. They drove on, for another fifty-six miles. Nearly dropping from exhaustion, they stopped, ate a little butter, and again roused the dogs. After continuing north for a few more hours, with a bitter wind in their faces, they saw unmistakable moving dots on the horizon, dark against the white. "The dogs dropped their tails and pricked up their ears," Rasmussen recalled. "We murmured the signal again between our teeth, and the snow swirled up beneath their hind legs."

The two weary travelers surged across the snow plain toward two fur-clad figures, one driving a dogsled and the other riding on it. The strangers had spotted Rasmussen and Brønlund in the distance and now turned around to race toward them. Rasmussen and the approaching man leaped off the runners of their sleds and ran alongside one another, as was the custom, greeting each other warmly while their dogs barked in excitement. The strangers, Maisanguak and his wife, Meqo, stared in astonishment at each other—astonishment that grew when Rasmussen explained who he and his companion were. Maisanguak yelled back to his wife, "White men! White men! White men have come on a visit!"

The couple were returning to their home, about fifteen miles up the coast of Melville Bay. Four other families lived there, in three stone houses and five snow huts, and even more people were at the beach at Agpat (Saunders Island), where the hunting was particularly good at this time of year. Maisanguak and Meqo were so excited that they decided to join Rasmussen and Brønlund and lead them to Agpat. They soon met two other men on sleds who joined the group, and they all proceeded toward Agpat. The drivers screamed, "White men! White men!" and people rushed from their dwellings to behold the spectacle. Rasmussen described the excitement: "Our dogs drooped their tails and pricked up their ears as a many-tongued roar from the land reached us. And then, like a mountain slide, the whole swarm rushed down to the shore, where we had pulled up—a few old grey-haired men and stiff-jointed old crones, young men and women, children who could hardly toddle, all dressed alike in these fox and bear-skin furs, which created such an extraordinarily barbaric first impression. Some came with long knives in their hands, with bloodstained arms and upturned sleeves, having been in the midst of flaying operations when we arrived, and all this produced a very savage effect."

THE EXPEDITION HAD reached the Etah Eskimos—Inughuit, Polar Eskimos, Polar Inuit or Thule people, as they have been variously called—who lived farther north than any other people on earth, in a land Rasmussen called "The Kingdom of the North Wind." They had reached the land of the "New People," a group cut off from the more southern Greenlanders by the two-hundred-mile ice barrier around Melville Bay. Even to Rasmussen, this first encounter with the Polar Inuit in Etah was a shock and a revelation. "Never in my life have I felt myself to be in such wild, unaccustomed surroundings, never so far, so very far away from home, as when I stood in the midst of the tribe of noisy Polar Eskimos on the beach at Agpat." While the children snuck glances from around sleds and huts, dashing away if any of the strangers looked at them, the men passed around, among themselves and to their visitors, a frozen raw walrus heart, each gnawing off a chunk of meat as a symbol of welcome and camaraderie.

Contrary to common belief at the time, the Polar Inuit were not entirely isolated from contact with the outside world. Whalers had periodically put into sheltered bays in the region for brief summer visits. Other explorers had been in contact with them, including the British captain John Ross, the first European to encounter these people, whom he called the "Arctic Highlanders," in 1818. The British mariners had traded some beads, cloth, mirrors, sundry metal utensils and knives for furs and meat. Later contacts included the Scot William Penny in 1850–1851, and Americans Elisha Kent Kane in 1853–1855 and Charles Francis Hall in 1872–1873, although their cultural exchanges with the Polar Inuit were limited. The American explorer Robert Peary had visited the region in 1892 and 1894 and later used the area as the base for his North Pole expeditions. Nevertheless, these Inuit were not accustomed to having Europeans arrive from the south by dogsled; this was the first arrival of Europeans by dogsled.

Rasmussen immediately noticed that while the northerners' language was similar to that spoken in southern Greenland, differing only in dialect and accent, their customs were different, causing occasional embarrassment: "On one's arrival at a settlement in Danish West Greenland, it is usual for the young women to help the newcomers off with their outdoor clothes. Now, for a moment, I forgot where I was, and as the Greenlandic custom is, stretched out my foot towards a young girl who was standing by my side, meaning her to pull off my outer boots. The girl grew embarrassed, and the men laughed. There was that winning bashfulness about her that throws attraction over all Nature's children; a pale blush shot across her cheek, like a ripple over a smooth mountain lake; she half turned away from me, and her black eyes looked uneasily out over the frozen sea."

"What is your name?"

"Others will tell you what my name is," she stammered.

"Aininaq is her name," put in the bystanders, laughing.

A jovial old man then came up to her and said with gravity:

"Do what the strange man asks you." And she stooped down at once and drew off my boots.

"Move away, let me come!" called out an old woman from the crowd, and she elbowed the people aside and forced her way through to my sledge.

"It was my daughter you were talking to!" she burst out eagerly. "Do you not think her beautiful?" and she rolled her little self-conscious eyes around.

But Aininaq had slipped quietly away from the crowd of curious beholders and hidden herself. It was only later that I learnt my request to her had been construed into a proposal of marriage.

RASMUSSEN HAD REACHED the land he was for many years to call home and to which he would often return. Once the New People had built a large snow house for their unexpected visitors, they helped to bring in the remaining sleds and members of the Danish Literary Expedition. Rasmussen and Brønlund spent the next two weeks shuttling between Etah and the caches of goods they had left behind, bringing exotic luxuries such as bread, preserves, canvas tents, tools and items Rasmussen considered indispensable, such as his phonograph and records. Although ice and snow lingered here in May, men and women threw off their clothes and played in the welcome warmth as the dogs sought relief from the heat by the ice edge, their tongues lolling in the sun. Moltke, who had been "transformed from a young, healthy man into a dirty skeleton," was slowly nursed back to health. Once the travelers were settled in the community and given food, rest and shelter, Moltke resumed sketching, now of the people and activities in this exotic land.

Not long after the visitors had settled in, a blood-curdling cry issued from the stone hut of a powerful shaman, Saqdloq. As he was the greatest and oldest member of the tribe, everyone rushed over to investigate. Saqdloq was about to conjure spirits, and a hush went through the gathered crowd. "Every face bore the imprint of earnest reverence." Rasmussen peeked in the irregular window to behold the weathered old man sitting on a bench and drumming.

"When he saw my face at the window he stopped beating the drum, laughed up at me, and said: 'All foolery, silly humbug! Nothing but lies!' And he wagged his head apologetically."

Someone pulled Rasmussen back from the window and ordered him to be quiet, as no one could interfere in a spirit conjuring. "All foolery!" the old man repeated, with what Rasmussen called "genuine Eskimo sham modesty. A magician always precedes his conjurations with a few deprecating words about himself and his powers. And the more highly esteemed he is, the more anxious he is to pretend that his words are lies." The drumbeat grew louder and was soon joined by a slow murmuring that also grew louder and stronger as the spirit song plodded on. Others in the crowd hummed along or issued grunts and exclamations with the rhythm. Soon Saqdloq began to moan as if under a heavy weight. The sounds of a struggle could be heard, followed by a screech. "Ow! Ow! It is impossible! I am underneath! He is lying on me. Help me! I am too weak, I am not equal to it!"

Finally, Saqdloq's shrieks faded into convulsive sobbing. But the drum beat on, with rhythm and power. Then it stopped and the crowd grew uneasy. The shaman released a series of staccato barks: "The Evil Fate, misfortune-bringing spirit, the white men!" and then made some garbled sounds.

"The white men brought the Evil Fate with them, they had a misfortune-bringing spirit with them. I saw it myself, there are no lies in my mouth; I do not lie, I am no liar, I saw it myself!" The people looked toward the newcomers. In a long and disjointed speech, punctuated by howls, moans and words in a secret spirit language, the shaman pronounced that the evil spirit had touched Harald Moltke and made him sick. It had tainted many of the dogs, too, accounting for their illness. Then followed groaning, heavy breathing, the sounds of wrestling and clacking of stones and the relentless pounding of the drum. No one was to eat dog's flesh, he proclaimed. But the shaman's wife had eaten dog, she claimed in a weak voice, and she was now ill. The shaman roared louder in ululating howls mixed with deep laughter. He could be seen, despite his advanced age, contorting around the small chamber "like a wounded animal." Then, at last, the ordeal was over.

Once the evil spirit had been exorcised, the visitors were officially welcomed to the community. In a short time, Rasmussen impressed them with his skills; he proved to be one of the best dog drivers around, and one of the most skilled caribou hunters. With his unique ability to forge relationships, he was quickly accepted. The Inuit regarded him, rather than Mylius-Erichsen, as the natural leader of the expedition because he was proficient in the skills that were critical for their survival. Rasmussen was a good speaker and storyteller as well, and he quickly learned the subtleties of their distinct northern dialect. Most important of all, he was a good listener. He spent countless hours crouched in the stone huts or snow houses of the oldest people, listening intently to their stories, hearing their songs and poems.

He never wrote anything down when listening, just concentrated and memorized; afterward, he would rush to his hut and record what he had heard in a notebook. Neither did he carry or use scientific instruments of any kind, instead relying on his hosts and his own travel and survival skills to get around. "It would have destroyed their confidence in him," wrote Freuchen, "and their feeling of equality to see him pull out a theodolite or another magnetic instrument." Much later, after many expeditions and years of living in the region, Rasmussen would claim with perfect honesty that "no hunter exists up there with whom I have not hunted, and there is hardly a child whose name I do not know."

The six southerners spent from May to December of 1903 in the Cape York District. Living with "the neighbours of the North Pole," they experienced all the seasons. As the sun grew stronger in June, the snow melted and the oceanside cliffs came alive with ducks, petrels, guillemots, razorbills, gulls and kittiwakes, quarreling and screeching in "one great roiling wave of sound" as they fought for nesting space on the innumerable ledges and cracks. There were over fifty breeding species of birds in Greenland. "Things are beginning to wake up out there. Summer is coming!" was a common refrain as driftwood fires were lit in anticipation of the first great bird feast. Occasionally, melting ice dislodged in mighty chunks from the face of the cliff, and as it plummeted, it sent up vast clouds of squawking birds. The children would dash to the stones below the cliffs to collect the birds killed by the falling ice.

"In the spring, there are no regular hours for sleep in an Eskimo camp," Rasmussen wrote. "Life goes on by day and night, if the weather is good. A large open fire, kept burning briskly, assembles the people round the open-air banqueting place, and the constant coming and going of men who are starting out on fishing trips, and of those who are returning, keeps up life and interest round the fire all the time." The fire pit was the perfect setting for the charismatic Rasmussen to meet people and talk to them, to learn of their activities and make plans to join them on their journeys.

In summer, the land was transformed under the perpetual sunlight into a lichen and wildflower carpet profuse with life. "The sun is scorching our faces," Rasmussen wrote, "and the sun's rays, which are flung back by the endless icefields, force us to close our eyes, so brilliant are they." Foxes, stoats and Arctic hares wandered the rocky plains. Hunters pursued caribou, while kayakers searched for walrus and seal.

In spite of the beautiful weather, Moltke's recovery was slow and he could still barely walk. The members of the expedition decided they would cut their trip short and try to return south before winter fully set in again. At first they hoped whalers might appear in the bay and take them south. But when half of July passed with no ship arriving, they knew they couldn't wait any longer. Rasmussen decided to head north, to find out about a small boat reputedly owned by a man who had received it as a gift from Robert Peary. The boat would enable them to sail south before Melville Bay froze.

On July 17, he and Brønlund and two young local Inuit, Sidtluq and Qisunguaq, readied their sleds and dogs for the journey. It was hard going from the start. Inland travel was rough at that time of year, and they made slow progress, clambering over rocky outcroppings and headlands, wading through glacial streams wild with the summer melt, and following the snakes of unmelted snow while searching for a path for the sleds. They brought only sleeping bags, a little clothing and some sugar and biscuits on this trip—no tent and no meat: "Men don't drag meat with them in the height of summer," Rasmussen observed. Although it was summer, they were stranded by several storms that kept them hunkered down in caves for days at a time. The few duck eggs they found were insufficient nourishment. Finally, they shot a caribou and ended their "starvation fare." They spent many days telling stories to pass the time during a series of unrelenting storms, until Sidtluq grew impatient and began yelling into the sleet, "Stop the rain! Stop the rain!" When Rasmussen asked him what he was doing, Sidtluq calmly replied that "up among the rocks there lived powerful spirits who can command the wind and stop the downpours of rain."

But the rain and sleet did not stop. It continued relentlessly, and soon the men's feet were swollen from damp and cold. Then Qisunguaq began yelling at Rasmussen, blaming him for the unseasonal storms because Rasmussen had taken some items from a grave they had passed.

"You are so strange, you white men!" he yelled. "You collect things you will never require, and you cannot leave even the graves alone. All this calamity is the revenge of the dead. Perhaps we shall die of hunger. Just because you took those stupid things!" Rasmussen tried to explain that he had done as they had told him—exchanging tea, matches, blubber and meat for the scratching-pin, needle-case and curved knife he had taken— surely the corpse would have been satisfied with these "gifts to the soul"? But Qisunguaq would not be placated so easily.

"The thoughts of the dead are not as our thoughts," he sighed. "The dead are incomprehensible in their doings."

"Stop, stop the rain!" Sidtluq again called despairingly up to the rocks.

Even Brønlund was growing bored and irritated with their forced inactivity, and he called to Rasmussen: "Tell tales, and do not stop till we have forgotten where we are and think we are with them."

Soon, Rasmussen recalled, "memory hypnotises us back to experiences that lie behind; and fancy draws us ever in the same direction back to vanished well-being, when we knew no privations; back to the delicacies of the Danish-Greenlandic kitchen, to the magnificent splendour of the shops. And thus, when one of us gets well under way with his narrative, we succeed in forgetting for a moment where we are, and friends, who perhaps think of us no more, Danes and Greenlanders, file past us, while the roaring stream outside thunders and swells with the rain."

When the sun finally came out on July 25, many days of hard slogging remained before they would reach the place where a boat might be found. On one occasion they clambered up over 2,000-foot cliffs, hauling the sleds and dogs up the rocks with ropes, only to find that their destination was blocked and they would have to backtrack. After two more days of sledding, this time over glaciers, they encountered people who fortunately had food to share. Eventually they came to the small bay, only to discover that there was no boat in the district after all. One wonders if Rasmussen had gone on this journey as much for the adventure as to investigate the dubious likelihood of finding a seaworthy vessel in such an unlikely place.

Once back in the Agpat region near Saunders Island, Rasmussen and his companions, using boulders from a nearby cliff, built a winter house near the village. With no boat, they would have to wait until Melville Bay froze over again before heading south. "Up there then, in that cave half-buried in the cliff, we were to await our fate, the Winter and the Dark. We were going to pass the next few months of cold and night far north of the civilisation which so many of us regard as a necessity of life. Our tiny winter lair was of cold stones, and we had no stove to warm ourselves with, and no fire. And we should have to procure our food from day to day. And yet," he enthused, "I felt a warming wave of joy rush through my body, the joy which those who live on their travels feel most keenly: excitement at the rich possibilities of life!"

By September the nights were lengthening, the new ice was forming, and the village was anticipating the return of the moon and the stars. To celebrate, Rasmussen invited all the "happy people" to his hut for a party. He brought out his hand-cranked phonograph, played recorded opera music and doled out tea and currant biscuits to his guests. Moltke fired off some magnesium shells for makeshift fireworks. "This may sound all very childish and foolish," Rasmussen wrote, "read among the manifold resources of civilisation; but to us, up in that little Eskimo camp, it meant a great deal. Our spirits rose high and we saw our strange existence in a very festive light. In this marvellous land you can hold a perfect bacchanalia on a few cups of tea and a little mouldy bread."

He had obtained the currant biscuits from Roald Amundsen, whose ship *Gjøa* was in the vicinity in mid-August, pushing through the ice-choked waters of Melville Bay to pick up a cache of supplies that Amundsen had commissioned a Scottish whaling captain to deposit for him before launching his epic voyage through the Northwest Passage. While *Gjøa* was in the vicinity of Dalrymple Rock, two kayakers came around a giant iceberg and began to wave and yell at the Norwegians. "We were very anxious to make the acquaintance of the North Greenland Eskimo," Amundsen recalled, "of whom many strange things are reported. They were extremely lively, jabbered both together, threw their arms about and gesticulated. There was evidently something particular they wanted to tell us, but we, of course, could not understand a syllable." Soon there was the sound of gunfire, and a flotilla of six additional kayaks rounded the iceberg, one flying a Danish flag. It was Rasmussen and Mylius-Erichsen, on tour with their Inuit companions. They all enjoyed a festive congregation of "joyous confusion" while the Norwegian explorers loaded their supplies and shared the currant biscuits with the two Danes.

IRONICALLY, IT WAS around this time, in the fall of 1903, that the first news of the Danish Literary Expedition reached Copenhagen. The Scottish whaling ship *Diana* reported on the "pitiful" state of health of the three Danes when it had dropped off supplies for the Amundsen expedition near Saunders Island at the end of June. While Rasmussen was on his northern excursion, Mylius-Erichsen met Captain Adams of the *Diana* on the shore and brought him to the village to meet Moltke, who was still partly paralyzed. When Adams returned to Scotland, he described the three Danish expedition members as "pathetic, filthy and unclean, while oddly enough the two Eskimos were scrubbed, combed and looked to be brave men." His comments, intemperate and vague as they were, provoked controversy in Denmark. There was no communication except by sailing ship back then, so as far as anyone could tell the entire party might either be dead by the time the news arrived or might have traveled south to Danish Greenland and safety.

From our twenty-first-century vantage point, expecting instant communication via satellite phone, when the fate of explorers is nearly always known, and help can be dispatched with comparative speed, this uncertainty appears unbearable. At the time, Captain Adams's report gave rise to a fog of unsubstantiated rumors, speculation and sensational claims, often designed to attract attention. What if the Danes and Greenlanders were in danger, or dying, or trapped? What if they were in fact in desperate need of rescue? But if they were really in such a poor state, why had they not returned with Adams on the whaling ship?

"THE LOWER THE sun circles towards the horizon," Rasmussen wrote in *People of the Polar North*, "the lovelier in its vivid colouring the Polar country grows. Light and darkness wrestle in blood-red sunsets, and the clouds with the light behind them, crimson-gashed, glide out into the night." He and his companions had spent nearly eight months in the Cape York region, living among the New People in all seasons before it was finally safe for them to cross Melville Bay again on their way south. Darkness had come upon them months ago, and gloom ruled the land much of the time. The "visiting month," November, had come and gone, and people went about their business in this darkest time of the year with a mixture of anticipation and dread. The members of the Danish Literary Expedition had inspected the bone runners of their sleds for damage, repaired them and cut new leather harnesses for the dogs that would pull them. Without these preparations, the dark season would be deadly.

Mylius-Erichsen and Rasmussen had done much writing and thinking; they had each formed the foundations of their respective books, and their minds were filled with new ideas. Now it was January 1904, and they would make their second attempt to cross Melville Bay. In early December, they had ignored warnings of poorly frozen ice, setting off with eleven people and nine sleds, each hauled by a team of six to nine dogs. It was a difficult journey in the cold and dark of winter, with eerie shadows looming on the snow and the appearance of strange ice formations. They were turned back by open water. Once again Rasmussen was in the unexpected position of making decisions for the entire party, which now included several northern Inuit who wanted to visit their southern cousins, as well as one Inuk who wanted to return to Denmark with him. In fact, several young men had expressed an interest in visiting Denmark.

One of these was Qisunguaq, the young man with whom Rasmussen had traveled north and spent days holed up in a rocky cave waiting out a violent summer storm. Rasmussen enjoyed Qisunguaq's company, and they had become close companions on several journeys. In *The People of the Polar North*, Rasmussen writes of how Qisunguaq spoke to him of his desire to travel to Denmark.

"You have masters in your country?" he asked Rasmussen. "A man of wisdom and power, who can think thoughts for other people as well as himself, and tell one what to do?"

"Yes, that is what a master ought to be," Rasmussen replied.

"I should very much like to have a master, and I should like to choose you," Qisunguaq said.

"Perhaps you would get tired of it, Qisunguaq," Rasmussen replied. "All you men up here are accustomed to be the masters of your thoughts and actions yourselves."

"Yes; but a master gives the one who helps him possessions. That is what the great Peary always did up here. And I am fond of you; and I should like to possess something." Slowly Rasmussen learned Qisunguaq's story. Although he came from a respected household, his father had died in a fall when Qisunguaq was young, and he grew up having to provide for his mother and two younger siblings. He had never been able to acquire his own dogs or gun, and consequently, although he was twenty years old, he had no wife. "The desire to become the owner of something had taken hold of him," Rasmussen recalled. Qisunguaq knew that the men who had ventured north with Peary returned with valuable items. He wanted some for himself, to share with his younger brother and to help him gain a wife. Rasmussen agreed to take him south when they departed in the fall. But Qisunguaq soon had second thoughts.

"Riches and possessions are death," he burst out. "I will follow you far away south," he went on, "and you will keep your word and give me precious weapons, I know that. But amongst strangers I shall die. My body will not know life in other countries; rich in gifts, I shall be obliged to sacrifice the breath of my life to strangers."

"The spirits of the dead have talked with me; my words are wisdom, like the speech of our forefathers. I have seen hidden things!" he shouted and then began to tremble. Qisunguaq had closed his eyes and clenched his fists. He soon began singing a spirit song, which ended in great fits of sobbing.

"I held him by the shoulders to quiet him," Rasmussen wrote, but "he rushed at me with a roar, and for a long time we struggled together, stumbling in the dark over the stones. He pressed his face against my neck, as if he were trying to bite me, and ground his teeth with rage." Was he wrestling with his fear? The question remained unanswered, and they traveled in silence for the remainder of the journey. When Rasmussen went looking for Qisunguaq in the fall, to ask the young man whether he still wanted to go south, Qisunguaq replied that he had changed his mind: he had gotten married and would be heading north instead.

Another young man, Osarkrak, was also an orphan who desired the material wealth that was unobtainable in his present circumstances. He was cross-eyed and had a leg that could not stretch out fully, forcing him to walk with a bent gait, "like a bear that balances on his hind legs." Despite this, he was a good enough hunter and an excellent dog driver, but still he could not find a wife because of his imperfection. As a youth he had wandered between families, often sitting by himself outside to eat the food scraps tossed to him from within. Mylius-Erichsen wrote that Osarkrak "was poor because his legs were paralyzed. For that reason he was not a good hunter . . . With his little sled, built of many, small, joined pieces of wood, and pulled by only three dogs, he continually visited the settlements. The dark season he spent with one or another family willing to mend his clothing in exchange for his catch." Osarkrak was determined to better his standing by journeying south with Rasmussen.

THE JANUARY JOURNEY south across Melville Bay was "a terribly bad one." The hunting was poor, and the travelers ran low on food. The dogs in particular were starving, until a polar bear appeared on the ice ahead of them and they shot it. In early February, the party reached a food cache it had placed on the trip north. A few days later, on February 12, the sun rose briefly on the horizon for the first time in months, and soon after, the men saw a Danish flag fluttering in the wind. They had reached Upernavik. It was feared that they had perished in the north, so their sudden appearance in the village was cause for celebration. They spent several months in Upernavik to recover their strength before conditions improved with the return of the sun and they could continue south to Ilulissat. There they visited

with Rasmussen's uncle Jens Fleischer; but as they found no ship
to carry them farther, they continued south by dogsled to board a
ship there. Moltke decided to wait for a ship in Ilulissat, returning to Denmark on his own. Although Rasmussen was reluctant
to leave Greenland, he was equally reluctant to remain in one
place for too long. He had already developed the nomadic urge
that would characterize his life.

Part Two

MIDNIGHT

SUN

4

THE NEW PEOPLE

I have a little song to sing,
The little worn song of another,
But I sing it as were it mine,
Mine own dear little song.
And thus singing it, I play
With this worn little song,
Renewing it.

—Recorded and translated by
Kaj Birket-Smith in Upernavik,
during the Fifth Thule Expedition

NEWS OF RASMUSSEN's and Mylius-Erichsen's return to Copenhagen preceded their arrival. Disembarking from the British ship *Fox II* on November 7, 1904, they were greeted by throngs of admirers on the Copenhagen waterfront, given ovations and lavish bouquets, and presented with countless dinner invitations. Even for Rasmussen, who was perfectly comfortable with crowds, the adulation was overwhelming. He wrote that he felt "exhibited" with all the parties, speeches and interviews, and it took a while for the excitement to die down. He and Mylius-Erichsen were pestered by reporters for months, although, to

Rasmussen's irritation, they showed little real understanding or appreciation for his work and were more interested in the sensational aspects of the expedition, particularly in his Inuk companion Osarkrak. What was his life in the north like? What did he think of Copenhagen?

Even so, Rasmussen was quite willing to provide anecdotes, opinions and interviews to the press. He clarified that the rumors of their poor condition in Greenland were false and that Captain Adams's lurid report was probably a reflection of his inability to conceive of Europeans living like Inuit—stripped of the trappings of European culture, with no modern means of travel or pre-stocked food supplies. Contrary to expectations, the Danish Literary Expedition had shown that it was possible to live off the land as the Greenlanders did, and in the future Rasmussen would seldom travel in any other way.

As a result of the publicity, he was no longer merely an ambitious youth with big ideas, but a genuine celebrity. The Danish Literary Expedition had ventured to the fringes of the known world, had traveled in this mysterious land populated by little-understood people, and had returned with intriguing and previously unknown information about them. They had claimed Greenland's northern territory for Denmark, as an extension of the southern colony, and had established cultural, commercial and political ties with the most remote group of people then known to exist. It was an exciting and brilliant accomplishment, and the expedition's members were on their way to becoming national heroes.

Despite a two-and-one-half year absence, Rasmussen quickly rejoined his old circle of friends—the poets, musicians, writers and actors whom he had always chosen as his companions—and renewed and expanded his correspondence with luminaries in the Danish arts community and others who shared his interests, such as Fridtjof Nansen in Norway and the writer Albert Engström in Sweden. All were part of his ever-broadening social circle. And he no longer had to ask for paying work as a writer: his opinions were sought after by newspapers and magazines. He was learning to use the press just as the press used him. About town, the now famous Rasmussen was frequently seen with his "heathen" friend Osarkrak, provoking even more publicity and sensational reportage.

Although Osarkrak was a celebrity in the Danish capital, he was not the first Inuit to visit southern lands. In 1897, Robert Peary returned from one of his North Pole expeditions with a group of six northerners to be displayed at the American Museum of Natural History in New York City. At this time, the people of the world's last remaining wild places were regarded as exotic novelties by the urbanites of America and Europe. Some viewed them as amusing spectacles of curiosity and wonder, others as a window into humanity's Stone Age past. Some zoos included humans, often Chinese or African Pygmies, in their exhibits. Over the centuries, other Inuit, too, had been kidnapped and brought back to Europe or America as novelties or entertainments, and usually they died without ever seeing their homelands again. For example, four of Peary's "specimens" died in New York within a year of their arrival; one survived in America and eventually returned to Greenland.

Osarkrak, however, had not been kidnapped, and his friendship with Rasmussen was genuine and reciprocal. He lived in Rasmussen's father's rectory, where all the members of the Rasmussen family could speak with him in his own language. Osarkrak was as curious about Rasmussen's new land as Rasmussen had been about Osarkrak's home, and he was on "the trip of a lifetime" with a devoted and sensitive host. Rasmussen attempted to answer his questions as best he could, as Osarkrak was especially interested in cars, trains and other "vehicles without dogs." He was also curious about the men and women he saw promenading down the street together, soldiers wearing identical uniforms and men raising their hats to each other, an act which he thought was a prelude to battle. He wondered how people could live in such crowds, like mosquitoes. But it was the exotic animals at the zoo—the lions, monkeys, elephants and other creatures that bore no resemblance to anything living in Greenland—that aroused his greatest curiosity. Rasmussen wrote up his conversations with Osarkrak as a series of vignettes, slyly posing questions about Danish society to people who never questioned their own habits or customs.

All the while, Rasmussen was working long hours between publicity stints on his book *Nye mennesker (The New People)*, published in Denmark in 1905. The following year, he published another book, *Under nordenvindens svobe (Under the Lash of the North Wind)*. Both volumes were combined, translated and published together in English in Great Britain and the United States under the title *The People of the Polar North* in 1908.

RASMUSSEN'S ABILITY TO make friends in new communities was one of the secrets to his success. In *The People of the Polar North*, he related the story of meeting a boy who appeared to be alone:

> "Who is he?" I asked an old woman, the first time I saw Kajoranguaq. He was worse dressed than any of the others, but his eyes rivalled the blubber of the lamps in their brilliance.
>
> "Oh, a poor little orphan fellow, who eats by the cooking-pots," she replied, flinging a bone to him. The boy seized it eagerly, and set upon it with his teeth; but the meat was tough.
>
> I had a rusty little child's knife from South Greenland in my pocket, and I presented him with it, to inaugurate our acquaintance. A gift always opens the door of an Eskimo heart.

It was assuredly the first time in his life that the orphan boy had ever had such an experience as to receive a present. He looked me up and down and shook his head. I assured him that I really meant it. Then, without a change of expression, he snatched the knife out of my hand and ran off. I did not think that I should see any more of him for the present, and was just going into our tent, when he came running up with a piece of walrus meat, which he pressed into my hand.

"You gave, see: I give too," said he, and his face shone with grease and pride. Of course he had stolen the walrus meat. But from that day forth we were friends.

Rasmussen knew how to get people to trust him, respect him and talk to him. Sitting with old people for hours, he would help them with their tasks and tell stories and jokes about his time growing up, always telling these tales in their own language. He had developed an intuitive sense of human nature and a deep understanding of Inuit culture, not only the rituals and customs but also an insight into why those rituals and customs came to be, and an acceptance of them even when they seemed cruel or violent by Danish standards. His penetrating character portraits are astonishing for their insight into human nature. His ear for words and sense for story captured the Greenlanders' worldview in a series of powerful vignettes, in chapters titled, for example, "The Orphan," "The Old Bear Hunter" and "The Magician's Last Great Inspiration." *The People of the Polar North* was fleshed out with Moltke's sensitive charcoal sketches.

Rasmussen drew from the Inuit intimate details that would never have been shared with strangers. When he mentioned that the Inuits' "gums were always dry with smiling," one elder from the northwestern rim of Hudson Bay commented: "Oh! You strangers only see us happy and free of care. But if you knew the horrors we often have to live through, you would understand, too, why we are so fond of laughing, why we love food and song and dance. There is not one amongst us but has experienced a winter of bad hunting, when many starved to death in front of our eyes." Rasmussen wrote how they were always keen to see happy people around them, to hear laughter in their homes, and were grateful for a jest or joke. A researcher makes himself one with his subjects, Rasmussen believed, and this was key to his insight. His sympathy, however, also came from a shared appreciation and desire for the simple life, which allowed him to admire a life stripped of the façade of civilization, exposing the raw human impulses that drive everyone.

Although his first major literary work lacked a distinct chronology or anchoring structure, Rasmussen is a minor character in many of the stories, a supporting actor whose role is to set up the performances of the others. Interwoven throughout the book are four distinct elements: the narrative of his own travels, the stories of people he met during his travels, details of Inuit customs and taboos, and their legends and folklore. He follows roughly the sequence of events of the Danish Literary Expedition's progress from south to north and back again along Greenland's western coast. His story is told with self-deprecating humor, candid appraisal of his own ignorance and an ear for anecdotes.

In one anecdote he relates how he was urged to take a wife and the underlying cultural reason for the advice, revealing a little more about both himself and the world than is evident at first. The *angakoq* (shaman) Sorqaq did not mince words when he told him: "You should understand that it is not the right thing for a man to travel all over the country, as you are doing, young and unmarried. You will get a bad reputation, and expose yourself to be made game of. See you, a bachelor is a man who is rejected because he is a poor provider. For a woman is one of the things that a man should have. Here, a woman is the first thing he takes; after that come dogs, kayak, and last and most difficult of all, a gun. All this you have already. But who is to look after your things, who will warm your bed, and caress you? Up here a young man always travels with a wife; sometimes, if necessary, with a borrowed one."

Rasmussen describes pleasures in the direst of conditions. "Some of the pleasantest memories of my travels," he wrote, "are the recollections of days when I have lain weatherbound on a desolate coast, far from the conveniences of the overheated huts. There grows up within you a feeling that you have just defeated the malice of the storm nicely when, despite an unexpected attack, you have been able to reach a satisfactory shelter, and you can rest at ease with a good friend, wrapped in soft skins with well-filled stomachs and delicacies to eat and laugh at everything. You feel yourself master of the situation."

The People of the Polar North reveals for the first time many aspects of northern Greenlandic cultures. When Rasmussen discusses, for example, food caches, it is to show that the land wasn't quite as desolate and untouched as it might seem to an outsider unfamiliar with the landscape and the people's customs. "When Eskimos, travelling from one fishing-place to another, meet with a quarry, they generally store the greater part of the meat in a deposit, as it is often a matter of difficulty to transport it. These stores of meat are regarded as places of refreshment for any travellers, and there are always enough of them scattered along a day's driving distance, to render it unnecessary for anyone to carry provisions for a journey, in the more frequented districts. The meat is stored under formidable piles of stones, to protect it from bears and foxes."

Other customs and taboos governing behavior are described in short interludes. An astute storyteller, Rasmussen knew not to clump the anecdotes together, however more comprehensive an approach that might have been. A woman, for example, "must never name animals which are used for food; if she does, they might bring some misfortune upon the hunters," whereas a man "must never talk to her of his hunting or fishing; if, after his arrival home, he wishes to mention dangerous animals to others, he must call them by other names. Thus *nanoq*, a bear, must be called *ajagpagtoq*; *auveq*, a walrus, *sitdlalik*; *uksuk*, a bearded seal, *takissoq*. He must never use *serratit* (magic formulae) to his prey."

Rasmussen also included the standard incantations to ward off bad spirits or for luck. When a hunter was creeping up to a seal basking on the ice, for example, he might chant silently to keep the animal from becoming aware of him.

> *Let me disappear*
> *Between the earth*
> *And the glacier.*

When it came to the ancient Inuit legends, Rasmussen provided context for the way these legends were told and remembered, describing the culture of storytelling that was so strong among the northerners, and then recounted many unusual tales of strange goings-on and mysterious happenings.

"These fables and legends are told in the houses during the polar night, when the Eskimos, after great banquets of raw, frozen meat late in the evening, are digesting their food and are heavy and tired. Then it is the task of the story-teller to talk his hearers to sleep. The best story-tellers boast of never having told any story to the end. The legends are known to all; it is the grandmother's business to teach them to her grandchildren. This is the first time that the legends of the Polar Eskimos have been put on record, and my principle, during my task, has been never to repeat any story until I myself had learnt it and told it. In this way I made the whole manner of the story-telling my own, and I have endeavoured, as far as possible, to give literal translations."

In the rich narrative tradition of the Inuit, where wisdom was expressed as story and metaphor, the inspiration perhaps came from the brooding darkness that pervades the land during half the year. Inuit oral traditions reveal an intricate system of beliefs in spirits, strange beings and magic, in which souls can travel between humans and animals and between animate and inanimate objects; giants roam the land, and terrifying flesh-eating monsters deceive and attack lone travelers.

Despite being raised in a Christian home, and though his own religious beliefs were often skeptical and ambivalent, Rasmussen never passed judgment on others' beliefs or on the powers of shamans. Never are any of the beliefs of the polar people he met presented as anything but entirely valid—his job, as he described it, was to learn and report rather than to instruct and correct. As a result, the stories have a rare vibrancy and authenticity, drawing readers, as they must have listeners, into a unique and fascinating world, into the lives and rich cosmology of the Greenland Inuit. The stories have an otherworldly essence; instead of portraying a marginal culture of people grimly struggling against nature, Rasmussen shows bravery, heroism and tragedy occurring in a mysterious and unexplained world. These stories, like all great myths, transcend the time and place they record.

One of the intriguing and arresting stories Rasmussen retold is of Navaranapaluk, who when she married went to live with a tribe that she didn't like and sought vengeance through deception and brutality:

> One day she was going to pay a visit to her relations, she drew a pair of mittens over her feet instead of boots. She did this so that her people might believe her new compatriots treated her badly. It was the middle of winter, and her relations were exceedingly sorry for her, when they saw her arrive on foot; and so they agreed to attack the tribe that she now belonged to.

They set off, and arrived at the village at a time when all the men were away; there were only women at home, so they fell upon them and murdered them; only three escaped. One of them had thrown over herself the skin that she was just dressing; the second had turned a dog's-meat trough over herself; and the third had hidden in a shed where meat was stored.

When the men came home they found all their women killed, and their suspicions were aroused when they found that Nava-ranapaluk was also missing.

And great was their anger, for the assassins had impaled the women on long stakes, so that the stakes pierced their bodies. At once they prepared to attack their enemies, and began to make large numbers of arrows.

The three women who were left plaited the sinew-thread with which the heads of the arrows were to be fastened on; and they plaited with such ardour that there was no flesh left on their finger-tips, and the bones projected. One of them died from loss of blood.

When they were well equipped, they set off, and hid behind large stones, above the houses of their enemies. The assassins, after their return home, had expected the avengers every day; so their women took turns to watch.

It is said that one old woman had a remarkable dream. She dreamt that two lice were fighting on her head. And when she told it to the others, they all thought that the avengers must be in the neighbourhood. So they all gathered together in one house to ask counsel of the spirits. And when the incantation was well under way, a dog on the roof suddenly began to bark.

The men rushed out, but by then their enemies had sur-rounded the house, and they accomplished their vengeance by shooting all the men down with arrows. It was only when there were none left that they chose wives from among the widows, and took them home.

Many of the Greenlandic legends Rasmussen recorded are similarly violent and disturbing. "The mind of the Eskimo may be calm and sunlit like the water of the deep, warm fjords on a summer day," he wrote. "But it may also be wild and merciless like the ocean itself, eating its way into the land."

THE PEOPLE OF THE POLAR NORTH became an immediate sensation. No one had read anything quite like it before. The content and subject matter were fresh and intriguing, and the writing masterful. The reviews were all positive, and Rasmussen was hailed as the champion of a new kind of anthropologist and scientist—as someone destined to clear out the musty halls of academia by venturing from the library into the field, exploring and returning home with the new information. His was a poet's and writer's approach, in which intuition, imagination and insight carried the day. His way of empathizing with "primitive" people revealed their culture as universal, a perspective that applied to humanity in general and spoke to life more broadly.

No longer merely a charming and entertaining companion at parties and dinners, after the publication of *The People of the Polar North* Rasmussen was a cultural celebrity, a public figure regularly sought out for official gatherings, for speeches and interviews by newspapers and magazines, the mass media of the day. Peter Freuchen recalled that "he was the most sought-after young man in Copenhagen, and he had many, many friends." Rasmussen's parents encouraged their three children—Knud; his sister, Me; and his brother, Christian—to invite their friends to the parsonage so that they could chat and play croquet there. His father, still the indulgent parent, pleaded, "Bring them home . . . We know there must be something worth knowing in all of them, even though it is often difficult for us to recognize what it is!"

One member of that large and fluid group was a friend of Christian's—a twenty-one-year-old medical student, Ellen Hallas. She and Rasmussen began a flirtatious relationship that continued, on and off, for years. "What was it that was so charming about Knud Rasmussen?" Ellen asked herself in a memoir of her time with him. "The confidence with which he met all the people, the goodness that actually radiated from him and characterized all his actions, his cheerfulness, chivalry, naturalness? I do not know, but he enchanted all the people who came into contact with him."

Rasmussen continued to enchant Ellen for the next several years, but he was too nomadic for a settled relationship. His first multiyear trip to Greenland had not cured him of either his love of that rugged island nor his wanderlust. In any case, his intentions did not seem serious, particularly when he informed her in a letter from Greenland that he had gotten a Greenlandic woman pregnant. It might very well have been true, but it might also have been a way to keep Ellen from feeling too strongly about him. It was his style to be direct and frank, and he made little effort to conceal behavior that would have been considered outrageous by the Danish moral standards of the day. In 1908, he was still flirting with her: "Ellen, alas, Ellen! I like you a little . . . I will marry when I get home, but not with you—God forgive me for it!" This was typical of his numerous relationships with women: full of admiration, teasing, and professions of love, but avoiding commitment. One could pass it off as the insensitivity of youth, but Rasmussen never seems to have entirely outgrown it.

He could not forget Greenland and its people, but neither could he dispense with the lively congeniality of Copenhagen. He was a hero in each place when he returned from the other. The fame, adulation and public pressure in Denmark drove him to the solitude and remoteness of Greenland, the source of his public acclaim, in a cycle that repeated itself for his entire life. He was celebrated in Copenhagen, and soon in other cities in Europe and North America, for his exploits in Greenland; he was celebrated among the Inuit for returning from the far south and from across the sea in Denmark.

Within a year of the Danish Literary Expedition's return to Denmark, Rasmussen was off on another trip back to Greenland. In the summer of 1905, under the auspices of Denmark's Ministry of the Interior, he toured the fjords of South Greenland to investigate whether reindeer herding, common in Lapland, could be introduced into Greenland to augment the local economy. Reindeer herding was big business in Alaska at the time, particularly the famous Loman Brothers enterprise in Nome.* To assess its potential, Rasmussen toured possible herding sites in Greenland with his friend Osarkrak and an experienced Sami herder. This was followed by a dogsled excursion north to Cape York, where he was met by more than two hundred cheering Inuit. It was a short trip, but it was free from logistical complexity and uncertainty.

Rasmussen was back in Copenhagen by the fall, and in January 1906, he made another trip to Lapland, returning to Greenland in the spring for a longer journey in which he planned to record more myths and legends. His sister, Me, came with him on the first part of this trip. Rasmussen had a warm and stable relationship with Me; indeed, he was close to all his family members throughout his life. Brother and sister toured the more settled regions of Greenland, visiting relatives and inspecting the

---

*A few decades later, the Canadian government implemented its own similar plans for reindeer herding in the North. This experiment proved successful over time; there is still a small reindeer business today in the Mackenzie Delta. See Dick North, *Arctic Exodus: The Last Great Trail Drive* (Toronto: Macmillan, 1991).

southern, more Danish-influenced communities, until Me returned to Copenhagen in the summer of 1907. Knud was forlorn and lonely when they parted ways in Tasiussaq, the northernmost Danish settlement in the Greenland colony. "In the winter we had worked together in Greenland, we had become so strongly attached to each other that now it was hard to separate," he wrote. "It was so strange now that my sister would be standing there on the ice and not following as she did before. She was the only person in the world I could not be without."

Rasmussen seldom stayed in one place for long. After leaving Me, Rasmussen dogsledded north to the Cape York region again. In early 1908, he crossed the ice to Ellesmere Island to interview a handful of Inuit who were hunting there. During this trip, he hunted and collected the furs of hundreds of Arctic foxes, amassing a small fortune because the pelts were extremely valuable. Hunting and all commercial activity was strictly regulated by the government in southern Greenland but not north of Melville Bay, where Denmark had no recognized territorial authority. The success of this venture gave Rasmussen not only a business idea that would transform both his life and the economy of northern Greenland, but also provided the additional money he needed to consider marriage.

Soon after returning to Denmark in August 1908, after an absence of nearly two years, he married. However, his bride was not Ellen, but rather Dagmar Andersen, another attractive young woman he had met around the same time. He had been consolidating his relationship with Dagmar even while continuing his ongoing flirtatious relationship with Ellen.

Dagmar was a counterbalance to Rasmussen: serious, reserved and sensible, she was as grounded as Rasmussen was flighty. Three years younger than Knud, she was the daughter of Niels Andersen, state councillor, chairman of an employers' association and one of the most prominent entrepreneurs in Denmark.

Well off and well connected, Dagmar was modest and unassuming. She did not immediately attract attention, though many considered her beautiful. She was an accomplished pianist and shared Rasmussen's love of opera. Her reserve was perhaps exacerbated by the glaucoma that hindered her eyesight. She was also an excellent secretary and had been reading and commenting on Rasmussen's manuscripts and letters for years, becoming immersed in his exotic world as no other woman had done. "In the gay crowd that surrounded Knud," Freuchen recalled, "she functioned as a breath of common sense without ever being cool or sitting in judgment on them; she was a wonderful human being."

Dagmar had taken an interest in Rasmussen and his Greenlandic adventures soon after the return of the Danish Literary Expedition in 1904. She wanted to learn about the Greenlandic world. In the fall of 1906, she had sailed to the remote West Greenland community of Uummannaq, where she became the housekeeper of physician Dr. Alfred Bertelsen, Rasmussen's former companion on the Danish Literary Expedition. These determined efforts were certainly an unusual initiative for a young woman of such affluence and status, and her posting with Bertelsen had probably been organized by Rasmussen or his father. When Dagmar returned in the fall of 1908, after two years abroad, she spoke tolerable Greenlandic and had developed an insight into Rasmussen's world.

Dagmar and Rasmussen corresponded frequently during the years of intermittent contact, when she was in Uummannaq and he was roaming around Greenland, first with his sister and then alone. He had spent part of his time in the Uummannaq district during the winter of 1907–1908 in order to visit Dagmar, on one occasion undertaking a weeklong journey by dogsled, with only a twelve-year-old boy for company. The boy, Ajako, later became a famous adventurer who accompanied Rasmussen on several lengthy journeys. On her return voyage from Greenland to Copenhagen, Dagmar had met an engineer and mine owner,

Marius Ib Nyeboe, and told him about Rasmussen's work. It was a contact that proved useful the following year, when Rasmussen was seeking financial backing for a business he had in mind for Cape York.

Their wedding on November 11, 1908, was an elaborate affair in an ancient church, attended by prominent members of Copenhagen's business and arts communities. Two Greenlandic Inuit led the couple to the altar. For their honeymoon, the newlyweds set off for a skiing holiday in Norway. But the honeymoon period didn't last long; Rasmussen was already planning another expedition to Greenland for the summer of 1909.

In many ways, theirs appears to have been an ideal match, each opening new worlds to the other and complementing each other's strengths. Although their relationship had its turbulent periods, Dagmar was always loyal, advocating for Rasmussen, working with him to promote his ideas and fame, perhaps knowing that this reflected glory from her husband might be her only reward for years of loneliness. She was, according to numerous sources, his comrade and champion—yet she did not share in any of his major adventures, remaining in Copenhagen during the years-long absences. Unfortunately, most of their letters were destroyed after Rasmussen's death, either by Dagmar or by their children.

Around the time of their marriage, the American edition of *The People of the Polar North* was published and hailed in the *New York Times* as "an important work" by "the only explorer whose journey has been made for the sole purpose of acquiring knowledge about a peculiar and somewhat mysterious branch of the human race." The book review and author interview also made an interesting claim that hinted at Rasmussen's grand plan, commenting that he "hopes to start on a six years' tour along the whole of the north coast of North America to make a further study of the Eskimos . . . traveling like an Eskimo and living very much like an Eskimo."

Rasmussen's growing fame in Denmark also paved the way for the publication of his book *Lapland*, from a manuscript that had sat untouched since he had written it years before. Now the manuscript had become a valuable commodity. It was hailed as a perceptive account of another remote people undergoing the rapid changes of modernization. The parallels between the Sami of Lapland and the Greenlanders were clear.

Rasmussen and Dagmar spent the remainder of early 1909 in Copenhagen while he laid plans for his next trip to Greenland. This time he had a more concrete objective than simply wandering from place to place and interviewing people. He spent four months that summer of 1909 visiting communities along Greenland's southern coast for the Danish government's Department of the Interior, helping to introduce a new set of laws for the island. He was also on a contract from the Greenlandic Lutheran Church to help establish a mission station among the Inuit of the Cape York region. His ship arrived in North Star Bay in northern Greenland on July 23, and within two weeks he had unloaded all the cargo and constructed two small buildings—a residence for the two missionaries and their families and a nearby storehouse. His assignment was to help the missionaries meet the local people. It was not to be a fire-and-brimstone mission; rather, Rasmussen hoped it would ease the transition of the Polar Inuit to a more settled life. His longer-term goal was to have a commercial trading post built in the region, and he hoped the mission would bolster the argument for having one.

Much as he admired the traditional ways of the Polar Inuit, Rasmussen believed that the material culture from Europe could bring them a better life. He never believed, as his government did, that they should be left isolated, as museum pieces, unchanging down the generations. Change was inevitable, and the increasing number of whalers in the wake of Peary's explorations was just the beginning. Rasmussen thought that by understanding their culture and helping others who encountered it appreciate the Inuit ways, he might be able to ease their transition to a life that would have to accommodate outside influences.

Those intrusions from the south were becoming more numerous and attracting a great deal of attention. While Rasmussen was in Greenland, Dagmar forwarded requests to him for information about a polar controversy that was becoming a sensation: after years of effort and competing expeditions, two men were each claiming to be the first to have reached the North Pole.

THE KINGDOM OF
THE NORTH WIND

And I think over again
My small adventures
When from a shore wind I drifted out
In my kayak
And I thought I was in danger.
My fears,
Those small ones
That I thought so big,
For all the vital things
I had to get and to reach.
And yet, there is only
One great thing,
The only thing.
To live and see in huts and on journeys
The great day that dawns,
And the light that fills the world.

> —Collected and translated by Knud Rasmussen
> on the Kent Peninsula, from *The Report of the*
> *Fifth Thule Expedition, 1921–1924*

BETWEEN 1886 AND 1909, the American naval officer Robert Peary led five expeditions in search of the North Pole, using Smith Sound, the channel between Greenland and Ellesmere Island, as his path to the north. An imaginative and stubborn man, Peary, like other contemporary explorers such as Roald Amundsen and Frederick Cook, was an avid adopter of Inuit customs and survival techniques to further his ambition. The Polar Inuit of Cape York were Peary's model. From them, Peary learned how to hunt, how to build snow houses and what fur clothing to wear. His 1908–1909 expedition consisted of twenty-five people, mostly local Inuit families, and 133 dogs to pull the dozen or so sleds. Peary paid well for their services, offering many items of inestimable value to people who were essentially living with Stone Age technology: metal knives, pots and utensils; wood, cloth, and primus stoves; and, most important, guns and ammunition. "There was hardly a rifle in the tribe when I first went there," Peary claimed of his early expeditions, but in less than a decade he had furnished most of the Polar Inuit with metal tools and firearms. These items improved their lives immeasurably, and the Inuit quickly became dependent on regular access to them.

Peary bragged that he was like a millionaire moving to a small village and offering to purchase a "Brownstone mansion and an unlimited bank account" for everyone. But the bank account was not unlimited. It would last only so long as Peary needed the region and its people as a base for his expeditions. In 1909, he announced that he had accomplished his lifelong goal of reaching the North Pole and departed the region for good. Peary's sudden departure left northern Greenlanders without a source for the manufactured goods upon which they had come to rely. His claim to have reached the North Pole was fantastic news at the time, though it is not universally accepted today.*

---

*The first undisputed expedition to reach the North Pole was Roald Amundsen's *Italia* airship expedition in 1926; the first expedition to set foot on the ice at the pole was the British explorer Wally Herbert's 1969 expedition.

Dr. Frederick Cook, a physician from Brooklyn, was also a contender for the North Pole. Cook, who traveled on an early expedition with Peary, had also been a mentor to Amundsen during the expedition of 1897–1899 on the ship *Belgica,* the first to overwinter in Antarctica. Cook now claimed to have reached the North Pole ahead of Peary. In the United States in particular, the competing claims of Peary and Cook were big news—two American explorers each claiming to have reached one of the world's great remaining geographical destinations. In Denmark, the news was exciting, as most of Greenland was Danish territory and Cook would be returning to Copenhagen by steamer. The city would be the first to see him after his sensational achievement.

Owing to his growing fame in the wake of the recent publication of the US edition of *The People of the Polar North,* Rasmussen's opinion was eagerly sought on the matter of the rival Polar claims. American reporters tracked him down in the fall of 1909, when he was still in Greenland. As the *New York Times* put it, he was "the only white man who saw Dr. Cook's start and the only one with a real knowledge of the Eskimo language who had been in contact with the Cape York Eskimos." It was one of the big controversies of the day, and Rasmussen was quickly drawn into it. As the polar regions were the last remaining large unexplored regions of the globe, any news about the apparent accomplishment was of great interest. The lives of the people who lived at the world's end were no less intriguing to the public. In Denmark, Rasmussen's press had all been positive; if not yet a national hero, he was well on his way to becoming one, thanks to the success of his books and his outsized public persona. Wading into the Peary-Cook controversy, however, introduced him, as it did Amundsen, to the more rough-and-tumble nature of the American press—less genteel, more inclined to fan the flames of controversy than to seek a resolution.

Although Cook was eventually discredited and his claim is now generally believed to have been fabricated, Rasmussen was inclined to believe him at the time, based on the evidence of Cook's Greenland Inuit companions. Rasmussen met him in the vicinity of Cape York before Cook departed for the pole in February 1908, with guides and hunters Ittukusuq and Aapilaq, and afterward in the fall of 1909, when Rasmussen was again in Greenland after his marriage. His wife, Dagmar, acted as his secretary and liaison during this time, receiving Rasmussen's dispatches from Greenland, which belatedly arrived by steamer, and communicating on his behalf with the American press via correspondents.

"I was never so much moved in my life as by the success of Cook," Rasmussen wrote to Dagmar in a letter she forwarded to a correspondent at the *New York Times* in September 1909. "For," he claimed, "I hoped to carry-off this triumph myself"—although there is no other record of this being Rasmussen's goal, before or afterward. If Rasmussen ever did have the North Pole as his objective, the news of Peary's and Cook's rival claims surely would have pushed him more firmly in the direction of cultural instead of geographical exploration, just as this same news compelled Amundsen to abandon his plan for an expedition to the North Pole and switch his attention to Antarctica in time to race the British explorer Robert Falcon Scott to the South Pole. "My husband," Dagmar claimed, "was the first to congratulate Dr. Cook, and he listened to the testimony of the Eskimos, which is by no means negligible. They do not understand the use of instruments, but they know how to make observations of solar light."

On September 25, Rasmussen published an article in Denmark's largest newspaper, *Politiken*, in which he claimed that the Inuit he had spoken to were certain that Cook had reached the North Pole, or rather that Cook and his Inuit companions had been gone long enough to have reached the pole. "I am informed by trustworthy members of the same tribe that their journey across the ice field away from land was so long that the sun appeared, reached a high point in the sky, and at last did not set at all and it was almost summer before they reached land again. So it is sure that the travellers were not compelled to turn back because of ice hindrances, but only because they believed the goal was reached."

In Denmark, and in Europe generally, the sentiment was initially in favor of Cook's claim. But this soon changed, particularly after Cook presented his first lecture in Copenhagen. The *London Daily Chronicle* reported: "People who would have staked their lives upon his honesty were now full of the most terrible doubts. The lecture was a fiasco of the first magnitude and seemed so obviously a story of the imagination, wildly improbable and unsupported by a shred of scientific facts, that those explorers who were present in this city of explorers and who stood by Cook now felt shattered in their belief." Cook's supporting evidence was universally considered to be flimsy and unprofessional, certainly unconvincing, and although he promised to provide additional proof later, his battle was already lost.

Rasmussen wasn't in Copenhagen at the time—he was still in Greenland, without any communication from the outside world except the letters he sent to Dagmar, which were months out of date by the time they arrived in Copenhagen. Dagmar nevertheless forwarded them to correspondents for major newspapers, particularly the *Washington Post* and the *New York Times*, where interest in the story was greatest, as both the claimants were Americans. Cook naturally was pleased with the apparent support of Rasmussen, "a man who had no occasion to defend me." But the controversy was virulent, and others accused Rasmussen of being imprecise. Cyrus Adams of the American Geographical Society dismissed Rasmussen's support of Cook and claimed that Rasmussen "is a sort of genius in his way. He is a dreamy, poetical, imaginative young man." Herbert L. Bridgman, secretary of the Peary Arctic Club, claimed that "Rasmussen made the mistake of taking the word of Eskimos who were not in a position to know what they were talking about." Rasmussen repeatedly stressed in his letters that his support for Cook was based upon information from his Inuit companions and not on any scientific data. His views, however, were starting to make him unpopular, as institutional support was quickly shifting toward Peary.

While Rasmussen was still in Greenland, many newspapers were waiting for his return, hoping that he would be able to offer insight into Cook's claims because he probably knew some of the men hired by the American explorer. The *New York Times* even reported—in what surely must be a record for fabrication on a slow news day—that according to the secondhand word of a ship captain, Rasmussen would probably be traveling to the United States immediately, along with two of the Inuit hunters Cook had employed. Instead, Rasmussen returned to Copenhagen on October 25 aboard the steamer *Hans Egede*, one of the more or less regularly scheduled ships that connected Greenland to the outside world. There he was able to catch up on the details of the controversy and clarify his opinions. "I read and examined Dr. Cook's original diary," he stated, "after his return in 1909 and found it correct and satisfactory in every detail." But, he reiterated, he planned to meet with two of Cook's Inuit assistants the following spring.

A week later, Rasmussen had clearly and publicly changed his mind. "When I saw the observations I realized it was a scandal," he reported after he had settled into life in Copenhagen and had time to visit the university and consult with members of the Danish Geographical Society. "My confidence in Cook had been based on personal impressions, on reports that I had received and also on the testimony of the Eskimos when they all said that he had made the trip from Cape Sparbo to Etah, and such a trip during the dark of winter would suffice to make a man famous. But the letters Cook sent to Copenhagen University are most impudent. No schoolboy could make such calculations. It is a most childish attempt at cheating. Cook has killed himself by his own foolish acts." The papers reported that "practically the whole of Denmark [was] in a somewhat humiliating position" because of the early support for Cook and the hasty bestowing of an honorary degree upon him. Not surprisingly, Cook later attacked Rasmussen in the *New York Times*, calling him "unmanly" for his reliance on the testimony of "savages and for tak[ing] cover under the verbiage of two half-breed missionaries. There is something irrational about Rasmussen's public utterances."

Controversy can be good for publicity, and no doubt this irony was not lost on Rasmussen. *The People of the Polar North* was now, in October 1909, according to the Literary News section of the *New York Times*, "receiving new attention, not only by reason of the part which the Danish author has played in the controversy over Dr. Cook's story, but because of the detailed accounts which Rasmussen gives of the Arctic tribes of Eskimos, whose co-operation has been such an essential factor in the operations of both Cook and Peary." The Peary-Cook controversy may have been annoying and frustrating to Rasmussen, with his name being bandied about in the American press for his conflicting opinions, but it also helped to secure his reputation outside of Denmark and gave him increased stature in North America and Britain as a Greenlandic and polar expert. At least twelve articles about him appeared in the *New York Times* alone, quoting his opinions and confirming his credentials. And his book was selling.

THE SCANDAL NOT only broadened Rasmussen's fame, it also brought him closer to Peter Freuchen, the man with whom he would embark on several of the greatest Arctic journeys of all time. Freuchen was a bearded giant, nearly six feet five inches tall, a jovial optimist with a self-deprecating sense of humor. He had dabbled in medical studies at his university before taking a job as a fire stoker on the ill-fated *Danmark* expedition, which returned to Copenhagen in August 1908 after a two-and-a-half-year voyage to northeastern Greenland. The expedition became a sensation because of the death of three of its members, two of whom—Ludvig Mylius-Erichsen and Jørgen Brønlund—happened to be Rasmussen's colleagues on the Danish Literary Expedition.

Rasmussen had attended the *Danmark*'s sailing in June 1906 and warned the party about the poor quality and improper style of their footwear. There were other organizational problems with the expedition as well: "I learned a lot about how not to start an expedition," Freuchen later commented. Although Rasmussen and Mylius-Erichsen had had an uneasy relationship on their journey together, neither willing to accept the leadership of the other, Rasmussen was asked to write Mylius-Erichsen's obituary. Rasmussen was also saddened by the death of his childhood friend Jørgen Brønlund. But he became friends with Freuchen as a result of Freuchen's friendship with two Greenlandic members of the expedition, Henrik and Tobias, who had visited Rasmussen at his father's home in Lynge and had praised Freuchen.

After Rasmussen married Dagmar but before he went to Greenland to help establish the mission station at North Star Bay, he and Freuchen spent considerable time together discussing Arctic expeditions, Greenland and related topics. The fact that Freuchen had learned some of the Inuit language and had developed polar skills was enough to commend him to Rasmussen. When Rasmussen returned to Denmark in the fall, Freuchen had reenrolled at the university to study chemistry and surveying, but once again he lacked the enthusiasm and the discipline to succeed.

The Peary-Cook controversy gave him the break he needed. With the sensational claims by Cook, followed closely by Peary, newspapers were desperate to fill their pages with commentary and stories even tangentially related to the Arctic and Greenland. There was a shortage of people with any knowledge or experience in these subjects. *Politiken*, which frequently ran Rasmussen's articles, was casting about for another writer and asked Freuchen, as a member of the *Danmark* expedition and as someone with knowledge and experience in northern matters, to submit something. Freuchen commented wryly: "This was the biggest news break of the year, and any slant we could invent was a story . . . Since we had no facts to give the public, I was asked to supply them." Freuchen was one of the first to sense that something was not right. After discovering many factual errors and dubious claims in Cook's diaries, he decided that there was no compelling reason to believe Cook's claim.

Through their continued involvement in Arctic affairs and their shared belief that Cook was a fraud, Rasmussen and Freuchen solidified their friendship. Rasmussen, having recently returned from Greenland, was also busy with meetings and writing assignments related to the Peary-Cook controversy. He made a surprising offer to Freuchen in early 1910: that they should sail beyond Melville Bay, where Danish authority did not hold sway, claim some land and set up a trading post. His reasons for the outpost were the same as those he had been arguing for years: there were valuable furs to be taken in the region (he had sold a small fortune in fox furs two years earlier); the Polar Inuit needed to be protected from the exploitative barter of itinerant whalers; and the Inuit should have a secure supply of the goods they had come to rely upon. The Greenlandic Church Society mission, which he had helped to establish the previous summer and which now housed two missionaries and their families, had little interest in promoting commercial activities.

After thinking about the proposal for a couple of days, Freuchen agreed to abandon his more predictable and stable options for the

future, claiming that "the spirit of adventure was in my heritage."
It seems improbable that two larger-than-life individuals so suited
to each other and to the seemingly crazy idea of an Arctic trading
post should have found one another in the same city; nevertheless,
it was the beginning of a fifteen-year partnership that would result
in some of the most thrilling and outrageous stories in the history
of Arctic exploration. The only obstacle, as Freuchen succinctly
put it, was—"as usual"—the lack of financial backing.

LONG BEFORE PEARY claimed to have reached the North Pole
in 1909, Rasmussen anticipated the downside both to Peary's
generosity and to the intermittent supply of trade goods brought
by other polar explorers and whaling ships. He believed that the
northern Greenlanders needed the protection of a nation-state
to help them make the transition to a market economy and prevent their exploitation. He feared that, sooner or later, the Polar Inuit would be abandoned and unable to obtain what they
needed. Rasmussen was also afraid that he, and Denmark, would
be preempted by the Norwegian adventurer Otto Sverdrup, who
had mapped most of the High Arctic islands between 1898 and
1902. Sverdrup had announced plans to set up a sealing station
on Saunders Island in northwest Greenland, giving Norway a
potential political claim to territory that Rasmussen felt should
eventually be governed by Denmark.

Whereas polar explorers such as Amundsen and Peary expressed their desire to see the Inuit shielded from outside influences and never "civilized"—a policy similar to the historic
Danish model for southern Greenland—Rasmussen was resigned
to the inevitable outcome of increased whaling and sealing expeditions, to northern Greenland being opened up to the world
of international commerce. If the process of "civilization" was

inevitable, he wanted to do what he could to make it less painful and more on terms controlled by the Inuit. He felt that this would best occur if the Danish rule that governed the southern part of Greenland were extended north to incorporate the Cape York region.

In early 1910, Rasmussen asked the Danish interior minister, P. Munch, to consider a series of proposals to construct a trading post at Cape York, to extend the traditional Danish monopoly on trade that prevailed in southern Greenland to the north, and to make all of Greenland subject to Danish rule. His letter outlined a business plan for the post and offered himself and Freuchen as its organizers and managers. After some deliberation, Munch informed him that the Danish government could take no role in any permanent settlement or trading post. The government was unsure what the international reaction would be to an assertion of Danish sovereignty in the region, and perhaps more important, Danish reluctance may have been due to the negotiations for the sale of the Danish West Indies to the United States at the time. As the United States might have had a territorial claim to northern Greenland based on Peary's many expeditions in the region over the years, Denmark didn't want to risk Greenland becoming part of the negotiations over the Danish West Indies (now known as the Virgin Islands). Interestingly, in 1916, when the sale of the Danish West Indies was finalized, the United States simultaneously announced that it supported the Danish position over the Norwegian position and would relinquish any further political or economic claim to Greenland.

Rasmussen shrugged off his nation's lack of interest, but Freuchen was a little less charitable in writing about it decades later. He recalled that he and Rasmussen "ran up against the bureaucrats who asked such asinine questions and made such stupid objections that we knew our chances in that direction were nil . . . During these negotiations I saw a good deal of human nature at its worst. My respect for the human race lessened." Eventually, Freuchen did admit that "this failure may have been partly due to my own lack of experience with diplomatic language. At one stage of our delicate negotiations I asked the Secretary of the Interior whether he really was 'such a nitwit' as he appeared to be." Whatever the reason, he and Rasmussen had to find another source of funds and backing.

To help drum up awareness and support for their project, Rasmussen and Freuchen decided to tour Denmark with a lecture-and-slide presentation. The "discovery" of the North Pole and its associated controversy had brought Arctic matters into fashion again, and an eager public awaited. Rasmussen and Freuchen were a pair of amusing impresarios who somehow turned every hurdle into fun. First they bought, on credit, a newly designed portable lantern slide projector. They had posters and advertisements printed, and rented lecture halls around the country, taking advice from a friend who worked in the theater as to where to start their tour and how to proceed. There is no doubt that the two had a flair for theater, and the tour began more as a comedy than as a serious presentation on the plight of northern Greenlanders. On the first leg of the tour, they barely had enough money left to purchase train tickets. Nevertheless, for their first stop they had filled the hall, and Rasmussen, who planned to give the first lecture, took the stage. When he signaled Freuchen to begin showing the slides, only a distorted black blotch appeared on the screen. While Freuchen, swearing under his breath, tinkered frantically, Rasmussen didn't miss a beat.

In his deep voice, Rasmussen intoned: "Yes, ladies and gentleman, I'm sure you've all seen pictures of Greenland taken during the summer midnight sun. But this evening we shall show you some realistic pictures from the period of darkness, when all contours merge, so that one hardly knows what is to be found quite nearby." That took care of the first slide. Then, Freuchen brought up the next lantern slide, a fuzzy, unfocused scene of women dancing. "A night polar bear hunt," Rasmussen proclaimed. "It is extremely dangerous to attack wild animals with no light to shoot by." The next was another blurry, indiscernible image: "A hunter patiently waiting over a seal's blow hole in darkness in an attempt to catch a seal for his starving children." The audience duly applauded the heroic effort of the valiant hunter. Rasmussen continued to bluff his way through a series of incomprehensible images. Then it was Freuchen's turn to speak, and the audience loudly called out to see what Greenland looked like in the daytime. Now the two explorers had to sheepishly plod on without any images at all. In the next two lectures, they tried to get the finicky projector to work, with mixed results, until they finally hired a trained projectionist for the remainder of the tour. They visited dozens of towns—"every community in Denmark," according to Freuchen—and although they didn't make a lot of money, they gained many admirers.

This popularity, however, did not extend to the views of the interior ministry when it came time to plan more seriously for the trading post. The ministry offered neither official support nor financing. Undaunted, Rasmussen began to search for investors. He succeeded in securing investment from Marius Ib Nyeboe, the Danish businessman whom Dagmar had met on her return voyage from Greenland two years earlier. An engineer who had worked on US railroads and who had financial interests in a copper mine in southern Greenland, Nyeboe not only urged Rasmussen to pursue the project but also offered his office as a business center and helped in the search for additional investors.

Rasmussen offered three goals for the venture: to secure the territory for Denmark, to finance and equip expeditions for the further scientific and geographical exploration of Greenland, and to help the Polar Inuit gain access to the goods they needed.* Rasmussen suggested that a certain percentage of the trading-post profits should go toward a fund to support the old and sick; then, once the loan from investors was repaid, the profits should be used for the development of the Cape York region; and finally, the Danish government should take over the business when it was willing to pay book value for the enterprise. This original business plan shows a lack of business sense hardly surprising in one so idealistic. Nevertheless, the board of directors eventually included Nyeboe and Christian Rasmussen, Rasmussen's father. Freuchen's girlfriend, Michelle Erichsen, convinced Adam Biering, a prominent and wealthy Dane working in Baku in the Caucasus and a friend of her father's, to donate a large sum to the enterprise, even though he had never met Freuchen or Rasmussen. Nyeboe supplied the balance.

Financing in place, the two adventurers chartered a small ship that was cheap enough, "but otherwise totally unsuited for any excursion to the Arctic." It was a three-masted, forty-nine-ton vessel with a sixteen-horsepower auxiliary motor that Rasmussen had somehow managed to insure. They loaded their meager supplies, boarded their crew of six, and set sail for Greenland on July 17, 1910, after saying good-bye to "our women," Dagmar and Michelle. They planned on being gone for several years, which raises questions about Rasmussen's relationship with Dagmar, to whom he had been married for only a year and a half. It must have been difficult in any event to be married to Rasmussen—he was often away, and Dagmar, having spent time

---

*Decades later, French anthropologist Jean Malaurie observed that because the trade had come from the people, in effect they had financed the study and documentation of their own culture. See Jean Malaurie, *The Last Kings of Thule: With the Polar Eskimos, As They Face Their Destiny* (New York: E.P. Dutton, 1982).

in Greenland herself, knew that her husband had other female companions. We can only imagine what Dagmar thought when her husband's ship cast off from the wharf in Copenhagen and chugged away under the power of its tiny motor. She was holding one seven-month-old infant and expecting another child. A multiyear trip to the farthest-north inhabited region of the world was a dangerous undertaking, even for one who had made the trip several times before.

Although she expressed frustration with her husband's eternal absences and reputation as a ladies' man, Dagmar was very much aware of his nature. She knew before she married him that he would never be entirely "Danish" and content to settle peacefully in Copenhagen. His exotic Greenlandic heritage was surely what had drawn her to him, as it had others, and with that fact came the reality that Greenland was very far away and, in those days, difficult to reach. Nonetheless, they remained together until Rasmussen's death, eventually having three children together: a daughter, Hanne, born in December 1909, whom Rasmussen didn't see again until she was three years old; another daughter, Inge, born in March 1911; and a son, Niels, born in March 1919. Inge and Niels were born while Rasmussen was away in Greenland. "The fact that Dagmar didn't want to come up here has been a deep scar in my happiness of being here," he wrote from Thule in a letter to Nyeboe in 1912, "and especially I suffer periodically a strong longing for my little girls, of which I have not even seen Inge." A few years later, it was not only longing that plagued him. To Nyeboe he admitted his fear that after being away for so long, he wondered whether Dagmar would still care for him.

When he was on long and dangerous journeys, Rasmussen often gained strength from imagining that his wife and children were living comfortably in Copenhagen. Although he worried about growing estranged from them, this never plagued him enough to keep him from embarking on his next adventure. Greenland was not only part of his identity, it was also the core of his professional distinction and the source of his income. Greenland and its native inhabitants, and later all the Inuit, were not only his past, but also his present and future.

WE WERE YOUNG and still believed that life would reward us with a reality equal to our dreams," Freuchen wrote many years later. He was seven years younger than Rasmussen and looked up to his thirty-one-year-old leader. In the months leading up to their departure for Greenland, their relationship with the Danish government had become so tense that they had been forbidden to stop at Godhavn (now called Qeqertarsuaq). Nevertheless, the ship with its crew of eight slipped out to sea, bound for Cape Farewell in southern Greenland. They then turned north along the west coast, sailing on to Disko Bay and Qeqertarsuaq, knowing that no one there could have heard of the prohibition. In Greenland in particular, Rasmussen did as he pleased, allowing full rein to his stubbornly independent streak, an independence that he tempered at least partially in Denmark. They stopped briefly to purchase a few supplies, and Freuchen bought some dogs—much to Rasmussen's disdain, as he had planned to obtain dogs from his uncle Carl farther north. They also brought on board Arnajark, a woman who begged to be taken north and offered to be their housekeeper. She was accompanied by a child, and Arnajark did become their housekeeper once they had built a house. This was typical of Rasmussen's generosity, Freuchen claimed, and he also noticed something else: everyone in Greenland seemed to know Rasmussen; they asked about his parents and siblings, they remembered him as a boy, or they knew his other relatives.

Leaving Qeqertarsuaq, the ship sailed up the coast to Qeqertaq, where Uncle Carl "ruled like a king," and another of Rasmussen's uncles, Jens, lived nearby. Rasmussen and Freuchen had brought some gin, normally a prohibited substance in Greenland, with them, and "the games and dancing lasted for days." There were games—target practice, wrestling contests, running and kayaking races—while Uncle Carl on violin and his daughter on accordion "played for us in the sunlight all night." Rasmussen got his dogs, the best in the world, so he claimed, and many other items as well. During a break in the festivities, he revealed another side to his character when he took Freuchen aside to show him some of the people who lived in poverty nearby. He admitted that it angered him that his uncle lived so well when such slums were so close, but he didn't see how he could do anything about it during such a short visit.

After spending more time than they had intended to at Qeqertaq, the crew set sail across Melville Bay, whose dangerous shores the Danish Literary Expedition had rounded by dogsled years before. Melville Bay was covered with ice several feet thick for eight months of the year and filled with ice chunks—some large enough to crush an ill-equipped vessel—the rest of the year, and for nearly two hundred miles the coast was banded by a long series of ice cliffs. Not only did no one live along this coast, but there was nowhere for a ship to land and no way to go around the bay on land. As it rounded Cape York, the ship was beset by a gale that spun it around and tore at its sails. The engine was too weak to control the vessel, and finally the rudder and the propeller were destroyed by ice. The ship drifted with the strong current between icebergs into North Star Bay, near where Rasmussen had helped to establish the mission the previous year. Some of the Inuit who were dwelling in the region had seen his ship the day before and had thought it would surely be destroyed by the grinding ice. Wondering how to search for the wreckage, they came out in boats to row the party ashore, cheering when they found out who they were rescuing: "If we had known Knud Rasmussen was on board, we would have realized he would make harbour."

Although his ship was badly damaged, Rasmussen nonetheless called for a celebration, telling his Inuit friends that he had been waiting for months to eat their delicious food. Freuchen was not so sure about the food as he was taken from hut to hut to sample delicacies that included various fermented or rotted meats, raw caribou and other foods that he would soon grow to love. They feasted until they "were stuffed and collapsed and slept until the captain of our vessel sent a messenger to ask how long we were going to keep him anchored there." They had not planned to build their trading post here in North Star Bay because Rasmussen didn't want to be too close to the missionaries. Fate, however, decreed otherwise; it was getting late in the season and the ship needed repairs. They would have to share the bay, a situation that Freuchen in particular grew to dislike.

The crew unloaded their equipment and supplies, dragged the ship onto the beach during a low tide, and repaired the rudder and propeller. In a few days they sailed away, leaving Rasmussen and Freuchen to set up their post. Rasmussen was in his element, giddy with excitement at the prospect of experiencing another Arctic winter, while Freuchen admitted to some trepidation about their situation: "two lone white men, in a little world of North Greenland Eskimos." And it was isolated. North Star Bay was ice free for only a few weeks in August each year. The only other way to communicate with the outside world was to dogsled across Melville Bay to Tasiussaq when the ice froze solid in December.

The territory the trading post was intended to serve was enormous, from as far south as Melville Bay to the last settlement far north along the band of rocky barrens between the sea and the vast inland ice fields. This region of northwest Greenland is now sometimes called Avanersuaq. It consists of a narrow band of stony land about two hundred miles from the north shore of Melville Bay, where the ice cliffs dwindle, to Smith Sound at the entrance of Kane Basin. The southern part of the district is punctuated by a series of fjords that end where tongues of ice from the great inland ice sheet stretch out to the sea. The sea forms the western border of this remote and isolated land, and the east is guarded by the impenetrable cliffs of the ice sheet that sometimes reach heights of up to one hundred feet, and rockbound moraines of glacial boulders. More than one hundred glaciers have been counted in the region; in summer, travel is nearly impossible because the snow turns to slush and rushing torrents of melting glacier water carve up the land.

When Rasmussen and Freuchen arrived at North Star Bay, barely two hundred people lived in the entire region. There were only about four families present when Rasmussen and Freuchen began to assemble their small prefabricated house on the northeast shore of the bay, at the base of Mount Dundas. Freuchen recalled that "it was not very big nor very comfortable, so we spent as little time in it as possible." Rasmussen wanted to name the place Knudshope, but fortunately Freuchen had a better idea: Thule Station, from Ultima Thule, the term ancient geographers placed on their charts to signify the farthest north territory inhabited by people. The settlement is now a US Air Force base, but for Rasmussen and Freuchen it was to be home for many years, the base from which they launched numerous remarkable expeditions, and a social and trading center for Greenland's Polar Inuit.

THE TWO FRIENDS immediately settled into life at Thule. Winter would soon be closing in, and procuring meat for themselves and their dogs was one of their first priorities. As fall progressed into early winter the news of their arrival spread. When a herd of walruses appeared across the fjord, the hunters paddled over to capture as many as possible—dangerous work, as an adult male walrus can weigh up to 1,500 pounds and its enormous tusks can easily smash a kayak. Freuchen described the hunting technique: first a hunter would throw his harpoon, attached to an inflated bladder, into the side of the massive beast. The walrus would typically dive and then be brought to the surface again because of the bladder. When it surfaced, the hunter would kayak toward the enormous thrashing animal to finish the kill. "It takes time, skill and bravery," Freuchen claimed with understatement. Afterward, the beasts were pulled ashore and butchered. Photos of walrus butchering from that time show men, women and children alike gathered around the massive carcasses, covered in gore, working furiously to process the meat and transport it to camp. Nearly the entire animal was used in some way—flesh and blubber for food, hides for shelter, bones and tusks for tools and weapons—and the guts were fed to the dogs. Such hunts were and remain a complicated business involving multiple family groups, requiring cooperation and planning to stockpile food according to the seasons.

Freuchen, who received several hundred pounds of walrus meat because he had thrust his harpoon into a walrus, made the mistake of thanking the primary hunter when accepting the meat. The man looked at him but said nothing until later, back at camp: "Up in our country we are human! And since we are human we help each other. We don't like to hear anybody say thanks for that. If I get something today you may get it tomorrow . . . Up here we say that by gifts one makes slaves, and by whips one makes dogs." The politics of dividing up meat was not always as perfect in practice as in theory. A boy was entitled to an extra share if he had dogs, even if the dogs were loaned to him by his father; but a man with daughters received no extra portion.

Freuchen, also known as Pitarssuaq, meaning "Big Peter," committed many faux pas in those first few months. Rasmussen knew these customs instinctively but others had to learn before they could be accepted. Freuchen later took pleasure in describing his initial social blunders and his amazement that Rasmussen, whom until then he had known only in Denmark, had an intimate knowledge of the minutiae and subtlety of the culture. Freuchen once asked some women to make *kamiks* (boots) for him, but they laughed and went away. Rasmussen, who overheard the exchange, explained that "it is considered worse for a woman to sew for another man than to sleep with him." Freuchen was supposed to ask the husband to ask his wife. On another occasion, when a group of men and boys were looking at a cartographic globe that Nyeboe had given them, Freuchen wandered up and presumed to tell them, in poor Kalaallisut, that the globe represented Earth and they were located on its surface near the North Pole. Rasmussen quietly advised him to stop, informing him that the old man knew exactly what he was doing and was giving the boys a geography lesson.

They spent the fall of 1910 hunting and storing the meat in large frozen piles outside their house. As word spread of the new trading post, many Polar Inuit came to visit the post and socialize with each other. Rasmussen always seemed to be the center of life there, arranging dancing and singing soirées. People would journey for days to visit him. "I never knew a man who could find so many occasions for celebration," Freuchen recalled. Rasmussen showed himself to be a natural leader, respecting the local customs and knowing how to insert himself into the proceedings and how to shift events in the direction he wanted. This was done not so much to gain an advantage, as he sought no real commercial advantage, but to maintain the social culture and avoid conflict.

Unnecessary discord bothered him, and he considered it wasteful and counterproductive. On one occasion, a murder occurred when a boastful and arrogant man threatened others in the community and stole their wives and food. Two men shot him, and the murdered man's brother announced that he was now compelled to kill the brother of the man who had killed his brother. Rasmussen decided he would settle the matter before a series of reprisals devastated the community. Inviting all the men to his house at Thule Station, he passed around tobacco and coffee and gave a speech in which he outlined the traditional customs and their inevitable outcome. He explained that he understood why the killing must be avenged to assuage honor, and that the stakes for murder had to be high to discourage murder; but then he proclaimed that having the ability to kill a man, but choosing not to, would show greater courage. He implored the men to reconsider: he needed them to bring furs to Thule Station; otherwise, the trading post would have to close and the whole community would suffer. Thus, they should put aside their fighting for both his sake and the community's sake. The ploy worked. Because Rasmussen straddled the worlds of insider and outsider, or Greenlander and European, he had an authority born of his impartiality. Both sides in the conflict agreed to pay him five fox furs to secure the brokered peace.

In mid-October, when the sun dropped below the horizon for the winter, "one might think the natives would regret its going," Rasmussen observed, but they rejoiced instead. "The long summer, with the sun always circling overhead, is tiresome. During the winter freeze travel was much easier and the disparate fjords were again united and travelers came up and down the coast visiting." Freuchen and Rasmussen each went on separate sled journeys in the late fall, because of their love for travel and because, as Freuchen put it, "the more we travelled and the more we made friends, the better our prospect of making our trading post a financial success."

It was not always easy going. In December, under a bright moon and calm skies, Freuchen and his three companions sledded across the frozen Melville Bay to Tasiussaq for supplies and news. When they returned three weeks later, never having reached their destination, they had lost one of their members. One of the sleds had broken through thin ice and Freuchen's companion Avatanguak froze to death. As they returned to the community at Thule Station, "according to Eskimo custom, we remained on our sleds with our backs toward the shore—a sign that someone had died and that our trip had ended in tragedy."

Rasmussen had remained at Thule in case any traders came by, but after Freuchen's return he himself set off for Tasiussaq, early in the new year of 1911, with a team of the best dog drivers. Minding the post was now an easy way to pass the time, because all the trade goods had been disposed of, and Rasmussen left Freuchen to recover and entertain any visitors. But Freuchen, having nothing to trade, grew restless and decided on a second expedition across Melville Bay. This time he made the journey without incident, and he and Rasmussen enjoyed the hospitality of the Tasiussaq post manager and his wife, later returning separately with supplies and trade goods. "It may seem strange to the average reader that Knud Rasmussen and I so constantly occupied our time with travelling in a land where travel was so hazardous," he wrote. "Perhaps the principal excuse for our excursions was to break the monotony which moves in like the Arctic's gray, impenetrable fog. Then one does not need much excuse to travel, or do anything out of the ordinary. Even certain peril was better than sitting about with no prospect of change in routine ahead of us."

Later in the winter they headed north, with a small group of Greenlanders, to Natsilivik, a community rumored to be the site of many strange events, including numerous murders. A young pregnant woman and her husband traveled with them. When a storm blew in from the ocean, bringing blowing snow and biting winds, they could find no shelter on the open landscape. It was at this point that the woman's baby was due. She could travel no farther. "The atmosphere was an unbreathable mixture of snow and blinding ice," the dogs were blown off their feet by gusts, and the people huddled together, yelling to be heard over the howl of the wind. They tried to build an igloo, but the snow was too dry and the wind too strong, so they overturned several sleds to make a barrier against the ferocious gale. The woman was in labor, and even Freuchen's limited medical training told him that her water had already broken—there would be no moving, bad weather or good. As she could not undress in the freezing cold, they slit a small opening in her pants and helped to hold her in a crouching position until the baby boy emerged. The new mother quickly "snatched the child inside her coat, wrapped some skins about him and soon had him warm and snug."

The distance between life and death was very narrow here, and this raw and elemental aspect of life in the North appealed to Rasmussen. It mirrored the land itself, where the rocky bones of the earth were laid bare, where animals were eaten raw right after their killing, where shelter consisted of rudimentary huts, caves or snow houses, and danger and death were never far away.

Rasmussen was often willing to go far out of his way in pursuit of stories. On one journey he made a detour to visit Semigaq, an old woman rumored to be both a trove of ancient lore and a great gossip. A storm was rolling in when he and Freuchen arrived at their destination, and the two travelers were invited into a hut to take shelter. Rasmussen asked about the woman, who lived there. "Oh, that poor old woman," replied the host. "She has very few relatives here and she is alone most of the time. She went out to look at fox traps before the storm started and she hasn't come home since; her traps are a long way from here. Everybody is sorry for her and now we think that it is better to commiserate with her once and for all and then never feel sorry for her anymore."

Rasmussen would not hear of this, and he and Freuchen set out into the storm to find her. Heading to the place near the ice edge where she was known to keep her traps, they found the crouching old woman, exhausted and chilled. "So, there you are," she said without surprise. The spirits of the cave had told her that Rasmussen was coming, she told them. When they returned her to her home, Rasmussen obtained a new dress for her, whereupon she informed him that she was coming to live at Thule. With that, she climbed up on Rasmussen's sled, crushing his camera, and refused to leave. When Rasmussen couldn't hide his annoyance, she loudly chided him that he had no business messing around with things that couldn't bear the weight of an "old half-starved woman." Semigaq lived with them for many years, telling Rasmussen numerous tales of the spirit world, of strange deeds and mysterious goings-on.

Rasmussen now had four old women living at Thule. Along with Semigaq, there was Vivi, whom they had brought north with them and who did their cooking; Arnajark, an elderly woman who had been Rasmussen's servant on an earlier expedition, and Aloqsiaq, a recent widow. They vied with one another to tell him more stories, for which he paid them with small presents such as tins, old tea leaves, cloth rags and scraps of paper. Rasmussen knew that when their storage boxes were becoming full, the women would leave soon after to distribute the gifts among their relatives. He spent extra time talking with them then, having them repeat their stories until he knew those stories by heart and could write them down.

RASMUSSEN, AND LATER Freuchen, did not give the trade goods away cheaply; the skins they traded for had to be perfect, and the traders were critical of poor cutting and sloppy cleaning. When they first opened the trading post, they received an inferior-quality skin, which Rasmussen pinned up on the wall as a joke. He never said who had supplied the skin, but word spread rapidly and seldom did the post ever have to display inferior skins in the future. Rasmussen knew Inuit culture; he understood that pride in one's prowess and in giving and receiving what one had earned was important. He could never publicly tell someone what to do or how to prepare a skin—it would be interpreted as a horrible slander—but he knew how to get what he wanted using the cultural norms of the people he lived among.

When their first spring in Thule arrived, Rasmussen and Freuchen prepared for the seasonal hunt on nearby Saunders Island, where walruses congregated after the winter, and for the arrival of the birds—auks, ducks and fulmars. There was great activity and celebration in the community as they replenished the food supplies. The ice lasted until July, followed by several weeks when slush made any type of travel difficult—neither dogsled nor sail nor paddle could get through—so Rasmussen and Freuchen settled in for the warmer days of the brief summer, with few visitors and little business to conduct. Whaling ships would soon be arriving, bringing news from home and perhaps more supplies. And one morning they did see a ship, far out in the bay. Knowing it carried mail, the traders paddled through the ice-choked water to meet it. The cargo included a letter from Freuchen's girlfriend, Michelle, who wrote that she wanted to join him in the Arctic and make a life together. Rasmussen had a letter from Dagmar about the birth of their second daughter, Inge.

They waited anxiously through August for the next ship, which would bring their badly needed supplies; they were nearly out of matches, nails and coffee. When a schooner finally arrived in September, Michelle was not on board, but a letter informed Freuchen that she couldn't leave the city; she had changed her mind. And thus passed the traders' first year at Thule. This annual routine of hunting, traveling and celebrating would repeat itself for many years, with only occasional breaks. Freuchen managed the trade and accounts and the mapping, while Rasmussen interviewed the Polar Inuit and pondered their myths and legends. He also began to wonder how the Inuit had peopled the Arctic. Where had they come from originally?

6

THE FIRST
THULE EXPEDITION

Far, far will I go,
Far away beyond the high hills,
Where the birds live,
Far away over yonder, far away over yonder.

Two pieces of rock barred the way,
Two mighty rocks,
That opened and closed
Like a pair of jaws.
There was no way past,
One must go in between them
To reach the land beyond and away,
Beyond the high hills,
The bird's land.

Two land bears barred the way,
Two land bears fighting
And barring the way.
There was no road,
And yet I would gladly pass on and away
To the farther side of the high hills,
To the birds' land.

—Collected and translated near Hudson Bay
  by Knud Rasmussen, *Report of the Fifth*
  Thule Expedition, 1921–1924

A S HE AND Freuchen prepared to spend their second winter at Thule Station, Rasmussen formed a new plan: the out-of-date newspapers delivered by the ship in September carried stories of a Danish expedition that had gone missing on the northeast coast of Greenland. Led by Ejnar Mikkelsen, the explorers were a year late in returning and no one knew their fate. Rasmussen sensed an opportunity to gain more publicity and recognition for his and Freuchen's trading venture at Thule, as well as acclaim for himself. A rescue mission to Greenland's east coast—later to be termed the First Thule Expedition—was just the sort of devil-be-damned undertaking to get headlines. Freuchen quickly agreed—after all, they had mostly been living off the land for the past year anyway, so how hard could this expedition be?

In the fall, Freuchen—who claimed to have become more "Eskimo" as time passed and who had no real plan to return to Denmark—married a local girl, Mequ. It was all very low key, at least until the wedding. Mequ, who was very shy, had been lingering around the trading post, giving small gifts to Freuchen, and although her clothes were ragged, one day she brought him a pair of gloves she had knitted—he had once given her a piece of bread. Sometime afterward, as Rasmussen and Freuchen strolled through the village, they saw Mequ standing outside her hut. Rasmussen casually said to Freuchen: "She is the only girl in Greenland who is good enough and smart enough and pretty enough to marry." The common practice of borrowing other men's wives was not a long-term solution to the desire for female companionship. Freuchen was to be stationed at Thule for many years, though Rasmussen planned on returning to Denmark more frequently.

Freuchen soon realized that Rasmussen was right, and that Mequ was "an extraordinarily pure and fine person." When the old woman Vivi and Freuchen were alone in the house one night, Mequ came to visit. Vivi asked Mequ to stay the night, and Freuchen invited her across onto his sleeping pallet. "That was all the wedding necessary in this land of the innocents," Freuchen commented. Not surprisingly, Rasmussen felt differently: he called for a celebration, with dancing. "Knud's will prevailed, as usual, and the festivities lasted several days," Freuchen recalled. Mequ changed her name to Navarana to reflect her new status.

Rasmussen's own domestic arrangements at that point are rather opaque. But, given the many years he spent living in the region without returning to Denmark, the somewhat fluid and informal nature of sexual relations among the Inuit at the time and his own admission that he had fathered a child with an unidentified Inuk woman, it is unlikely that he was living a chaste or celibate life. It would have seemed strange to the Inuit if he had refused female intimacy, and it was not in Rasmussen's character to do so. Many of Rasmussen's contemporaries hint at his promiscuity in the Arctic and in Denmark; on one multiyear expedition he traveled with Arnarulunguaq, who was widely accepted as being his mistress and whom he teasingly called "my little woman." Rasmussen always loved living in the Arctic—the roaming, the adventure and the freedom from the constraints and conservative morality of early twentieth-century Copenhagen— and sexual freedom was undoubtedly part of these pleasures.

IN DECEMBER 1911, Rasmussen and Freuchen decided on a sled journey south to Tasiussaq, and then to Upernavik, to meet with Danish colonial officials and discuss their planned expedition. They liked to travel together, and this year they were joined by Navarana, who was a superior dog driver. On December 13, just before they left, Rasmussen organized a Christmas party featuring an artificial Christmas tree. Even the missionaries attended, although there was some grumbling about Rasmussen changing the date of Christmas. The feast consisted of canned roast goose and cakes, followed by rousing renditions of Danish Yuletide songs.

They departed the post on December 15, a dark day (as usual) but for the sliver of the new moon under a vast dome of stars. While traveling on the ice of Melville Bay, the expedition came upon a strange scene—an entire school of narwhals had become trapped in the water around an ever-shrinking hole in the ice; clustering around it, the desperate animals took turns coming up for air. It was too far for them to travel to a larger area of open water. As word went out, hunters congregated for the kill—the narwhals would soon be dead anyway, from drowning.

So the slaughter began, and it continued for two days— harpooning and dragging the hapless creatures from their breathing hole, which made room for others to crowd in for air, which in turn caused water to slosh up and around the hole, shrinking it further and sealing their fate. "The poor animals had a bad time . . . it was almost an act of mercy to kill them," Freuchen recalled. "I stood beside the blowhole and watched the steam from their blood and heard the desperate breathing of the unfortunate beasts." The butchered narwhals lay strewn across the ice: meat, blubber, bone, hide and ivory tusks separated into piles. Rasmussen noted that there were hundreds of the valuable tusks in the store that year. Sold as unicorn horns in medieval times, the tusks were still valuable in China for their purported medicinal properties.

With mixed feelings about the hunt, the travelers harnessed their dogs and continued on to Tasiussaq. At that time the Danish colonization of Greenland was mainly complete in the south, where Christianity dominated and most people had been baptized, although local spiritual beliefs and traditions had not been entirely extinguished. The Polar Inuit north of Melville Bay were only just beginning to be exposed to the cultural pressure to conform. On the party's arrival at Tasiussaq, the villagers ran out to meet the sleds, chanting, "The unbaptized are coming!" Navarana had no idea what they were talking about, but she had heard rumors that northerners were frequently looked down upon in South Greenland because they were not baptized. Recognizing an insult, she proclaimed: "One gets the idea here that something smells of urine!"—a reference to the southern tradition of keeping buckets of urine handy "for everything from driving ghosts out of their dwellings to washing their hair, and keeping it inside until the stench brings tears to the eyes," Freuchen related. Thereafter, Navarana made this announcement whenever she was about to enter a dwelling where she felt she might be insulted.

Receiving no news of the lost explorers, Rasmussen proceeded south to Upernavik, where the travelers were received as honored guests. They were provided with beds covered with white sheets and ate while sitting at a table with white linen and cutlery—customs they had all but abandoned since arriving in Greenland. There was dancing in the evenings, and "the place rang with our shouts and laughter." The Danish officials in Upernavik confirmed that some Danish explorers had died while trying to substantiate Peary's geographical claims in northeastern Greenland, but the fate of the rest was unknown. Now Rasmussen was determined to cross the Greenland Ice Cap. Of course he and Freuchen were supposed to be running a trading post—they had debts and investors—but they felt that the moral imperative to help their countrymen overtook mere commercial considerations, not to mention the publicity and attention the effort would bring.

They stayed several weeks at Upernavik, awaiting the proper ice conditions, before setting off for the north again in early February with loaded dogsleds. The sun had returned, and the sky was already bright at noon. The return to Thule included the discovery of dead bodies floating in an open patch of water and their own near tragedy when an exploding iceberg hurled them to the ice and showered them with shards. When they arrived at Thule in March, many customers were waiting for them. They did their business quickly, as they had other plans: they were preparing for a grand journey.

PREPARATIONS FOR THE expedition included selecting two skilled and reliable comrades to join them. In early April, after some discussion, Rasmussen selected the new expedition members. The first man chosen was Uvdloriaq, an Inuk in his late thirties, a superior hunter known for his "ingenuity and perseverance" and ability to "completely ignore sleep and hunger and all kinds of exhaustion." Uvdloriaq was also Freuchen's father-in-law. The other member of the group, Inukitsoq, a man ten years younger, had traveled with Peary on two polar expeditions and was known as a "tenacious and good hunter and dog driver . . . with a warm and good humour that never allowed him to falter in any situation." Uvdloriaq and Inukitsoq were eager to explore the farthest regions of their land—the areas where no one ventured because there were no animals to be hunted, and thus no food. In addition to experiencing wanderlust, the two men possessed unusual courage to be willing to brave the crossing of the terrifying ice cap, known to Polar Inuit as the spirit-infested *Sermik-soak*. Legend had it that East Greenland was populated with fantastical monsters, crazed people who ate stones, and dog-sized rabbits.

Rasmussen's original plan was to follow the coast around the northern tip of Greenland, in order to stay close to hunting grounds, but after consulting a map, Uvdloriaq suggested they cut straight across the ice cap. It would be a short cut, he claimed; after all, "the icecap is only a road without rough ice." Apart from the expedition members having insufficient provisions, lacking snow goggles to prevent snow blindness, and encountering no game until they reached the eastern coast, Rasmussen supposed it could be done. "If you can navigate us across," he told Uvdloriaq, "we'll look out for the food." A simple plan. But the food Rasmussen had stocked consisted largely of biscuits and oatmeal—which they all disliked—along with his personal tobacco supply. They had enough meat for one month, but the journey was expected to take five months and cover a distance of at least 1,000 miles.

The provisions they were able to assemble consisted of 130 pounds of biscuit, about the same amount of oatmeal, 20 pounds of coffee and tea, 12 cans of milk, 5 pounds of sugar, 10 pounds of butter, 5 pounds of honey, and 20 pounds of blood pudding. They also packed 105 cans of kerosene, 35 pounds of tobacco, two primus stoves, several blubber lamps, 300 pounds of walrus meat with blubber, a four-person tent, skis and snowshoes, extra underwear, coats and sleeping bags, as well as tack and harnesses for the dogs. Their weapons included Winchester carbines and enough ammunition to last them for about six months, as well as various styles of harpoons. They had spare seal hides, fishing gear, extra wool, drills, saws, knives, nails, axes, pots, cutlery, and a collection of books and scientific instruments, thermometers, barometers, telescopes, and a theodolite.

Yet, although their four sleds were each loaded with about six hundred pounds of provisions and equipment, the food they carried was barely enough to feed them, even assuming that all went according to plan. Perhaps to fortify the group, Rasmussen organized a feast as a send-off, serving a northern delicacy for which he was beginning to develop a taste: pickled walrus liver, or *quongulaq*. The giant liver had been aged in a bag of blubber in a shaded spot for a year, until it turned as green as grass and tasted like spicy curry. It was so potent that it could bring tears to the eyes.

ON APRIL 16, 1912, thirty-four sleds and 360 dogs and their handlers congregated on the white, stony plain outside Thule Station. With a shout, the unruly congregation set their sleds onto the ice to follow the coast north to the Clements Markham Glacier, where they would turn inland and ascend the ice cap. There, most of the drivers would turn back, and only fifty-three dogs and four men with fully stocked sleds would head east into the interior. A photograph of the scene shows the multitude of dogs and their heavily laden sleds shooting across the plain, ascending the frozen desert of ice and rock toward the unexplored interior of Greenland. The giant boulders and ice chunks cast long shadows in the bright sunshine of early April. Rasmussen's journal entry captured his exhilaration at the event: "Hello comrades, happy men on the eve of cheerful discoveries. The morning brings alive the dream of the great unknown, and with the sun we rush to meet our destiny! Out of breath, full of zest for the dawning day . . . Can anyone be richer?"

The sun was a low and swollen orb circling between the horizons. They sweated their way up the glacier, over slippery ice and around deep crevasses. Rasmussen felt like "a free man." He urged his dogs to greater exertion, loudly singing American football songs and opera arias, accompanied by the patter of hundreds of feet and the rasp of the sled runners hissing over the soft snow. As they ascended the great Greenland ice dome, there were many days of uneventful slogging when they could cover only thirty-five miles, but on other days they traveled as far as sixty miles, propelled by Rasmussen's humor. Each day they thawed walrus meat for the dogs and constructed an igloo to sleep in; if the snow was not suitable, they slept in their tent. Some days they kept traveling until they could go no more, avoiding sleep until a storm arose and made them stop.

On April 19, Rasmussen scrawled in his diary his impression of the daily monotony and the temperatures that hovered as low as −22° Fahrenheit (−30° Celsius): "Around me I see only the white desert, the glacier, which draws in deathly cold and blinding snowstorms. It overwhelms me and the ice dazzles the eye with its white monotony. Only when the sun is out is there heat, bathing the silent landscape in a wistful peace." Sometimes a solitary raven would fly silently overhead, across the "one hundred mile wide road" to the east. "It is with strange feelings that under such conditions we go into a large and unknown land," Rasmussen wrote, "and can be swallowed by bleak loneliness. There is a seriousness about these vast wastelands that involuntarily creeps into one's mind. Hour after hour without hearing any sound, without seeing any living thing, and you work in these solemn surroundings so long that you stop and wince at the sound of your own footsteps. In each mountain ridge I saw only hope."

Greenland's ice cover is more than a mile thick in some places. When the travelers reached an altitude of 7,000 feet on their journey up and over the ice cap, the sun's rays pierced like "white hot metal in our eyes." Yet their faces froze while their skin burned from the ultraviolet rays until it peeled, hanging in ragged splotches, raw and bleeding. Ice needles shredded the poor dogs' feet, and one dog team was blown into the air "like flour in a mill." The four men looked like ghosts driving ghost dogs, covered in crystalline powder that shimmered in the sun. Amid the "vast desert of cold and dead" that was the heart of the ice cap, Rasmussen dreamed of the lush green forests and fields of Denmark. Yet it overwhelmed him "with a kind of mystery, this great white being that lets the fine white snow drift over me, this ocean of unshakable calm that has its own breath. It triggers the awareness of half-forgotten mythological visions: Ragnarok! Now I understand the imagination and the dreams in the old Nordic mythology."

Endless days of pushing into endless white nothingness made the travelers lose focus and hope. The wind was constantly in

their faces until they reached the height of land of the great ice
dome and began their descent to the east coast. As the snow was
now too soft to make igloos, they slept in the tent, which offered
scant protection from the elements. During sleep breaks, the dogs
were tethered by walrus-hide ropes so that they wouldn't wander off, but they soon became too exhausted even to try getting
away; they simply curled up together and slept huddled in a mass.
The men were constantly thirsty, yet Freuchen complained about
Rasmussen's tea-brewing skills: "He thought that tea should be
boiled and of course that's wrong." Soon their food began to run
low and they were reduced to gulping hot pots of melted and
slightly diluted fat and blubber: "We drank it like sweet milk."
When they had eaten all their lamp blubber, they grew lean and
silent.

Freuchen's duties included taking daily measurements of the
sun's position and the temperature, and estimating the distance
they had traveled by reading the odometer connected to his sled.
He would then do the mathematical calculations to determine
where they were. All this squinting into the sun finally took its
toll, and Freuchen developed snow blindness. While Uvdloriaq
also developed a minor case, it was Freuchen who became debilitated. His eyelids became so swollen that he could not open
them. He was essentially blind, and he silently celebrated when
a gale kept them inside the tent, huddled together for warmth.
Even this was a mixed blessing, because they had decided that
they would eat only on travel days. Freuchen's measurements,
however, indicated that they should sight land soon.

Because they had nearly run out of food, Rasmussen offered a
different sort of sustenance. Every morning, while they lay "freezing on the ice in their sleeping bags," he would leap up and begin
singing. And every evening he read from various novels to entertain them. Uvdloriaq and Inukitsoq grew suspicious when the
plot seemed improbable, asking if the stories were true. When

Rasmussen admitted that it was all fictional, they lost interest; only true stories were worth paying attention to—a curious reaction, considering the mythical nature of much of their own folklore. Perhaps they thought their own stories were true stories and not metaphorical.

Before setting out on the expedition, the men had spent days making special runners of frozen walrus hide to help the sleds glide when the snow grew soft. Now these runners became food for both them and their starving dogs. Far from letting the situation get them down, Inukitsoq and Uvdloriaq joked about their starvation, recalling how much fat and blubber they had cached on the west coast—all that food, and no way to get it! Periodic starvation was part of the Polar Inuit annual routine, and the uncertainty of not knowing where their next meal would come from was an issue they dealt with their entire lives. Eventually, Rasmussen and Freuchen also became hardened against the cold, wind and pain and focused on only one goal: getting off the ice cap, reaching land again and hunting for fresh meat before they became too weak to do so.

When they finally saw mountains in the distance, they faced the problem of going not too slow but too fast.

The downhill slope increased, and soon they were sliding out of control through the soft snow. A dog stumbled, the sled ran over it and crushed it, yet the sled couldn't slow down. There was also a strong wind at their back, and with no way of stopping they feared flying off an ice ledge at the foot of the glacier. Fortunately, the careening sleds and howling dogs slid to a stop on the ice at the edge of a cliff with a fifty-foot drop to the rocks below. Behind them was the vast desert of the ice cap; below, a stony plain of heather and dwarf willow poking through patches of snow that lingered in early May, offering the possibility of food.

The cliff was a terrifying prospect, a maze of chasms and ledges, but Uvdloriaq scouted and found the best way down. The team used walrus-hide ropes to lower themselves, their dogs and sleds to the ground. Freuchen went first, accidentally impaling himself in the thigh with his harpoon tip when it snagged on an ice outcropping. Warm blood trickled down his leg, soaking his pants. Such an injury, so far from shelter and safety, could mean his death. Some of the dogs grew impatient with the roping procedure and leaped off the cliff, crashing to their death among the jumbled ice blocks at the base, where Freuchen lay in pain. The newly dead were immediately fed to the remaining dogs, who devoured them in a frenzy of wild hunger.

Once the men had descended the ice wall, it was as if they had entered a land of "tropical" warmth, Rasmussen wrote, that made them "lazy and sleepy . . . everything in us was prepared for frozen mercury." They bandaged Freuchen's leg, moved onto the plain, and set up camp. It was now May 9 and light all the time, with the sun rotating in a tight disc above them. They had traveled 650 miles in twenty-six days, including days with storms that kept them from leaving their shelter. They still had fifty dogs, although others were soon to die. The surviving dogs recovered their health and became frisky in the soft heather tufts, and the men rejoiced at feeling soil under their feet and breathing the scent of living things. They stripped down nearly naked and lay in the sun and warmth. After a while they collected twigs and driftwood for a small fire. They brewed coffee and made porridge, thinking of the enormous distance between them and any other human beings.

In mid-May, as the three others set off to hunt, Freuchen was left in camp to recover from his snow blindness and wounded leg. "One must walk far and bravely before you get to where musk oxen live," he knew. The hunters split up and fanned out across the terrain, the better to spy any game in the gently undulating valleys, and fortunately they did. Rasmussen recorded Inukitsoq's story of his successful hunt: "My [Inukitsoq's] attention was caught by some strange black stones, [at] which I directed the telescope continuously. They were very far away, but as I became more and more aware that it might be a musk-oxen, I let my gaze rest on them uninterrupted. It was strange that the black stones were similar, they had exactly the same form—and then, well, then it came: One of the stones began to move and walked slowly beside the other!" Inukitsoq crept slowly closer over several hours, trudging downwind through a canyon toward the small herd of eight animals. Then he let the dogs loose on the herd to force them into a defensive circle.

Inukitsoq was "completely transported to the stone age by facing such prey," Rasmussen observed. While the dogs held the animals in place, Inukitsoq shot them all and then rushed back to the others to get help transporting the carcasses back to camp. With so many dogs to feed in addition to themselves, and already so close to starvation, they needed the meat of two musk oxen each day. Adult musk oxen stand between four and five feet at the shoulder and weigh between four hundred and five hundred pounds. They hunted several more in the coming days. But still more dogs died, nearly daily, from being swept away while crossing glacial rivers and other mishaps, and they were fed to the others. The four explorers decided to break up one of the sleds for firewood, as there were now only enough dogs for three teams.

They continued to hunt but saw no further signs of game, and soon they were reduced to eating rabbits and ptarmigan raw— they had used all the wood and eaten all their cooking oil. On one occasion, the others went ahead of Freuchen to scout while he, still feeling his injury and his eyes not yet fully healed, made his way slowly through the fog. He heard his dogs snarl, and the ropes on his sled went limp, so he opened his swollen eyes just enough to see the dogs clustered and feasting on a carcass of some kind. Dashing forward, he pushed them aside and grabbed a gnawed femur, believing it to be from a cache of musk oxen left by the others. He returned to his sled and ripped the flesh off the bone, enjoying the aroma of what he believed was raw musk ox. Then he felt something peculiar at the end of the bone. After "an unusually unpalatable mouthful," he pried his aching eyes open to see the nails of a dog's foot nearly in his face. When he caught up with the others, they roared with laughter at his sad tale.

The group soon reached a beautiful chute bounded by sandstone cliffs covered with sparse grass, willow and heather. Many small creeks ran down it, fed by glaciers melting from the spring sun. The valley, which they named Zigzag Valley because of its many turns, was sixty miles long and appeared to be devoid of game. Travel was hard through patches of deeper soft snow, and soon the men and their dogs were exhausted and starving again. One day they solemnly stripped the remaining walrus-hide runners from their sleds and gnawed on the "abominable" hides for sustenance. Then they once again fed the dogs some of their fallen comrades. The world seemed bleak and desperate. "Can anything be sadder when travelling than waking up to a storm," Rasmussen wrote. "When you know yourselves surrounded by hungry dogs and have to go up into the mountains to hunt?" They continued to trudge over a terrain of small sharp stones that tore the soles of their boots. Each day they fruitlessly scouted for musk oxen, while subsisting on a few grouse that they managed to shoot.

The dogs went days without food, and soon tried to eat their own harnesses, until "the snow was finally quite red from the blood from their gums." When the ragged band of adventurers finally did come upon a small herd of musk oxen, the dogs went crazy. They attacked, "joined in a circle, barking and howling, with dripping tongues and evil grinning teeth, their eyes burning with the animal longing for blood," Rasmussen recalled in his diary. Before they could shoot the musk oxen, the dogs "flew at the poor beasts sinking their teeth in, taking a hold of the belly and seemed to want to eat into the living animal." When the musk oxen were dead, Freuchen slit their bellies open to release the gas and cut out their hearts and a few other prime cuts to share, before retrieving the rest of the meat. Their spirits revived, they followed the desolate valley through the mountains and around several small lakes, "oblivious to pain and fatigue, because you know that giving up here is the path to destruction."

On June 1, the men emerged from the valley, coming out on the coast near Denmark Inlet. As the water in the inlet was still frozen, they decided to sled over the ice to make good time heading north. After a while, they noticed something on the shore: an old sled runner stabbed into the ground. Upon closer examination, they discovered the remnants of a camp. It was a summer camp from the *Danmark* expedition, of which Freuchen had been a member, although he had remained on the ship. According to custom there should have been a note, but the men could not find one.* They found no traces of the men they were looking for.

It was a desolate spot for a camp, with no game and no possibility of finding any, given the terrain. There were no clues as to the whereabouts of the lost men, and eventually Rasmussen concluded that they must have traveled south. But finding them really wasn't Rasmussen's ultimate purpose; it was merely his excuse for crossing the ice cap instead of tending to business at Thule Station. He left a note in a cairn, detailing their departure, their time of travel and their plans to travel north. "It is always so still and silent when passing places where others have struggled in vain for life. And here, where it was about friends, our feelings were strong in our minds—old times when we shared the same

---

*They later learned that a note had been written but was removed by Ejnar Mikkelsen, and that he had violated tradition by not leaving a new note explaining his actions.

possibilities—both Uvdloriaq and Inukitsoq had known Mylius and Jørgen."

Eventually, Uvdloriaq shot a seal out on the ice, and they all feasted on the quivering fat, tossing chunks to the dogs, who soon groaned with overconsumption, causing Uvdloriaq and Inukitsoq to laugh as if it were some great joke. "The Eskimos laughed out loud with joy once again at the glistening fat, this was certainly something other than the dry, aristocratic musk ox. The liver we ate raw, and as we gradually got the pot boiling, there were good pieces of meat covered with fat." They continued to explore the land to the north by sledding along the frozen coast to Independence Fjord, named by Peary when he observed the frozen inlet from a nearby promontory on American Independence Day in 1892. They followed the frozen waterway inland with Peary Land, Greenland's northernmost region, which was then believed to be a separate island, to the north of them. On June 6, they encountered herds of musk oxen dotting the green lowlands and stopped to hunt. After a successful hunt they rushed up to the fallen animals and, according to Freuchen, "lay down and sucked the fresh milk from the udders of the cows. The taste was heavenly." Rasmussen was more philosophical, musing that "again I was fascinated by the atmosphere that travel gives to men, a mood that stems from the variability and unpredictability, which you submit to: yesterday we were miserable and hungry, with no prospect of obtaining food, today we are in the middle of abundance and unconcern."

The next week they decided to venture inland from Independence Fjord, walking over "sharp, weathered stones that make our soles almost numb," and climbed every mountain within reach to enjoy the panoramic views. They found the unmistakable stone rings of an ancient encampment, proof that people had once lived here, at least temporarily, though Rasmussen and the others had thought themselves the first to visit the land. Ages ago, tents had been pitched here, and when the people departed they left behind two long straight tent poles, made from trees that must have been brought from somewhere since there was no other pole-length driftwood in the vicinity. Uvdloriaq and Inukitsoq each wondered what they were doing so far north; how did these people live? Rasmussen, too, wondered. How did they get to this exceedingly remote northern spot, isolated from all the other habitable regions of Greenland? Rasmussen noted that the Inuit were always pushing on to new lands, "and today we see the Eskimo tongue spoken from Asia's shores by the Bering Sea and completely over to the east coast of Greenland . . . they stopped only when, on one hand they were met with people stronger than themselves, and on the other they came to the 'world's end' facing the vast ocean."

Amid these musings, the kernel of an idea began to form. Might these ruins be proof of an actual migration route?

"The Eskimo are an exploring people," Rasmussen observed, "always longing for a change and a surprise. A people who like moving about in search of fresh hunting grounds, fresh possibilities, and 'hidden things.' They are born with the explorer's inclination and thirst for knowledge, and they possess all those qualities which go to make an explorer in these latitudes." Rasmussen may also have been referring to himself and his almost painful longing for something intangible—the wind spirits or the bird's land—a never-satisfied ache to be roaming, searching for distant images in his mind.

WITH ONLY TWENTY-FIVE dogs remaining, the explorers continued sledding up Independence Fjord under sunny skies. The days were hotter now; the ice became weaker and corroded, with pools of water and slush making travel harder for the dogs. They were following the frozen inlet that led like a highway into the interior of northern Greenland. Near the end of June, they reached a point where it was clear that Peary Land was part of Greenland and not a separate island, as Peary had maintained. Inukitsoq laughed out loud at the idea of "the great Peary" making such a major error. "Peary Channel" was in fact a glacier at the top of the inlet.

The end of June was the height of summer, and the explorers had to start thinking of recrossing the ice cap by ascending the glacier that Rasmussen named after his patron and business partner, Nyeboe. It took five brutal days to climb three hundred feet. The dogs were weary, the sleds were heavy, and the steep climb nearly finished them all off. They were running low on food again. One day, Rasmussen, the smallest of the men, charged ahead of the others, dragging his sled by a sling across his forehead. He didn't stop until he reached the top of the glacier seven hours later. The others agreed that he was the master traveler and none could duplicate his feat, but with rations reduced to one stale sack of oatmeal and their boots worn through, it was hard to work up enthusiasm for the accomplishment. They again resorted to eating raw hares, including one that had recently given birth. Rasmussen sucked on its udder to gain the fleeting taste of milk, announcing, "Sleep is milk, and milk is sleep"—recalling his days as a penniless journalist in Stockholm. Soon after, several of the few remaining dogs tumbled into a crevasse and yet more were swept away while crossing an ice-choked river.

Continuing west, Uvdloriaq went ahead to scout the route and came upon an oasis of alpine flowers and grass. They entered the undulating land, its yellow fields banded by blue glaciers in the distance. Fortunately, "Poppy Valley" was dotted with herds of grazing musk oxen. There was even the sound of bumblebees, attracted by flowering bell heather, red saxifrage, yellow poppies and lousewort, sprouting from mere handfuls of soil and the plentiful musk ox manure. The explorers remained there for several days, hunting musk oxen before pushing on over a glacier and into another verdant valley—with knee-high grasses and ice-free lakes with salmon, it was a true "paradise in the Arctic." They stayed there for three weeks, fattening up the dogs for the return crossing of the ice cap, which lay on the other side of this valley.

Here, too, they set to hunting musk oxen, placing the great slabs of meat on the sleds. Once, as they hiked across the valley with the twenty remaining dogs running free and chasing musk oxen, four were killed by the oxen when the beasts charged in defense. When the men finally caught up to the herd, they discovered that they had only seven bullets with them, but there were nine musk oxen. The curious thing about musk oxen is that they never abandon their fallen comrades; they form a defensive circle to fend off attacks and will never retreat, and even a single standing musk ox will remain standing to protect its fallen comrades. This is an excellent strategy against attacking wolves, who lack the capacity to kill an entire herd and often leave it alone. But not so much against humans. It was impossible to take a few animals and leave the rest—the whole herd had to be killed in order to eat. The men shot six of the nine musk oxen before running out of bullets. But there could be no retreat; they needed the meat in order to survive the trek across the ice cap.

Rasmussen decided to try his luck as a toreador. He grabbed a rifle and attached a long knife to the end of it. While Freuchen and Inukitsoq danced and waved to distract the shaggy beasts, Rasmussen charged a musk ox. He rammed the makeshift spear between the animal's shoulders, killing it quickly, and leaped away before the others could attack him. He did this three times. Rasmussen didn't enjoy killing for the sport of it, but he had the ability to take stock of a situation instantly and do what was required. And he had the physical stamina and skill to make it happen.

He also retained his droll sense of humor. Later that night, after they had feasted, they chatted while sitting on stones in front of their tent. Musk ox meat had been their main food for two months now. Rasmussen asked the other three:

"If you could choose and could have anything in the world, what would you like to have for dinner tonight?"

The two Inuit said nothing. Freuchen said, "Well, I don't know; I really don't know. It's hard to say."

"What would you say to a delicious piece of boiled musk ox meat? Could you imagine anything better?"

The travelers continued to lounge in the grassy valley they called "the Camp Under the Big Stone," recuperating before the final trek home. Now, with only sixteen dogs remaining, they burned a third sled because not enough dogs remained to haul it, leaving only two sleds for the return journey. It was so warm that they slept outside, without sleeping bags. They were well fed, languid, content. "In such moments of relaxation," Rasmussen wrote, "I can feel a heartfelt joy at the free life that comes with the journey."

ONE DAY, DURING their stay in the Camp Under the Big Stone, Rasmussen felt a "weird" pain in his leg and Freuchen noticed him limping as they butchered the musk oxen. He did less work than usual. That night, Rasmussen woke Freuchen up to complain that he could not sleep and there must be a rock under his sleeping bag. It was then that Freuchen knew something was wrong. The next day Rasmussen couldn't walk properly and had a fever. Freuchen suspected that he had some form of sciatica from being continuously wet and cold for months and sitting on cold stones, though sciatica doesn't usually cause fevers. As Rasmussen could barely move, they decided to let him rest for a few days. He was rarely sick, but when he was, it was serious.

On July 22, while Uvdloriaq remained with Rasmussen, Freuchen and Inukitsoq set off to find a cairn that Peary had erected at nearby Navy Cliff. They wanted to leave a short note about their trip in the cairn, which Freuchen had spotted by using his theodolite and telescope. After crossing several freezing streams and climbing a mountain, they scrambled to its peak. It was inspiring to be standing in the same spot where, years earlier, Peary and the Norwegian explorer Ejvind Astrup had surveyed the vast land. Unfortunately, when they returned, Rasmussen was still in agony, biting on a piece of hide and sweating. He was in too much pain even to enjoy the pouch of tobacco that Freuchen had saved for him, now that he had run out of his own supply. Rasmussen argued that Freuchen and Inukitsoq should recross the ice dome, leaving him and Uvdloriaq at the camp and returning with help in the spring. They all admitted that it was a good plan, but they refused to leave Rasmussen.

In early August, the dogs plump and the sleds piled with musk ox steaks, they decided to load Rasmussen onto a sled and transport him across the ice dome. Uvdloriaq and Inukitsoq began carrying the gear and food up to the edge of the ice, where the sleds could be driven more easily. Freuchen, by far the biggest of the four men, carried Rasmussen, moaning in pain, up the incline on his back. When they laid him on top of the meat supplies on Uvdloriaq's sled, "his face was as white as the snow, and his lips were pressed tight together on the pain." They traveled only six miles the first day, carefully easing Rasmussen's sled through the stream beds and over ice hummocks. When Freuchen asked him about the pain, he muttered so blandly that they nearly laughed: "Shut up and go ahead."

On each of the following days they tried to cover at least fifteen miles while ascending the glacier. A famous story about Rasmussen's endurance recounts that at one point, the sled hit a bump and Rasmussen fell off it and onto the snow. He bit down on the leather strap in his teeth and muttered the strongest complaint he could muster: "This is unpleasant." As he slowly improved, the dogs once again wearied and began to die. One dog gave birth on the trail to nine puppies, whereupon the others rushed in and ate eight of the pups; the mother then devoured the ninth herself. This was not unusual for the dogs; Amundsen reported the occurrence in his travels through the Northwest Passage and in Antarctica.

After two weeks of hard skiing and sledding toward the center of Greenland, the expedition again found its supply of musk ox meat nearly depleted. The men grew hungry on half rations, but they kept their spirits up with talk of feasting and of the meat caches they would find along the west coast. When they stopped to take stock of their remaining food, however, it amounted to dried musk ox strips, musk ox bladders filled with tallow and marrow, the contents of a musk ox stomach that tasted like a sour salad, a pouch of used tea leaves and several racks of dried musk ox ribs covered in tallow. It was not enough. Laconic and downtrodden, they weakly pushed on, muttering only a few words: "scrambled eggs" or "pancakes." Before sleeping, Rasmussen began to read aloud from a housekeeping magazine that he had brought along, lingering over the menu items and discussing the merits and drawbacks for hours each night. Uvdloriaq and Inukitsoq again saw the humor in their foodless predicament, chuckling and shaking their heads when they described the mountains of food they had cached, food that included seal meat and blubber. No one mentioned the *quongulaq*, the pickled walrus liver that had brought tears to their eyes at the start of the expedition.

Nevertheless, with fall approaching, there were compensations: "In camp we have an uncommonly beautiful moon lighting the northeast with wonderful, delicate yellows, white and heavy, blue-black clouds roll across the country—exceedingly picturesque by contradiction." After twenty-five days of sledding through steep gorges and around crevasses, braving wind and storms, the men and their dogs completed the dangerous descent from the ice cap, reaching the west coast in mid-September. To their dismay, it was a place they didn't recognize. Freuchen had made a slight error in calculating their position while traveling across the featureless expanse of the ice cap, and they were, according to their best estimates, about thirty miles north of where they had planned to arrive. Their long journey now became even longer, and the lengthening nights forced longer rests each day but made their hunger worse. Freuchen's legs became stiff and swollen, and his boots had to be cut away from his feet because of the inflammation in his tendons. In constant pain, he was soon unable to walk and lay on a sled pulled by the faltering dogs. Rasmussen could now ski and walk a little.

One day, they divided and ate the last of the musk ox. They had no food left; even the loathed old oatmeal was now gone. "Only two things were certain," Rasmussen wrote. "We had nothing to eat but eleven lean and hungry dogs, and the dogs had nothing to eat." Uvdloriaq and Inukitsoq immediately set off hunting and found several rabbits, and that evening the men burned their skis to make a fire to cook them. Freuchen, who didn't smoke, produced another hidden stash of tobacco for his gleeful companions. Huddled in their tent, trying to ignore their shrunken bellies, they plotted cheerfully about saving some tobacco for their return, to impress their friends with how well they had fared. To arrive home after five months of dangerous travel through unknown lands and still have tobacco would be quite a feat, and "the boys howled with delight" at the thought of it, Freuchen recalled.

Somewhat revived by the rabbit meat, the next day the expedition again set off south along the glacier, now with only eight dogs and one sled, which had Freuchen riding on it. They were "growing weaker by the moment." After a long day of travel, they crested a small glacier to see, far off in the distance, the fjord and the tiny specks that were "the beautiful view" of Thule Station, of home. The next morning, they found that yet another dog had died. With weary and painful strides, they shambled off the glacier and onto the gravel, walking on stones and grass for the final ten miles of their journey. Freuchen and Inukitsoq were both limping now, slowly stumbling behind Rasmussen and Uvdloriaq. Just outside the community, they regrouped. They washed themselves as best they could in a stream, changed into clean, unworn clothes—sealskin furs and shiny boots that they had saved for this moment—and strode into Thule together, firing a rifle and unleashing the dogs to announce their arrival. "It was a September evening and dusk had settled above the sea and coastline." The bay was calm, with a few icebergs glowing brightly with the evening colors.

Several men rushed from their houses and stood before the ghostly figures, laughing for joy. The four travelers had been presumed dead. Inukitsoq had one more surprise for them. He reached into his pouch and waited for the dramatic moment: "Have a smoke," he said to the astonished onlookers. "And then," Freuchen wrote, "there was feasting in Thule! All night dancing and heavy eating. People came running with huge slabs of whale hide and rotten bird meat and other delicacies," which they enjoyed while Rasmussen regaled the community with the tales of their adventures.

7

BEFORE THE EYE OF DAY

Glorious was life
In summer.
But did summer bring me joy?
No! Ever was I so anxious
For the skins and rugs for the platform.
Yes, I was ever anxious.
Ayi, yai ya.

> —"Dead Man's Song, Dreamed by
> One Who Is Alive," by Netsit, recorded
> and translated by Knud Rasmussen,
> *Across Arctic America*

R ASMUSSEN AND FREUCHEN did not head back to Denmark immediately with the news of their historic trek. The season was too far advanced for ships to arrive or leave Thule, and by the time they could have dogsledded south across Melville Bay to Tasiussaq, the bay would have been too frozen to catch a boat there. Yet there wasn't much to trade in their store. While they had been away on their adventure on the ice cap during the summer, the supply ship had been unable to get through the ice in the bay. So, with little trade or travel possible, they recovered from their months of privation and settled into a comfortable winter at Thule, recording their observations and collating Freuchen's barometric, cartographic and temperature measurements. They resumed their familiar lives among the Polar Inuit. Freuchen was glad to be welcomed back by his wife, Navarana. And Rasmussen? How could he not have been thinking about his family back in Copenhagen, his three-year-old daughter and the new baby girl he had never seen? Perhaps to console himself, Rasmussen began writing an account of their adventure.

In December, as soon as the ice on Melville Bay was solid enough, they sledded south to Tasiussaq to get supplies. At the time, neither Rasmussen nor Freuchen felt their expedition had accomplished anything special; they had failed to discover any information about Ejnar Mikkelsen, and no one other than a handful of Inuit knew anything of their accomplishments. "No radios broadcast our progress from day to day [broadcast radio didn't become common for nearly a decade], no newspaper headlines screamed our achievement. No organization offered us prizes, no cigarette companies sought us out to endorse their products," Freuchen later recalled. If everyone on the expedition had died, it would have taken years for anyone to find out.

But as the months passed, they felt that perhaps they deserved some recognition. After all, the feat had been accomplished only once before, by Rasmussen's boyhood hero Nansen, and then it had occurred much farther south and in only one direction. Perhaps they could even raise a little money to help out their floundering trading post. In April, the two adventurers, along with Navarana and Rasmussen's hunting companion Ajako—a teenage boy who was "virtually Knud's adopted son"—set off south through Danish Greenland to Holsteinsborg, about two-thirds of the way down Greenland's west coast, with the intention of catching the first ship to Denmark. Navarana accompanied them only as far as Tasiussaq, where she would await Freuchen's return.

The tour, through the relatively civilized south, was a pleasant trip full of "adventure and fun." Rasmussen, Freuchen and Ajako stopped in many communities as they pushed south on the six-hundred-mile dogsled trip. The greatest celebration was at Rasmussen's Uncle Jens's home, where they were serenaded all night by a chorus of singers, who, along with most of the community, were given mugs of strong coffee to ensure their energetic participation in Rasmussen's arrival. Dancing competitions, wrestling matches and shooting contests were held in their honor. The party used up Rasmussen's entire liquor supply, which displeased his Uncle Carl, whom they visited afterward and who had been anticipating a few drinks.

In the settlement of Ritenbenck, while staying in the post manager's home, they met a young man new to Greenland who didn't know he was speaking with two knowledgeable and respected Greenlandic explorers. The man began boasting about his knowledge of the local people and his important position with the government, claiming that because he was a government employee, the natives would have to obey him. Nevertheless, as a lark, the explorers consented to his joining them on their journey south. Freuchen referred to this bureaucrat only as "the royal assistant" in his account of the trip, but he referred by name to the man's half-Danish, half-Inuit guide, Karl Tygesen. Rasmussen and Tygesen, who had a great sense of humor, took an instant liking to each other and secretly agreed to a deception, assuring Freuchen that "a trip with the young man would be better than a circus." Rasmussen instantly understood the royal assistant's character and knew exactly how to take advantage of the newcomer by playing up to it. Throughout the journey, he pretended that he knew nothing and would defer to the royal assistant's knowledge of and insight into Greenland. As they traveled south, Rasmussen pronounced that they should elect the young man as the leader of their party, a prospect that greatly pleased the gullible civil servant.

When they had ascended the first hill on their journey, the royal assistant puffed at the top as they admired the view and exclaimed at the size of the mighty hill, suggesting that the others had probably never climbed one so large on their dogsleds. Exchanging smirks, the three quickly agreed that they had never been on such a hill, and Tygesen pretended to be on the verge of exhaustion from the climb. Rasmussen and Tygesen claimed that they needed some stimulant to get over the next hills—it was a Greenlandic tradition, as surely the royal assistant knew. The man, himself feeling tired and gratified that the others did as well, dutifully produced a bottle of liquor and some homemade cookies he had brought from Denmark and shared them out. Soon the bottle was empty and most of the cookies eaten. Freuchen, who didn't drink, went ahead as a scout to make sure they didn't get lost. Each day, a version of this farcical scenario played out, with the pompous Dane being deceived and mocked by his traveling companions.

Once, they came upon a hunter along a particularly remote stretch of coastline. The hunter had only seal meat to offer them, and the royal assistant declined because seal meat wasn't eaten by the "better class" of Danish officials in Greenland. Rasmussen claimed that he had eaten a little of it several years before and that it could almost be called food, but it needed to be washed down with a glass of gin. Rasmussen cooked, as he usually did, and then while they ate ravenously, the royal assistant turned green and decided he would eat some canned sausages instead. Rasmussen, as the cook, offered to heat the sausages but slipped and "accidentally" dumped the entire tin of sausages into the seal broth. Nevertheless, the young man remained in a good mood and "told us more about the land and natives than we could ever hope to know," including a shocking tale he had heard from one of his friends—that "the savages" would sometimes actually eat warm raw seal liver.

Freuchen proclaimed that such an outrageous tale must be false, while Rasmussen went outside, cut out a seal liver from an animal, sat down at the table and noisily devoured it, with blood dripping down his chin.

Another day, Rasmussen and Tygesen snuck into the royal assistant's baggage, siphoned the gin from several of his prized bottles, refilled them with water and brought the contraband to a dancing party. When the water-filled bottles later froze and burst, they sympathized, saying that it must have been a faulty batch of gin, but not to worry—surely such an important man had a large supply. Rasmussen and his two co-conspirators kept up their charade for nearly a week, somehow never giving themselves away, until the royal assistant finally left them at his destination. Although it was easy to argue that the boaster brought it upon himself for being so arrogant and insulting to the Greenlanders, the duration of the mockery seems almost cruel. It was not good to be on the wrong side of Rasmussen when it came to belittling his fellow Greenlanders.

When they arrived in Holsteinsborg, Rasmussen hired two boys to look after their dogs, and on April 16, 1913, he, Freuchen and Ajako boarded the ship *Hans Egede*. During the voyage they learned more about the Danish expedition to northeast Greenland that had inspired their own trek. After traveling south along Greenland's east coast, Mikkelsen and his companion had been rescued by a Norwegian seal-hunting ship. There was also news that the king of Norway had died. But the truly shocking news was that they themselves were presumed missing. It was claimed in the Danish press that there was no way they could have carried the provisions or equipment required to cross the Greenland Ice Cap and return safely. Prominent explorers had pronounced that it would be impossible for the expedition to succeed, and that it was a foolish and dangerous thing to have attempted.

Rasmussen and Freuchen had a good laugh and then realized that if they were presumed missing, no one knew that they would be arriving in Denmark. When the ship put in at the Faroe

Islands, they rushed to the telegraph office to assure their families and inform Denmark of their impending arrival. They looked so scruffy that at first the telegraph operator refused to send their messages collect, as they had no money to pay him. However, once the operator saw that many of the telegrams were addressed to the new king, to newspapers and to the geographical society, he snapped to attention and sent the messages with no further questions. "And now, on a nice cool May evening, we cruise into Skagen," Rasmussen wrote. "After three years we see again the flat Danish beach rising from the horizon. The mind rushes toward everything ahead, the waiting, the longing." With beating heart and tense nerves, he prepared to live his other life for a while.

THE RECEPTION AWAITING them in Copenhagen was small but enthusiastic, attended by joyful family and friends, eager purveyors of publicity and government officials with their "long and windy speeches." The explorers spoke and toasted the crowd with tall glasses of beer and then went to their parents' homes, Rasmussen to be reunited with Dagmar and his children. But after only a few hours, Freuchen recalled, Rasmussen telephoned him and asked about his plans for the evening. "It wouldn't be you and me if we didn't do something," he said. "It doesn't look as if anybody is going to do anything for us, so we'd better do it for them." So, instead of settling down to a quiet return, they telegrammed invitations to their friends and many prominent people in Copenhagen for a great celebration at the city's finest hotel. Freuchen, practical as always, asked who would pay, as they had no money. "You and I," Rasmussen replied. "If we crossed Greenland and came back alive, it would be too bad if we couldn't tackle this!"

The party was later described by Freuchen, perhaps with some exaggeration, as the greatest social event the city had ever seen.

Many prominent individuals came, as well as Rasmussen's old confreres from the arts and literature worlds. Starting out as a sedate affair in the dining hall, it quickly degenerated into a chaotic melee. Rasmussen donned his bearskin kamiks and a costume similar to the one he wore when in Greenland. Leaping on the table, he launched into a rousing speech about his adventures over the last three years and exclaimed how much he had missed his friends. The waiters rushed over to remove the expensive tableware before he could crush it, and then there was dancing, led by Rasmussen. After a few hours, to ensure the party's energy didn't wane, he dashed into the hotel's main dining room and urged the other diners to join in the celebration, which lingered late into the night.

The next afternoon, as Rasmussen, Freuchen and Ajako wandered through the city, Rasmussen complained that they had not received the rousing welcome he had hoped for, that other expeditions—ones that received government support—seemed to get much more attention. Of course, these expeditions were well publicized in advance, which helped build anticipation for the explorers' return, whereas in this case few people even knew they were on an expedition until the day before they returned. Rasmussen was discovering that it was difficult to manage publicity in Denmark from the wilds of the Arctic.

In the weeks that followed, however, interest in Rasmussen's and Freuchen's travels grew. Geographical societies from around the world were requesting more information. The *New York Times* zeroed in on the titillating news that Freuchen had married an "Eskimo girl" (true) and that Rasmussen's mother "was a full-blood Eskimo" (which was not true). The publicity inspired Rasmussen to approach the Carlsberg Foundation for a grant to help defray the expenses the expedition had incurred in crossing the ice cap. The amount he applied for, $700, was so small that the directors of the institution were embarrassed and asked how

anything of great scientific value could be accomplished with so
little money.

But making do with little was exactly what Rasmussen had
been doing all his life when traveling in Greenland. He knew—he
had seen the archaeological evidence—that people had been doing, and were continuing to do, this sort of travel all over the land
of the Inuit. Rasmussen simply applied modern goals and ambitions to a fundamentally ancient method of travel and subsistence.

The foundation's members said it was unprofessional and dangerous to travel as Rasmussen and Freuchen did, yet it was well
known that people regularly died on so-called modern expeditions. Rasmussen was a dreamer and fundamentally unprofessional, according to the criteria applied by established institutions,
but he had achieved incredible feats of endurance and survival
while developing grand goals for future expeditions. He was determined to do them by dogsled and to hunt for his food, the way
the Inuit had always done, professionalism be damned. Both he
and Freuchen felt they had overcome great hardships and discovered new things about northern Greenland, but some of their
peers did not view living poorly in the hinterland as particularly
noteworthy. In thinking about their situation, Freuchen observed:
"It is dangerous for a man to isolate himself from daily criticism
and changing values." Perhaps their fame was merely a flash in
the pan, a poor foundation for a respectable career.

But despite these concerns, during their first visit with the new
Danish king, Christian X, they were undaunted and cynical—
they were not about to show deference to a powerless hereditary
monarch. Perhaps sensing this, the king seemed a little peeved
that Rasmussen had named a new land for him without first having consulted him to determine whether the land, perhaps even
the gesture, were suitable. Rasmussen, with his fluid tongue, assured the king that the gesture was indeed intended as a compliment. The king mused that perhaps the land was not grand

enough to be worthy of his name and that he could not accept the compliment until someone of authority went "up there" and inspected the land. Growing angry, Rasmussen declared: "I know it is not permitted me to contradict a king," and then proceeded to contradict him. "I say it is worthy of you because I know the land better than you do."

AFTER ONLY FIVE weeks in Denmark, Freuchen became bored with Copenhagen and sailed back to Greenland and Navarana, taking Ajako, who was desperately homesick, with him. Freuchen would continue to run the trading post until Rasmussen returned. Nyeboe, "the brains and working force of our committee," who continued to finance the operation, purchased a small three-masted sailing schooner, *Kap York*, to solve the supply issues they had been having with the larger, irregularly arriving ships.

Freuchen and Ajako arrived in South Greenland at Ivigut, where there was a cryolite mine, and nearby, a copper mine owned by Nyeboe. They planned to wait there for the *Kap York* to take them north, but they became bored when it didn't arrive on time—the motor had failed—and instead begged a ride on one of the few motorboats in Greenland. At Egesminde (Aasiaat), about halfway up the coast, Freuchen said he was awakened during the night by "a number of girls squealing in my room" and demanded to know what they wanted. "It is Knud! Your Knud!" they exclaimed—and sure enough Rasmussen was waiting in the harbor, proudly sitting in a new motorboat. Hearing that Freuchen and Ajako had been stranded by the *Kap York*'s delay, and growing tired of conservative Denmark, Rasmussen had boarded a steamer and arrived in time to help the captain repair the *Kap York*. Finding that his comrades had already departed, he purchased another motorboat and rushed north along the coast until he caught up

with them. He couldn't resist the temptation to follow and perhaps travel with them the whole distance, around 2,500 miles, to
see his beloved Thule Inuit once again.

When the *Kap York* arrived in Tasiussaq, the trio unloaded
their goods onto Rasmussen's newly purchased and much smaller
motorboat and then used it to transport the goods to an island in
the south of Melville Bay, before the ice became too thick to navigate. On the island of Bjorneborg, Rasmussen and Ajako killed
twenty-two bears and cached them before heading north to get the
extra sleds needed to transport their goods the remaining distance
to Thule. When the *Kap York* returned to Denmark, Rasmussen was not on board, though he had promised Dagmar that he
would return with the ship: Dagmar in fact had sailed to Julianehåb (Qaqortoq) to meet him so that they could return to Denmark together. When Rasmussen changed his plans, he sent her a
note by kayak. It never reached her, and no one in the community
had heard any news of him. Left alone in the isolated town, Dagmar grew frustrated and sailed for Denmark without her husband,
whom she had seen for only a few months in the previous three
years. According to Freuchen, Rasmussen was in "hot water," and
Dagmar "did not recover her sense of humor until the next year."

Rasmussen remained stranded in Thule until the spring of
1914, which suited him fine, as he had many plans. During the
winter of 1913–1914, he and Freuchen learned that they were no
longer the only "white men" in the district. An American expedition, headed by Donald MacMillan, under the auspices of the
American Museum of Natural History and the American Geographical Society, was searching for Crocker Land, a territory
east of Ellesmere Island that Peary claimed to have seen on his
expeditions. The MacMillan expedition's ship was frozen in the
ice near Etah, at the extreme northwest of Greenland. Rasmussen knew the presence of the ship would interfere with the region's trade, as the local people would have another set of goods

1. Scene of Jakobshavn, now called Ilulissat, from the early 20th century. The Rasmussen household, by far the largest home in the region, is in the left foreground.

2. Knud and his younger siblings Christian and Vilhelmine. The photo is taken in Copenhagen in 1891 when Knud was 12 years old, just before his family returned to Greenland, leaving him at a boarding school.

3. Knud posing with Laplanders, or Sami, on his journey to northern Scandinavia, circa 1901.

4. Members of the Danish Literary Expedition before the trip, circa 1905. Clockwise from left, Harald Moltke, Knud Rasmussen, Ludvig Mylius-Erichsen, Dr. Alfred Bertelsen.

5. Members of the Danish Literary Expedition lounging in a snow hut, Christmas 1902, sketch by Harald Moltke.

6. Traveling camp of the Danish Literary Expedition, painted by Harald Moltke, circa 1903.

7. Knud posing with Arnajark outside Thule Station, circa 1911. Rasmussen encouraged many old women to visit him for extended periods of time so that he could hear all their stories.

8. Peter Freuchen and Knud, like two heroes from mythology dressed for the icecap, circa 1912.

9. View of Thule Station, or Thule house, in summer, circa 1912.

10. The expedition ship *Danmark* at Thule harbour with the distinctive Mount Dundas in the background, circa 1916.

11. Peter Freuchen and Navarana inside Thule Station, circa 1915.

12. Dagmar and Knud in Lynge with daughters Hanne and Inge, 1913.

13. Rasmussen and Inukitsoq consult a map during the Second Thule Expedition, 1916.

14. Musk oxen hunting on the Second Thule Expedition, "They approached us slowly and fearlessly, with bowed heads and shiny eyes."

15. Ajako at Beaumont's Cairn in northwest Greenland, circa 1917.

to trade for. Most disturbing to him was the expedition's partial objective, which he learned of from Dr. W. Elmer Ekblaw, a Swedish American who visited the Thule Station. Ekblaw and his crew planned to locate and remove a giant meteorite from somewhere in northern Melville Bay and transport the rock to the American Museum of Natural History in New York, where it would be displayed alongside two other north Greenland meteorites that Peary had already removed. Before the traders' arrival, these meteorites had been the Inuit's only source of iron.

Ekblaw's visit occurred when Rasmussen and Freuchen still had about forty loads of goods on the island of Bjorneborg that would have to be brought over to Thule across the ice of Melville Bay. As it was the middle of winter and hunting was difficult in the polar night, Ajako had gone to retrieve a walrus flipper he had stored on nearby Saunders Island. This was to be their meal. They had no other food to offer their distinguished guest, Dr. Ekblaw, and Freuchen suggested to Rasmussen that they admit they had nothing to eat apart from the old flipper and ask Dr. Ekblaw to bring his own food. Rasmussen was appalled. Never show your poverty, he said, it would only multiply in the visitor's eyes and give you a bad reputation. He had a better idea. In Freuchen's recollection, Rasmussen put on his smile and went to meet the eminent doctor.

"We are delighted to see you and are especially pleased to be able to serve you a very rare dish! Have you ever tasted real Eskimo rotten food?"

"I haven't tried it yet," Ekblaw said, "and I'm not sure that I would like it."

"Marvellous! I am so happy!" Rasmussen cried. "We can give you an especially light walrus flipper, without too much or too little flavour. How wonderful that we have saved this for the occasion."

Rasmussen continued to talk, never leaving time for Ekblaw to get a word in as the rotten walrus flipper was ceremoniously brought into the main room and chopped with an axe into suitable portions. Ekblaw looked horrified, and the smell was none too appetizing. "How lovely!" Rasmussen exclaimed. "Yes, it is exactly as I said—good, very good! No one could help liking it, and I can see that you appreciate good food—rotten meat with the Eskimos, fruit in the tropics, and pâté de fois gras in Paris." Noisily smacking his lips, he consumed a portion of flipper. "I am giving you an especially good piece of strongly smelling meat; it has had neither too much nor too little of the summer's heat."

Ekblaw, aware of the need for courtesy and observing the evident relish of his hosts, had no way out and began to daintily nibble the lightly rotten meat. When he expressed his tentative pleasure with the delicacy, Rasmussen was delighted and quickly hacked off another portion of flipper, ignoring Ekblaw's protests, and placed it on the poor man's plate. Freuchen recalled that "the blubber was green with maturity—almost the same as Ekblaw's face by now."

"Take it, take it!" Rasmussen said. "No modesty here. I knew you would like it, and you have not disappointed me. Take it and eat it; it may be a long time before you eat such a meal again!"

Once Ekblaw had finished, somehow without vomiting, Rasmussen proclaimed: "We Danes always used to take coffee after our meals. But you will admit it would be a pity to drink coffee after such a meal as this. It would not only run counter to custom, but would also kill the taste we still have in our mouths." Of course, they had no coffee—it was still with their supplies south across the ice of Melville Bay. But Rasmussen enthusiastically talked on, gradually bringing the conversation around to the topic of the meteorite.

The meteorite was already claimed, he bluffed; he had claimed it for the Danish Museum, and so Ekblaw and his companions had no right to remove it—they were just too late, unfortunately.

He then agreed to take Ekblaw, who graciously acknowledged Rasmussen's prior claim, to the meteorite so that he could take a chunk of it back to his museum in New York. (Rasmussen had in fact never seen the meteorite, so he later had to offer a new rifle as a reward for someone to show him where it was.) The next morning, Ekblaw surprised them by treating them to a breakfast of biscuits, butter, canned milk, syrup and canned salmon—"Ah, how it tasted!"—as a way of thanking them for their hospitality. The evening had surely been memorable for both the conversation and the food.

DURING THE NEXT few weeks, there were still forty to fifty sled loads of supplies to be hauled from the informal depot on Bjorneborg Island in Melville Bay to Thule, a daunting task. The men made dozens of trips back and forth across the dangerous ice of the bay under a dome of darkness. When someone came to trade, Rasmussen exclaimed at the fine dogs they possessed and said he wanted to witness how the dogs could haul, and he convinced them to deliver their fox skins directly to Tasiussaq. He then noted that it would be foolish to travel with an under-loaded sled, so he would be grateful if they would bring a few additional crates with them on their return journey. When they grumbled about the time and effort involved in making such a journey, Rasmussen offered them access to his cache of bear meat on Bjorneborg Island to feed their dogs. So, in effect, he would be saving them the expense of feeding their own dogs— and wouldn't it be a grand adventure! Rasmussen "loved to manage people," Freuchen recalled, "to praise some, scold others. He knew them all, and knew how to keep them going." Not until the end of March were all the supplies loaded into their storerooms at Thule. That accomplished, Rasmussen finally departed south again to Holsteinsborg, sledding most of the length of Greenland once again so he could catch an early season ship to Denmark.

Rasmussen arrived in Copenhagen on June 28, 1914, barely one month before Europe lurched to war. Earlier in June, a Danish millionaire named Ole Olsen had agreed to finance a two-year expedition to the North Pole, to be led by Rasmussen the following year. Rasmussen would make Thule his base, and he would be accompanied by a staff of scientists. But although Denmark remained a neutral country throughout World War I, this expedition never happened because of the war. Instead, Rasmussen completed writing his account of the First Thule Expedition, which he had begun composing in Greenland. After he had been in Copenhagen for several months, reacquainting himself with his wife and daughters, he sent a letter to Freuchen in Greenland. Mailed in the early fall of 1914, it didn't arrive until April 1915.

Although it had reached south Greenland by mid-October, the letter had worked its way north slowly by dogsled and kayak, arriving just before Freuchen was to set off on an exploratory expedition to chart part of Greenland's northern coast. Europe was engaged in "a terrible war," Rasmussen wrote. "Yes, pessimistic men even maintain that it might last until October, although it is hard to believe that such mass murdering will be tolerated that long. But inflation will come, so please take good care of your things and explain to the people up there that this fall the world is experiencing the greatest fright in its history." He added that he might not be able to get the annual supply ship up to Thule because of the war.

Later, Rasmussen learned that while he was in Copenhagen, many of his Inuit friends in the Thule district were concerned for his safety during the war. "We know that Knud is down there in the white man's world, and he usually manages to set things right no matter what is wrong," Freuchen recalled one man saying.

Others suggested that if only the ice would permit a ship to arrive, they could gather perhaps ten or even twelve men together, arm themselves, and sail to Denmark to put themselves under Rasmussen's command and help end the war.

Rasmussen now could do nothing but wait, which may have been a good thing. Instead of rushing back to Greenland in pursuit of more adventures, he settled down to write. He was also much sought after as a lecturer and speaker, his fame and profile rising with each trip he made. In 1915, he had two books published: *Before the Eye of Day* and *My Travel Diary*. *Before the Eye of Day* is a short literary book that explores his increasingly intimate relationship with the Polar Inuit, with whom he now enjoyed considerable standing for his leadership, daring exploits and tribal fellowship. A collection of his impressions of the northland, it portrays the peoples and their simple and harsh, yet also rich and fulfilling lives.

The realistic portrait includes several haunting tales of starvation and death that underscore the whims of nature and the uncertainty that regularly, if not frequently, befell the people of Greenland, including one story in which starvation killed most of an extended family and a mother had to kill her own little boy to end his suffering. "The memory of these two months of starvation during the severe cold had set such a mark on her light heartedness that she could still shudder violently as if she were still in the middle of a battle with death every time she thought back to those days."

The Arctic was a cold, unforgiving and desolate world that could grind down a person and end their life on a whim, but as Rasmussen was writing, the Great War ground down Europe with the same random and pitiless suffering. The south may have had a more forgiving climate, but it had its own unstoppable powers of destruction. Rasmussen's point was clear for those who chose to see: do not be so quick to condemn the savagery of others.

The disarmingly named *My Travel Diary* is an energetic account of his adventures crossing the Greenland Ice Cap in the First Thule Expedition. "Those who hope to find exciting entertainment will be disappointed," Rasmussen wrote in the book's introduction. But it wasn't true, and he undoubtedly knew it. The story is a constant string of adventures, blended with musings about the origin of the "Eskimo race" and the nature of life. Typical of Rasmussen, he never dwelt upon himself. He never praised his own efforts and stamina, bravery or work, or complained about his discomfort. The praise and accolades went to his companions—Freuchen, Uvdloriaq and Inukitsoq. The many life-threatening situations were related in a jaunty but matter-of-fact manner. A full picture of how Rasmussen organized and led the expedition, inspiring the others to greater exertion and determination, becomes evident only from reading Freuchen's accounts of the same journey. *My Travel Diary* is very different from Rasmussen's previous books, but it nevertheless became a classic of Danish exploration literature. Oddly, it has never been professionally translated into English.

"A journey has ended. A new one already opens its horizons," is the last sentence of the book. Rasmussen had been thinking for some time about the lonely collection of tent rings he had seen in Peary Land and had been ruminating on the implications of this abandoned human habitation site. Where had these people come from? But now he broadened his musings, and a larger question arose: how had Greenland come to be peopled in the first place, and when? The search to answer these questions led him to conceive his next great adventure.

GROUND DEARLY
PAID FOR

"Do you see that?" she asked.
"What?"
"That out there over the sea. It is the Dark coming up, the
great Dark!" she said gravely, and crept away home.

—Knud Rasmussen,
The People of the Polar North

RASMUSSEN DREAMED OF Greenland throughout 1915, while enjoying his celebrity as an author and his daily life with his family. He and Dagmar had commissioned a country home to be built in the hilly country of Hundested, about forty miles northwest of Copenhagen. The now-famous house was designed by a prominent Danish architect in an English cottage style, with somewhat whimsical curves, bay windows and a thatched roof. Surrounded by large grounds with a clear view of the open sea, the house would become Rasmussen's secluded workplace and the family's summer getaway when it was completed in 1917.

In early January 1916, while these plans were under way, Rasmussen received an invitation to travel to New York City and tour several other cities on the American lecture circuit. For an inveterate vagabond who had been grounded in Denmark for a year and a half, the offer was tempting indeed, and he accepted it. While he waited for his ship in London before crossing the Atlantic, he and an old friend wandered to Victoria Station to welcome some of the returning soldiers. Living in neutral Denmark had allowed Rasmussen to avoid direct contact with the devastation wrought by the conflict. Now, among the nervous jostling crowd, wounded, haunted men shambled from the train, hoping for a brief respite from the muddy trenches of the war front.

"Hundreds of gray-dressed soldiers swarmed out of the sealed-off outer platform," Rasmussen wrote. "I was immediately aware that everything that I was seeing really was real. The people here were not men who sought to attract attention with facile war cries or songs. They were serious men who had come from places where they had seen experiences that had taken them from their cozy homes and thrown them into a barbaric world where singing bullets were the only music." Rasmussen was overcome with the scene and its implications, and had an epiphany about the true implications of the war. "While the storm raged around me, and men gave their lives freely and honestly . . . I stood there, a man young and strong enough to act, ready to go away to a foreign country to talk the time away and tell stories about a journey I had once succeeded at but had long since ended."

An image of Greenland's mighty, snow-encrusted mountains came to his mind, "the great country where I belonged," with a lone sled track leading away into the distance. The wind whispered to him that the time was for action, not for talking. He longed to again test his strength, not against other people in war but against nature, to engage in a new battle in the name of science. He canceled his American lecture tour and returned to Copenhagen from London.

After two months of frenetic planning, he was ready to leave for Greenland. Owing to his powers of persuasion and the timely need to aid some fellow Arctic explorers, he was on the first ship allowed to pass through the North Sea. Both Donald MacMillan's Crocker Land Expedition and the relief party sent out to rescue it, headed by E.O. Hovey, were still trapped in the Arctic ice after three years. The *New York Times* reported that the American Museum of Natural History had commissioned Rasmussen to help the beleaguered American explorers, who were running low on supplies, to travel south across Melville Bay and then to southern Greenland, from where they could sail to Copenhagen and on to New York.

On April 18, 1916, Rasmussen and a companion disembarked from the steamer in Godthåb (Nuuk) to set off on the epic journey to Thule. Speed was of the essence; he had promised Dagmar he would spend only one summer in Greenland and return on the last ship of the year in the fall—although, given his past broken promises, one wonders what she really expected. Rasmussen's companion, specially selected for this adventure, was Lauge Koch, a twenty-three-year-old geology student who hoped to discover coral specimens that would reveal something about the age and composition of northern Greenland's geology. Koch was, according to Rasmussen, "broad of shoulder, strong of build, tough, and showing the consciousness of his strength in the way he walks, like a young Great Dane." A photo of Rasmussen, Dagmar and their children with Koch on the dock in Copenhagen before the two men departed confirms this generous description.

The Greenlander Tobias Gabrielsen, a longtime friend of Rasmussen and Freuchen, was also part of the team. Their plan, not yet known to Freuchen, was to explore and map the unknown coast of northern Greenland and to create a rough chart of the shores of Melville Bay. Although the bay had been crossed often in winter, its coast had never been mapped. Rasmussen also hoped to search for archaeological evidence of ancient human migration routes, such as tent rings and house sites that might reveal secrets about the ancient Inuit. This was the first of Rasmussen's expeditions to have official state backing and financial support, in addition to the support of the American Museum of Natural History. The trip north began right after the men disembarked from the ship and involved travel by dogsled, umiak (an open boat larger than a kayak), kayak, motorboat and, finally, hiking. By May 4, the party had reached the Devil's Thumb, a prominent landmark at the southern end of Melville Bay, and began their first task. For the next month and a half, until June 15, they worked their way north along the coast, sketching a rough chart of the ice and rock cliffs that formed the eastern edges of Melville Bay.

When Rasmussen and his companions showed up in Thule, it was a total surprise to Freuchen, and they were joyously received. A storm kept them from hunting at Thule and the dogs were already exhausted, so Rasmussen postponed the northern expedition until the following year. He and Freuchen happily settled into their old routine, a routine broken by the birth of Mequsaq, the firstborn son of Freuchen and Navarana. Rasmussen, being an "expert" on children, as he had two of his own at the time, advised Freuchen to get water and brew coffee—this, after all, was what he had done when Dagmar gave birth to Hanne.

As summer faded into fall, the expedition's supply ship had not yet arrived. When a ship finally did come, it brought news that the original supply ship had been sunk by German U-boats in the North Sea. The other surprise was the ship's passenger, the Swedish botanist Dr. Thorild Wulff, a thirty-nine-year-old newcomer to the Arctic. He had spent the past ten years in Japan, China and Indonesia and had developed an unfortunate sense of superiority over people whom he called "the natives." He wanted only to collect plants while the ship unloaded its small cargo at

Thule and took on the stranded Americans of the MacMillan expedition. But now another setback: ice prevented the ship from leaving, so Freuchen allowed Wulff to stay at Thule Station. Rasmussen responded to Wulff's enthusiasm in searching for unknown plants by inviting him to join the expedition, which was now planned for April 1917.

It was a crowded winter at Thule, with all the visitors and sailors living nearby. Rasmussen and Wulff decided to winter at Tasiussaq instead, which may have pleased Freuchen, who felt that Wulff was "not fit to consort with the Eskimos." Wulff viewed the Inuit as uncivilized and himself as superior, and tried to order them about. On at least one occasion he tried to physically punish one of them, until Rasmussen berated him and he went off grumbling. On another occasion, when the party stopped to observe the first cresting of the sun over the southern horizon—a momentous occasion—Freuchen and two Inuit doffed their hat and mitts. Wulff, however, laughed and refused. One of the men explained, "We think that if we do this we shall not die at least until the sun returns next year. Even if it does no good, we enjoy life so much that we do anything to keep it." Still Wulff refused.

Wulff annoyed and disturbed Freuchen, who brought him along on several winter sled journeys to get him into shape for the spring expedition. Freuchen said Wulff was weak and a complainer, shivering all the time, lacking in stamina and mumbling about heart troubles. And clearly he was not suited for arduous journeys, barely traveling for four hours before refusing to go farther. He screamed with fear at crevasses and ordered Freuchen around: "You got me into this, now get me out. I decide how fast we travel, and you can't leave me here alone." Freuchen informed him that Rasmussen wouldn't tolerate his complaints. When Wulff still refused to get going, Freuchen threatened to whip him and began snapping the whip in the snow around where Wulff slumped. When they finally returned to Thule after a twenty-day trip, the Inuit were surprised to see Wulff. They had given him up for dead. "Well," one mused, "the year is not yet gone."

RASMUSSEN'S PLAN WAS once again to hunt and live off the land, a dangerous gamble at the best of times, and particularly so in the unknown land of Akia, "the country on the far side of the Great Glacier." But this approach appealed to Rasmussen for several reasons: it gave him greater freedom to make decisions regarding the objectives and destinations of the expedition as well as improving his ability to respond to changing conditions. Not carrying all the required food meant lightly loaded sleds, which in turn meant faster travel and longer travel days. But it also meant more unpredictability, which allowed for greater adventure. Rasmussen liked to rely on luck and intuition and enjoyed the thrill of making serious, perhaps even life-and-death, decisions under pressure and he reveled in the spontaneity. He had confidence in his skills and abilities, and he loved to test them.

As an illustration of this, Freuchen remembered one horrible crossing of Melville Bay during a vicious storm. "Rasmussen blossomed under the gruelling routine. I can still see him standing in the middle of Melville Bay, the going bad through deep snow or rough ice, the dogs balking, the Eskimos disgruntled, no dog food, no fuel or provisions, and home far, far away. Then he was the gayest and most at ease." Rasmussen usually chose companions who shared this spirit of adventure and his ability to withstand extreme hardship. For this, the Second Thule Expedition, he elected, once again, to take along Inukitsoq; his longtime hunting companion Ajako; Nasaitordluarsuk, whom everyone called Bosun; the West Greenlander Henrik Olsen; and Lauge Koch. Freuchen, much to his disappointment, would have to remain at Thule to deal with the additional men from the ships and to man the store.

The one surprising addition to the party was Thorild Wulff. Given what he knew of Wulff's attitude toward the Inuit and his traveling capabilities, Rasmussen must have attached much weight to Wulff's scientific credentials, perhaps expecting that they would enhance the expedition's reputation, leading to greater respectability for Rasmussen's work and additional future financing. Rasmussen did make all the members sign a document proclaiming that the Inuit were "members of the Expedition with equal rights and duties to the scientists, and no man but the leader must have command over them . . . There must be no difference in standing between the Eskimos and ourselves." Clearly, there was at least one expedition member who needed this to be spelled out, someone who might have been educated to believe he was within his rights to command "the natives." Wulff seems to have been lacking in insight into his own unsuitability for the arduous journey, either out of pride, scientific zeal, or a belief that Rasmussen would look out for him.

The expedition set off from Thule on April 6, 1917, with a cavalcade of seventy-two "impatient dogs" and six sleds, initially augmented by twenty additional sleds and 282 dogs to haul food supplies partway north before turning back. Rasmussen was again exhilarated at the prospect: "The weather is glorious," he wrote in *Greenland by the Polar Sea*, "with a high sun above the white snow: the ice-mountains of the fjord gleam in the light and the basalt of the mountains out towards Cape Parry flash in merry colours." His plan was to follow the coast north, which would be more challenging and time consuming than ascending the glacier. But on the return journey he intended to cross the ice cap for speed. A successful crossing of the glacier would involve obtaining a great deal of meat beforehand, to sustain the men and their dogs on their journey on the ice, so they would need to find and hunt many musk oxen on the coast. "The risk you run in such a hunting expedition," Rasmussen wrote, "was quite clear to me; but the mind never occupies itself with the dangers when one is setting out. Every Polar traveller is aware of his risks when he leaves his home to set foot on unknown shores; and thus it was also with us."

Freuchen, no doubt with some regret, watched them go. "Time after time while they were gone I thought of them fighting their way up there," he remembered. Life went on at Thule Station as spring passed into summer and summer into fall. With the supply ship sunk, it was a hard year and food was scarce: the ice was thick, and the breathing holes of the seals froze over. Other animals proved elusive and ammunition was running low, so shooting birds was not an option. The new arrivals in the community meant there was less meat to go around, and they had barely kept themselves and their dogs alive through the summer. Worried about the fate of the expedition, Freuchen wanted to plan a trek north to lay caches of meat for his friend. But he had no meat to spare, particularly when he saw how thin his wife and young son had grown during the harshest season anyone could remember.

One day an old woman named Inaluk, "the most gifted conjurer" in the region, was visiting the station. In midconversation with Freuchen, she left the house and went outside, and Freuchen followed her out.

She began to chant as she swayed back and forth. "Those who have been on the Eastside are back," she intoned. The travelers would return soon, "but two of them are missing."

Freuchen was terrified: "Is Knud missing?"

The woman gave him a disdainful look: "Who suggests that the Ice Cap and lack of food could bother Kunuk?"

That night Freuchen lay awake reading and wondering what to do. Should he set out to help, or be patient? And then the door opened and Rasmussen walked in, looking worn and exhausted. He had "the look of the ice cap upon him," Freuchen wrote.

"It has been a terrible summer," Rasmussen said, "with starvation and hardship."

"Are you all here?" Freuchen asked.

Rasmussen slowly walked into the kitchen to get some food. "No," he said. "Two are missing."

The two friends stayed up all night talking while Rasmussen related the tale of the ill-fated expedition.

THE TRIP HAD started off well enough. In the first month they sledded from Thule Station up to Sherard Osborne Fjord, about six hundred miles north. By then the additional supply sleds had returned to Thule and only Rasmussen and his mates continued along the coast. They explored a series of fjords along Greenland's north coast—Victoria Fjord, Nordenskjold Fjord, De Long Fjord—and discovered and named J.P. Koch Fjord. Rasmussen, as usual, had a great appreciation for the luminous beauty of the glistening ice sheets, brooding mountains, rocky outcroppings, and curling tongues of glaciers lolling out across the plains. He pondered the sites of ancient, abandoned encampments as well as more recent places of heroic struggle, such as Dr. Elisha Kent Kane's ordeal in Rensselaer Bay, and Charles Francis Hall's grave in Thank God Harbour. "The ground on which we stand is dearly paid for," Rasmussen observed. "Its exploration has cost the life of many a brave man of iron will. But for each one who fell there were others who offered to take his place; thus our knowledge of the northernmost regions of the earth moves farther and farther north."

But the snow was deep in places, the wind harsh and relentless, and the going exhausting, wearing down the strength of dogs and men. The "endless white ice steppes" and stony terrain were only patched with snow, making sled-hauling arduous. And the hunting was erratic: musk oxen and seal were scarce. On May 27, Rasmussen, ever bright and optimistic, was determined to celebrate with a special feast and opened a can of pineapple. His thoughts drifted to Freuchen, whom he imagined was stoically manning the post and missing the adventure. In a notebook, with a flourish of his pen, he named a nearby cape Peter Freuchen Land, "after my beautiful and hearty friend."

On June 21, the longest day in a perpetually bright summer, the explorers reached the most northerly point of their journey in De Long Fjord. The return trip was treacherous because of meltwater and slush ice that compelled them to wade in glacial water for up to fourteen hours each day, heaving and pushing the sleds across paralyzingly cold rivers. Their waterlogged and puffy clothes disintegrated, and the constant cold kept them shivering. The dogs struggled on, their feet shredded by the shards of ice, leaving a trail of blood on the snow as they limped onward.

Food was inadequate. Rasmussen dreamed of eating the special cakes his mother baked for him: "There you go my boy; eat all you like," he dreamed her saying. But as he raised the cake to his mouth, he awoke "to all our misery. My companions are lying asleep, the wind is whipping the drifting snow around our tent, and an exhausted dog is lying out in the drifts, whimpering pitifully."

He tried to sing in his usual hearty way, but the others failed to respond. "We try to stimulate each other by poking fun at the miserable appearance many of us present [but] there is nothing for it but sucking nourishment from one's humour during these days." Throughout, Wulff was difficult: he lacked the stamina for the journey and was disliked by the Inuit, if not by Rasmussen as well. On one occasion he roused himself to give a brief lecture on lichens but then retreated into morose silence.

At the end of July, the expedition's food supply was disastrously low; they had been feeding the weaker dogs to the others and occasionally eating the lean, sinewy meat themselves. Before heading back onto the ice cap and returning to Thule, they needed to stock up on musk ox meat. They separated, heading in different directions to hunt for days at a time. Henrik Olsen, "the kindest and dearest of men," failed to return from one of these hunting forays, and his companions could not locate him, despite days of searching. They did come upon three wolves, one with blood smeared on its snout. Rasmussen suspected that Olsen had been eaten by the wolves, who perhaps had found him napping. One of the wolves later followed Rasmussen's tracks, seemingly hunting him, too.

The bedraggled party reached the edge of the ice cap on August 5 and began the 450-mile journey back to the west coast. The route included a 4,000-foot climb and descent. By now everyone was subsisting primarily on dog meat, even the dogs. Nonetheless, progress was steady, and by August 21, they were in sight of the Humboldt Glacier, a huge tidewater glacier on Kane Basin about halfway through their journey. Here the terrain became rougher and they again had to wade through freezing streams each day. Koch suffered a tooth abscess that was so painful he could hardly chew, and half his face was swollen. Wulff developed an infected abscess in his rectum that made each step a spike of hot pain.

There was "no sign of life, not a bird, not a plant [to soften] the impression of this utmost desolation . . . a land without a heart," Rasmussen wrote. By August 24, they had eaten their last remaining dog. With the coastal mountains in sight, Rasmussen and Ajako, who were still in relatively good health, decided to walk and ski ahead the final 150 miles to Etah and return with help.

WHEN RASMUSSEN WAS collecting stories for *The People of the Polar North*, his first book on Greenland, he recorded the tale of the sorcerer Sorqaq's miraculous escape from death on drift ice. Sorqaq had become stranded when the ice he was on floated out to sea. But the wind shifted direction and brought the ice, with the sorcerer on it, back to shore. "On the fifth day I was driven to landward by a south west wind," Sorqaq recalled. "But when people saw me come drifting in on the top of an iceberg, they very nearly ran away; they thought I was a sea-monster. Sorqaq, of course they thought, had been seal-catching in the hunting-grounds of the dead long enough—heh! heh!" Rasmussen found Sorqaq's observation on the fickle nature of Arctic life noteworthy. "Yes, death follows men about," Sorqaq intoned. It "dogs men's footsteps, and is never farther away from life than his shadow from a man!"

After Rasmussen and Ajako had left, the others were to make their way over the rim of the ice cap, following an agreed-upon route. Although they were starving, Wulff refused to eat the dog meat and kept trying to lie down, refusing to get up until they lifted him by the arms. On several occasions the others had to recross freezing streams to retrieve Wulff and drag him through them. He was moving so slowly that the others, half starved and limping, found the ordeal even more trying. Muttering that he would rather go to his grave on the ice cap than continue in this debilitating and painful manner, Wulff said he had nothing to live for anyway. On the afternoon of August 29, he asked Koch how far they had traveled that day.

"About two and a half kilometers," said Koch.

"How much farther must we go?"

"About seventy."

This further discouraged Wulff, which had not been Koch's intention. Koch had thought an understanding of the great distance remaining might stimulate Wulff into action, but instead the botanist became even more despondent. He refused to eat any of the rabbits that Nasaitordluarsuk and Inukitsoq had hunted. For the remainder of the day, each time they stopped it took him hours to get up again even with great urging by the others. "This walk is worse than death," Wulff claimed. "It is like walking to one's own funeral." He was too weak to carry his botanical collections and notebooks any farther but insisted that he would not go on without them. Finally he looked at the others and said: "This is the end. I will not go any farther."

Nasaitordluarsuk, Inukitsoq and Koch could not stay without food in a land with no game. Wulff urged them to leave him alone; they heated some water for tea, collected some grass for him to lie on, and promised to return as quickly as possible. Then the three men set off eastward, following Rasmussen and Ajako.

Rasmussen and Ajako had reached Etah on August 30 and arranged for hunters with food to race back on five fast sleds and find the stragglers. They were themselves too weak to travel farther. The rescuers reached Koch, Nasaitordluarsuk and Inukitsoq on September 4, but when they arrived at the spot where Wulff had been left, they found no trace of him. Rasmussen suspected Wulff had roused himself for one final effort to follow the others and had gotten lost. Eventually, they found his journal. In it . Wulff had written: "I await death with a perfectly calm mind and my heart is at peace. Up to the last I have honestly striven to honour our name and hope that the results of my work may be saved."

ONCE THE SURVIVORS had regrouped at Thule, they felt the need to put to rest the ghost of Wulff's death, which hung particularly over Koch, who had made the ultimate decision to abandon Wulff. Rasmussen suggested they visit a magistrate in Godhavn (Qeqertarsuaq), hundreds of miles to the south. He knew there would be an inquiry to determine whether the death was accidental or otherwise, and hoped that if the matter were dealt with quickly in Greenland, by someone who knew Greenland's fickle conditions, the matter could avoid the Danish courts—and the Danish press. They split into two parties for the long journey to make the hunting easier. While Rasmussen and his companions had no difficulties, Freuchen, Navarana and Koch experienced brutal conditions and near starvation.

While in Godhavn, however, Koch decided he would not submit to a Greenland magistrate's authority but would prefer to go directly to Copenhagen. Some other scientists had advised him against seeking out a Greenland magistrate. Rasmussen was understandably annoyed, and his relationship with Koch was permanently affected. The two men never adventured together again, and rarely spoke; and when Rasmussen died many years later, Koch, who had become nearly as famous as Rasmussen for his own scientific expeditions, wrote a critical obituary wherein he attacked Rasmussen's scientific credentials and claimed that Rasmussen could do little else than tell stories and drive dogs. Rasmussen maintained that Koch was right to leave Wulff behind in order to save his own life, although Rasmussen may have privately thought that he never would have abandoned a comrade; after all, he had refused to leave any of his companions on any previous expeditions and they had refused to ever abandon him.

Nevertheless, Rasmussen was in fine form on the return trip from Godhavn to Ilulissat. En route they stopped to visit an official in Ritenbenck, and when they heard he was absent, Rasmussen invited his party into the official's house despite the feeble protests of the housekeeper. They devoured the hindquarters of a caribou and then Rasmussen went to search the larder. He returned with a triumphant grin, exclaiming "He has wine! Wine in wartime!" and they drank it all before leaving. They then stopped in Ilulissat for several more days of partying before

Rasmussen boarded a ship for Copenhagen. He arrived in the spring of 1918, two years after he had departed and a year and a half later than he had promised Dagmar he would return. He found that his mother had died the previous July, while he was traveling on the ice cap.

The war ended on November 11, 1918, the day after his father died in Lynge. Although the death of his parents must have been devastating, Rasmussen never wrote about it. His son, Niels, was born a few months later, in March 1919. Rasmussen settled once again into the life of a celebrity, lecturing on his explorations and writing another book, *Greenland by the Polar Sea*, an account of the most recent adventure, published in Denmark in 1919 and in England in 1921. The tone of this book is more formal and clear, less poetic and whimsical than that of his previous books, emphasizing scientific goals and accomplishments rather than philosophical musings and tales of adventure. Perhaps the deaths of Wulff and Olsen led him to deemphasize the wing-and-a-prayer nature of his exploits and focus on the expedition's contributions to science.

What became known as the Second Thule Expedition brought much new geological, botanical and archaeological information to the world, but Rasmussen knew there would be scrutiny of his leadership of the expedition: whether he had been reckless or irresponsible was an open question, one that might overshadow the expedition's scientific accomplishments and tarnish Rasmussen's growing reputation. For Rasmussen, the notion of an expedition was to challenge himself and revel in the Inuit lifestyle of hunting and adventure. Not everyone shared these objectives or was suited to the lifestyle. Wulff was such a person. Surely Rasmussen suspected that Wulff would be a problem before they set out—the evidence of his unsuitability was readily apparent—but Rasmussen wanted Wulff's scientific credentials and contributions to the expedition's findings, and perhaps he hoped the man would buck up or find extra reserves of strength. Rasmussen had asked Freuchen soon after his return whether his friend thought him responsible for Wulff's and Henrik's deaths in any way. Despite Freuchen's assurances that he bore no responsibility for Wulff's demise—it was, after all, Koch's decision to abandon Wulff—Rasmussen was the expedition leader.

In *Greenland by the Polar Sea*, Rasmussen went into considerable detail to explain how previous expeditions, such as those of George Nares and Adolphus Greely, much better equipped and therefore laden with provisions and supplies, had failed to explore Greenland's far north, its remotest region, thus necessitating his plan to travel light and live off the land. Clearly, he was trying to defend himself against accusations of recklessness and negligence. "What is called good equipment could not get them ahead. Their heavy baggage did not permit them to get about . . . In other words, that which under all other circumstances was to be looked upon as a decided advantage, rich and good equipment, is here a weight that does not permit the explorer to move as quickly as the travelling season demands." It was a well-reasoned argument, and probably an accurate one; but it was also the first time Rasmussen had had to justify himself in such a fashion: "Thus for us there was no alternative. The experiences I had gained in 1912 during the First Thule Expedition gave me the right to assume that such a plan could be justified."

It is also likely that Rasmussen sought to further his reputation as the international authority on the "Arctic Highlanders." As their cultural historian and spokesperson, he sought to fit the role the press was creating for him as a respectable member of the scientific and social establishment. In *Greenland by the Polar Sea*, he itemized the scientific equipment, objectives and details of the expedition, listed the credentials of its members, and identified those on the "scientific committee" who had become his advisers, a group that consisted mostly of university professors. He defended the expedition's traveling "in Eskimo fashion," claiming that this was not done for the obvious reasons of efficiency or because he had grown up with this mode of travel and thus it was dear to his heart, but rather to lend a kind of authenticity to the journey, while "at the same time we can attend to our scientific interests." Rasmussen and his men were no longer regarded as companions on an adventure, but rather as expedition members with job titles and descriptions.

Because "it cannot be presumed that all who may read this book know anything about the Polar Eskimos," in *Greenland by the Polar Sea* he gave a sketch of their daily lives and spiritual beliefs. These are the most enlightening parts of the book. In spite of Rasmussen's humble introduction and disclaimer, the book is replete with his usual wit, sharp observations and musings. But the evidence of a more respectable Rasmussen is also evident, perhaps because he was now forty years old and felt the weight of fame and responsibility. He knew that to achieve his grand ambition, leading a multimember party that would traverse the entire homeland of the Inuit from east to west, he would have to become a public figurehead worthy of government support— serious, sober and with scientific objectives.

A TIME FOR DREAMING

When living this primitive life, one develops a quite extraor-
dinary feeling of well-being in the heavy, dozing satisfaction
that leads to sleep and dreams. You take your rest when it
offers itself, and you take it thoroughly, and drink it in in deep
draughts; that storm and misfortune must be slept through, is
the sound principle of the Eskimos. Then, they can take a brush
[a blow], when necessary, and there are few of us civilised
men who have as much staying power. The chance and haz-
ard of existence brings many surprises, and you soon learn to
seize and enjoy what life offers.

—Knud Rasmussen,
The People of the Polar North

THE YEAR 1919 was an excellent one for profits from Thule
Station. The price of furs had not declined after the war,
as Rasmussen had feared, but had soared, and the company had
plenty of surplus cash. He used the money to build the *Søkon-*
gen (*Sea King*), a sturdy vessel designed especially for sailing
through icy waters. Rasmussen was now organizing what were
to become known as the Third and Fourth Thule Expeditions.
The Third was merely a depot-laying mission for Norwegian

175

explorer Roald Amundsen's planned polar drift from Spitsbergen to Alaska. Amundsen assumed that his ship *Maud* could not make the journey in one stretch without refueling, so he was anxious to have a supply and provisioning cache. His representative, Godfred Hansen, arrived in Upernavik to be met by Freuchen, who escorted him to Thule and helped him set off on dogsled for Cape Columbia, on northern Ellesmere Island. Although the bulk of the expense was covered by the Norwegian government, Rasmussen helped plan the expedition and placed Freuchen and the company ship at Hansen's disposal, asking some of the Inuit to help. In the end, however, the cache of food and supplies proved unnecessary—Amundsen's ship never progressed farther than Alaska because the pack ice was too thick and unpredictable.

The Fourth Thule Expedition was Rasmussen's own brief journey to East Greenland to hear and collect more stories from the Inuit. It had nothing to do with the trading post, other than the fact that the trip was financed with Thule Station's profits. That summer, Rasmussen took the regularly scheduled steamship from Copenhagen to Julianehåb (Qaqortoq), and from there he traveled in a smaller boat around the southern tip of Greenland and then north along the east coast to Angmagssalik. Although he had earlier heard some strange and macabre tales from people who had once lived there, this was the first time he had visited the region. He didn't know these people, and they lived lives as secluded and remote as those of his beloved Polar Inuit. Hearing that the old pagan culture had not yet been crushed by missionaries, Rasmussen was anxious to visit them before their memories of the old days were lost. Ironically, for part of his time in Angmagssalik, he lived in a church attic. While they crouched in the attic around a small oil lamp for light and heat, he interviewed a former angakoq named Autdaruta. The news of this visit spread, and the people of Angmagssalik gathered below the two men in the church attic to listen while they talked about the old days.

When Rasmussen returned to Denmark from his summer's sojourn, he immediately set to work writing up his findings. The resulting book, *Myths and Legends from Greenland*, was published in three volumes in Danish, beginning in 1921. Rasmussen collected these stories to illustrate the elusive essence of the old culture, untouched by the modern economy and untainted by Christian missionaries, who had a dim view of the old traditions and beliefs. Especially appealing to Rasmussen were tales of shamans visiting the land of the dead, legends of strange beasts that dwelt in the murky shadows during the dark season, and stories of journeys to visit the moon or the ocean spirit. He wanted to hear of flesh-eating giants and bears the size of mountains, of malevolent storm birds and ravenous human-hunting dogs, of bears and seals who talked and who plotted revenge when the required rituals were not performed. He searched for insight into this world of the Inuit and its metaphors and signs, its mosaic of magic and mystery. The angakut were the keepers of this knowledge.

Angakut were believed to have supernatural powers. These varied slightly from region to region, but they all had the same basic function and purpose in society. They understood and navigated the spirit world by entering into trances to do battle with evil spirits or the ill intentions of other angakut to steal souls. They could visit the spirit world and return with wisdom or advice. One of the primary jobs of an angakoq in traditional Inuit society was to cure sickness; this was done by curing not the body but the soul, by battling with the evil spirits that were causing the sickness—the Inuit believed sickness was a manifestation of some crime or sin or the influence of a malevolent spirit.

An evil angakoq could create a *tupilaq*—a hell animal, or monster of vengeance. To do so, the angakoq would search for the bones of various dead animals and assemble them into an ill-shapen blend of his own design and then cover the grotesque skeleton with an old hide. He would conceal it in a cave or other suitable place and then spend days conjuring until the unnatural beast came alive and set off to do its evil deeds. If a hunter accidentally harpooned the tupilaq, for example, he might become paralyzed or cursed with other bad luck. Rasmussen found tales dealing with the malevolent actions of tupilaqs in communities throughout Greenland and the Northwest Passage region of North America.

In most cases, the stories told by an angakoq, the traditional stories that had been passed down for generations, were allegorical; the purpose of the story was to convey some wisdom about life and morals through metaphor. In one story, an angakoq's journey to the land of the dead showed him people in varying stages of decay. The lesson was to let the dead have their peace: when one mourns the dead for too long, they don't decay properly in the land of the dead; and they cannot come back into power until they are forgotten. Many of the tales from the mythic realm are meant to inform daily living. Rasmussen understood the cultural trappings of the angakoq's journeys and the cultural importance of the stories, the lessons they were meant to impart.

Neither Rasmussen nor Freuchen believed the angakut to be frauds or to be deliberately deceptive. Often, they witnessed the power of an angakoq's hypnotic trance and incantations to cure illness or at least remove pain. That Rasmussen could convince an angakoq to reveal his abilities and methods, and could convince others to tell him of an angakoq's power, shows the deep level of trust and respect the Inuit had for Rasmussen. That trust was not misplaced: regardless of Rasmussen's personal beliefs—and there is no evidence to suggest that he believed in the literal truths of these magic-infused legends and tales—he knew they were true to the people he was interviewing, the people with whom he was living and traveling. In recounting the old beliefs and stories of the people who experienced supernatural interventions, Rasmussen wanted the reader to see that they are neither false nor forced. He was never judgmental, condescending or dismissive of others' beliefs, even if they weren't true for him.

The traditional culture of the Greenlanders was certainly governed by a different morality than the one that governed early twentieth-century Europe and America. Among the Inuit, theft, lying and deceit were considered to be serious crimes, for example, but murder was not necessarily so; sometimes it was even required as punishment. In the absence of a central authority, those who committed a crime against the group, such as stealing meat or killing another with whom they disagreed, had to be punished by selected members of the group. Because there were no jails, serious crimes were punished by the offender being killed during a hunting "accident" or in some other unofficial manner. Sometimes the treatment of the less fortunate was appalling, by modern standards; orphans or the elderly might be abandoned, or pushed off the ice into freezing water, or denied food. But Rasmussen had seen and experienced enough of what life in Greenland could be like—the brutal, meaningless starvation, unpredictable death by accident, drowning and freezing—that he could understand how and why these practices developed and how they helped smooth the working of Inuit society under certain conditions. The society had no surplus, no ability to support the very young or elderly, who were incapable of contributing or of surviving arduous travel.

While the elders talked, Rasmussen quietly sat, sipping tea or eating. He offered no opinion. He accepted and he remembered, and he wrote later. No one else could have accomplished what Rasmussen did, coaxing the buried stories from people who had recently been told by others that it was all wrong, or blasphemous, or foolish. Although not considered "scientific," his ethnographic collections are a priceless contribution to world culture

and far outstrip the more solid accomplishments of the Second
Thule Expedition's cartographic and geographical exploration,
all of which was repeated later by others with more precision
and greater accuracy. The collections of myths and legends that
Rasmussen rescued before they slipped into oblivion—forgotten
by the older generation and repressed by missionaries—would
not otherwise have survived. It was on this trip to East Greenland that Rasmussen renewed his desire to explore this fading
world further. Did the indigenous people of the Canadian Arctic
and Alaska have the same stories, beliefs and taboos as those in
Greenland?

In 1920, WHILE he was living in Copenhagen and Hundested,
Rasmussen became a member of the Greenland Commission, a
Danish government council tasked with considering the future
economy and political structure of Greenland. His responsibilities
included numerous meetings as an expert on the language and
customs of the people. The committee work could be tedious, but
it was good for his reputation and a strong position from which to
influence policies that would benefit the Greenland Inuit. It was
a more official, governmental role for him, and he was now being
taken seriously as an authority on the Inuit, as having valid and
useful opinions on how the colony should be governed.

Clearly some colonial policies needed revisiting. The recently
milder climate had decreased the seal population and was causing
hardship in the Inuit's livelihoods as well as food shortages. At
the same time, fish stocks were increasing. Greenland remained
a closed country, still requiring visitors to have a special Danish
government permit, but the pressure to open up the land was
increasing and was sure to bring economic and social changes
to the residents. When the commission's report was released in

1925, it not surprisingly recommended that Greenland be made into a modern society in which people were allowed free passage to and from the island, and that it move toward an economy based on fishing.

The Danish colonial structure had a great deal of paternalism and subtle racism. It was not malicious, merely condescending. Commercial trade for goods manufactured outside Greenland was controlled by government monopoly, and the types of goods available for sale was strictly regulated. Only muzzle-loading guns were permitted—never breech-loaders, for example, because the Inuit would presumably go crazy shooting each other. When the first motorboats were brought over from Europe, the pilots had to swear never to let the Inuit near them, in case they should stick their hands in the motor. Freuchen remembered that he and Rasmussen were not allowed to import kerosene, due to fear that the Inuit "would amuse themselves by throwing burning matches into the barrels." When he tried to explain the foolishness of the notion, a government official told him to be quiet.

Freuchen commented that the Danish officials "had never tried to sit in a kayak or stand by a blowhole or fish cod in order to provide for a family at the incredibly low prices producers were offered at that time." Nor were they compelled to work as domestic servants for the officials for "starvation wages." There was a belief that the Greenlanders were lazy, or somehow like big, coddled children, in need of protection and guidance in how to live their lives. Church ministers and junior government officials would presume to order them about "for their own good." When traveling with Navarana in southern Greenland, Freuchen recalled that he would be offered a seat at the dining table of a government official while his wife was asked to eat with "the natives" in the kitchen. He refused, soon coming to the conclusion that the person being insulted and ordered about "was often more dignified than the one who was debasing him."

Although both Rasmussen and Freuchen felt that Denmark's colonial power in Greenland was not entirely a bad thing, these practices still annoyed them. Most Inuit showed great patience in the face of verbal abuse from colonial authorities. Once, Freuchen overheard a hunter being yelled at by the wife of a colony manager. The man stoically endured the barrage and then replied in Greenlandic, a language she didn't understand: "Alas, you are a child in the country, and a child in your thoughts. It is impossible to be angry with a child; it would be a loss of dignity!" Rasmussen lacked this Greenlandic trait. He could become nasty toward people who were rude, insulting or condescending to Greenlanders; he would leave them on the trail, trick them out of their liquor or food, or subtly mock them while maintaining a jovial façade, as he had done with "the royal assistant." Yet he believed that a "civilizing" influence was the inevitable way of the future—he tolerated institutionally what he opposed individually.

IN DECEMBER 1919, it became Freuchen's turn for a break from routine, so Rasmussen arranged a one-year holiday for him and engaged a temporary replacement to manage Thule Station. Freuchen duly arrived in Denmark with Navarana and their two children. After only a few weeks, however, he was tired of his former home and the way his wife was treated, everyone staring at her and talking slowly and loudly to her as she went about her business in Copenhagen. Although his parents were happy to see their grandchildren, Freuchen wanted to return to Thule and shorten his "holiday." But one day in early 1920, he collapsed in the street. Passersby, thinking he was drunk, ignored him until finally the police bundled him off to the station, where they recognized the symptoms of the Spanish influenza that was then sweeping Europe and the world.

16. "Portaging" the sleds and dogs across ice-hummocked terrain during the Second Thule Expedition.

17. Dr. Thorild Wulff, looking exhausted as he prepares to cross a freezing stream.

18. The expedition fording St. George Fjord, one of many freezing crossings that slowed and weakened the party.

19. Members of the Fifth Thule Expedition to Hudson Bay and Baffin Island. Clockwise from top left: Kaj Birket-Smith, Therkel Mathiassen, Helge Bangsted, Jacob Olsen, Peter Freuchen, Knud Rasmussen, Peder Pedersen.

20. Construction of The Bellows on Danish Island, Hudson Bay, 1921.

21. Knud ready for adventure near The Bellows, photographed by Leo Hansen.

22. Arnarulunguaq, the most traveled woman of her people. From the Thule region she accompanied the Fifth Thule Expedition to Hudson Bay, and then with Rasmussen dog-sledded the entire Northwest Passage to Alaska, returning to Greenland via Seattle, New York and Copenhagen.

23. The poet Netsit, from Bathurst Inlet along the Northwest Passage, a region renowned for poets and singers.

24. Arnarulunguaq, Rasmussen, and Miteq alongside their massive sled at Point Barrow, Alaska, near the end of their great journey.

25. Rasmussen, Arnarulunguaq and Miteq in Washington, DC. Photo by Leo Hansen.

26. Rasmussen is the guest of honor at a ceremonial gala in Copenhagen after he returned from his great sled journey, circa 1924. Amongst the dignitaries seated next to Rasmussen are Danish prime minister Thorvald Stauning and Peter Freuchen.

27. Rasmussen receiving an honorary Doctorate from St. Andrews University, Scotland, in 1926.

28. Rasmussen and some members of his East Greenland expedition, 1931–1933.

Spread by soldiers returning from the war, this terrible disease claimed somewhere between 80 million and 100 million people over the next few years, including, as they would later discover, many in Greenland and throughout the polar region. Freuchen was ill with it in a Copenhagen hospital for many months; his hair fell out and he became so weak that he could not walk. Because it was believed that he was dying, he was placed in near isolation. Worried that Freuchen might never recover, Rasmussen visited him frequently. Eventually, he told Freuchen that he and Nyeboe had hired a replacement to manage Thule Station.

Then, to everyone's surprise, Freuchen began a slow recovery and in the spring of 1920 was released from the hospital. Although he could barely walk and spent most of each day resting, he and Rasmussen began working together to plan the grand adventure that would become known as the Fifth Thule Expedition. It was Rasmussen's ambition to answer all the questions he had wondered about for nearly two decades, questions about the origin, language and culture of the Greenlandic people. It was an expedition he had been dreaming of since early 1910, when he published in the *Geographical Journal* in London his idea for a "Project of a Danish Expedition to the Central Eskimo." He suspected that the North American and Greenlandic Inuit had to have emerged from the same culture, but he wanted proof.

The Fifth Thule Expedition would be a large undertaking. No longer would it just be Rasmussen and Freuchen on a youthful adventure, living off the land; indeed, it was possible that Freuchen would never fully regain his strength. It had been over ten years since they had founded Thule Station, and now they both had wives and children as well as other responsibilities. The scientists they would be recruiting would have little skill or experience in Arctic travel, and with the shadow of the Second Thule Expedition's deaths hanging over the preparations, youthful exuberance and traveling light would have to give way to careful planning

for large numbers of people and equipment. By anyone's standards other than Rasmussen's, however, it would still be a lightly
equipped expedition. No other person then alive had the experience to lead an ambitious expedition such as this, with the requi-
site skills and cultural knowledge to make sense of the findings.
Rasmussen would have to bend his own preferred style to the task,
but he was ambitious and willing to compromise to achieve his
dream. The Fifth Thule Expedition would be an important scientific undertaking that would cement his reputation, elevate him
from his image as a wild risk-taker and prankster into a respectable member of the intellectual and scientific establishment—an
explorer rather than a mere adventurer, and someone to be taken
seriously.

The Fifth Thule Expedition would also be expensive, and to
finance it Rasmussen secured a significant contribution from both
the government and various private sources. Thule Station was
the guarantor for the shortfall, from its future profits. Rasmussen was to be the overall leader and ethnographer, and Freuchen
the cartographer and zoologist, in the greatest and most ambitious sled journey ever conceived. Two young Danish scientists
were brought on: Kaj Birket-Smith as ethnographer and Therkel
Mathiassen as archaeologist, cartographer and geographer. Helge
Bangsted was to be the research assistant. The party would also
include a new feature—a cinematographer—Leo Hansen, who
would accompany them for the first year to capture in moving
pictures some of the traditional life activities of the Inuit. The
Inuit contingent, which would provide hunters, dogsled drivers,
and seamstresses, was to consist of Navarana; Iggiannguaq and
his wife, Arnarulunguaq; Arioq and his wife, Arnanguaq; Nasaitordluarsuk and his wife, Aqatsaq; and the boy Meteq. As Rasmussen wanted, the party would be half Inuit and half Danish.

Rasmussen was counting on both Freuchen and Navarana to
participate in the expedition. Navarana, also still in Denmark,

needed to return to Thule as soon as possible to organize the sewing of all the clothing that the expedition members would need for their many years of travel. She set off for Greenland in the spring, taking their son, Mequsaq, with her but leaving their little daughter, Pipaluk, behind with Freuchen's parents. Rasmussen continued to process the reams of paperwork and documents related to financing and equipping the expedition. He also had to complete numerous applications for international travel, since the expedition would leave Danish territory to enter Canada and then the United States, and possibly even Russia. It was one thing for Inuit to wander in their traditional homeland but quite another for Danish scientists to cover the same territory, even if their expedition was scientific rather than political. Rasmussen was also putting the final touches on his book *Myths and Legends from Greenland*, which would be published after his departure.

The *Søkongen*, the new ship he had ordered for Thule Station, also needed some adjustments. Captain Peder Pedersen, longstanding captain of the supply ships that serviced Thule Station, would be the captain of the *Søkongen*, charged with picking up the Inuit expedition members in Greenland and then transporting the entire party and its equipment to an undetermined location along the northern shore of Hudson Bay in Canada.

Freuchen, who could still barely walk, retreated to a farm outside Copenhagen to recuperate. But within weeks, Rasmussen sent him an urgent telegram: he had word from Pedersen that the *Søkongen* had been damaged in a storm and was in Norway for repairs, and then had been damaged in another storm and had put in to Scotland for more repairs. It was getting late in the season, and the ship would not reach Tasiussaq until September, when it would be too late to cross Melville Bay to Thule. Rasmussen's telegram informed Freuchen that Lauge Koch, the geology student who had accompanied them on their previous expedition, had asked for assistance in transporting some supplies for his own expedition north of Thule. Despite their chilly relationship, Rasmussen agreed to help. The situation was urgent, and in typically Rasmussen-like fashion, he decided that the solution was for him and Freuchen to leave immediately to solve the problems.

It had been nearly a year since Rasmussen had been in Greenland, and the thought of waiting until the following spring was too painful. Within a day, he and Freuchen had boarded the last scheduled steamer for the year and were on their way to Upernavik and a logistically complicated season of voyages. The *Søkongen*, now repaired, arrived from Scotland, picked up Rasmussen and took him north, while Freuchen boarded Koch's overloaded ship and piloted it across Melville Bay. They regrouped at Thule. There, Rasmussen made arrangements for the following summer's expedition, speaking to the people he wanted to recruit as expedition members. Then he sailed south again. Freuchen followed soon after, leaving Navarana in Thule.

To complicate things further, both Freuchen and Rasmussen would spend the winter of 1920–1921 in Copenhagen. They still had the final preparations, meetings and paperwork to finish and a lecture tour planned, something Freuchen hated and Rasmussen loved. These busy final months were also taken up with an outrageously complicated series of meetings and letters with officials in London and Ottawa, regarding the delicate issue of Canadian sovereignty in the Arctic.

THE PREVIOUS SEASON, a whaling captain had reported seeing 150 dried musk ox hides at Thule Station. Apparently, the animals had been hunted on Canada's Ellesmere Island by Inuit from North Greenland, who were in the habit of making annual trips across Smith Sound to Ellesmere Island to hunt for polar bears and musk oxen. In the wake of MacMillan's Crocker Land Expedition, which had wintered near Etah in northern Greenland and hunted on Ellesmere Island, there had been a significant decline in the number of animals. As a result, the Canadian government had recently added a clause to its Northwest Game Act prohibiting musk ox hunting, except for subsistence. In July 1919, it had sent official notice to the Danish government via the British Foreign Office in London, requesting that the Danish government do something to stop the hunting of musk oxen on Ellesmere Island. North Greenland wasn't technically under Danish sovereignty, so the request was passed on to Rasmussen.

Rasmussen replied that Inuit in the vicinity of Thule were compelled to hunt on Ellesmere Island because the American expeditions had nearly depleted the caribou population in North Greenland and that in any case, Ellesmere Island was part of their traditional hunting territory. His letter had the unfortunate effect of ruffling the feathers of a Canadian government insecure about its northern territorial claims. "It is well known," Rasmussen wrote, "that the territory of the Polar Esquimaux falls within the region designated as 'no man's land' and there is therefore no authority in the district except that which I exercise through my station." He was referring to northern Greenland (as there was no permanent human population on Ellesmere Island), but Canadian officials misconstrued his letter to mean that he viewed Ellesmere Island as a "no man's land" and that Danish sovereignty might extend there. Could the Fifth Thule Expedition, financed in part by the Danish government, be considered an attempt to claim Ellesmere Island for Denmark?

Twitchy officials in Ottawa had been nervous about Canada's sovereignty in its Arctic since 1880, when the Arctic islands were transferred from Great Britain to Canada. Sovereignty was maintained by occasional government proclamations and formal declarations, but in the early twentieth century, the Arctic was seeing more visitors, and most paid little heed to the distant proclamations of a southern government that had no presence in the region. In 1900, Otto Sverdrup sailed his ship *Fram* on a Norwegian expedition that wintered on Ellesmere Island, near the island he named Axel Heiberg Island, planted a Norwegian flag, and claimed the territory for Norway. It was, however, a claim the Swedish government (which ruled Norway until 1905) never pressed. Between 1903 and 1906, Roald Amundsen sailed his ship *Gjøa* on the first successful navigation of the Northwest Passage without notification to or permission from the Canadian government, and American whalers had been overwintering and trading with the local people for decades. Although the Canadian government had sent out a handful of expeditions to explore and chart some of the Arctic islands in the region, there was clearly some confusion about sovereignty. When Rasmussen's letter arrived in 1919, it touched a nerve.

J.B. Harkin, an official with Canada's Department of the Interior, became convinced that Rasmussen's expedition was a secret effort by Denmark to promote Danish sovereignty in the Canadian Arctic. The opinion that Rasmussen was a Danish agent was disingenuously and erroneously echoed by the explorer Vilhjalmur Stefansson, resulting in a diplomatic miscommunication that required Rasmussen to devote many hours of letter and telegram writing and travel to London to obtain permission to enter Canada and avail his expedition of the services of the Hudson's Bay Company, the only source of supplies and communication in Canada's Arctic. He repeatedly stressed that the Fifth Thule Expedition was entirely scientific and that it had no commercial or political aspirations. Rasmussen was still trying to sort it all out mere weeks before he was set to sail for Greenland. An interesting footnote to the whole affair is that it inspired the formation of the Eastern Arctic Patrol of the Royal Canadian Mounted Police and the first Canadian government outposts on

Ellesmere Island. Ironically, the Inuit assistants to the RCMP were hired from North Greenland.

IN LATE MAY 1921, Rasmussen said good-bye to his three children, the youngest then just over two years old, and sailed for Greenland. Freuchen had left Denmark earlier to help shoot some footage for the film of the expedition. Rasmussen and the expedition scientists arrived in time for the grand celebration on July 3 of the two-hundredth anniversary of the missionary Hans Egede's 1721 arrival in Greenland to Christianize the Inuit. The king of Denmark sailed to Nuuk for the party, his entourage arriving with a flotilla of kayaks and boats escorting them into the harbor. It was the first time a Danish king had visited Greenland, and Rasmussen thought it a good omen. A three-day celebration followed, with numerous religious processions, in which the Greenlanders showed the pompous and pretentious Danish royal delegation how to celebrate properly, at least according to Rasmussen. "Knud was in his best humor," Freuchen recalled. Unusual delicacies were presented to the celebrants, including coffee, cookies, figs, prunes and cigars.

Dagmar had accompanied Rasmussen on the journey, to see him off on what they knew was to be a multiyear adventure. After the celebration, the expedition members boarded the *Søkongen* and sailed up the coast to Ilulissat, to load bales of dried fish for the dogs, and then on to Uummannaq. There they met Navarana, who had traveled south by dogsled. She brought with her all the skin clothes the expedition members would require. Rasmussen, as usual, organized another party, but Navarana felt tired and ill and went aboard the ship to sleep.

They sailed farther north to Thule to pick up the six Inuit expedition members and the dogs. On this trip, Rasmussen heard the rumor that the passenger ship *Bele*, in which they were transporting some supplies, had run aground. He also became concerned that Dagmar might be stuck in Greenland for longer than she had planned, leaving their children in Denmark without either parent. When he noticed the king's ship sailing past on its way south, he ran up the signal flags. The royal steamer cut its engines and waited.

"Very serious trouble," Rasmussen shouted. "We need help."

An officer yelled across for him to row over and tell them the problem. Rasmussen called back: "You send over a boat. It's easier for you."

The king's officer sent a boat over to retrieve Rasmussen, and as soon as he climbed aboard the steamer he strode directly to the king. "As Your Majesty is the protector of our expedition," he said, "I am sure it would disappoint you to see the whole project fall through. We must have more supplies to replace those that went down on the *Bele*. Besides, I would like my wife to return on your ship."

The king was shocked, but after a little more of Rasmussen's flattery he readily agreed to the request. As Freuchen observed, "Knud thought there was never any point in being too modest and subservient." Once he had the assurance that additional supplies would be forwarded to Thule and Dagmar had safely boarded the king's ship, the *Søkongen* sailed on toward Upernavik, where it met up with Mathiassen, Birket-Smith, and Leo Hansen, the motion picture cameraman Rasmussen had hired.

It should have been a time for celebration, for the expedition was well under way, but Navarana's condition became worse and she had to be carried off the ship. It was not a slight cold that had latched onto her, but the Spanish influenza that Freuchen had contracted the year before. Freuchen remained in Upernavik to take care of Navarana, while Rasmussen and the others continued north to Thule to pick up the Inuit expedition members and bring them south. There, Rasmussen learned that his old companion Ajako had died, and when they returned south in August, it was to find Navarana dead and Freuchen despondent. In her final hours, Navarana had fretted about her children, who were not with her—Mequsaq was in Thule and Pipaluk in Copenhagen.

When Freuchen went to bury Navarana in the graveyard, the priest refused to allow her to be interred. Because she had died a "pagan," he refused to say a sermon or ring the bells, and he threatened the Inuit with the horrible fate of dying without being baptized, using Navarana as an example. Many of the people who knew Navarana hid behind houses and rocks, peering at the tiny funeral procession, too fearful of the power of the church to be seen showing sympathy to a pagan. Rasmussen later wandered with Freuchen up the stony hill to her grave and said his farewells. Then he and Freuchen sailed south.

Rasmussen and Freuchen had an uneasy relationship with the missionaries who lived near Thule Station. Although the missionaries attempted to undermine local culture and traditions, Rasmussen reluctantly accepted them because he believed that the Inuit could not remain in isolation forever. Freuchen, on the other hand, married as he was to an Inuit, and a pagan, too, had little patience for the missionaries' autocratic and domineering behavior, and he went out of his way to defend the Inuit against the rough handling and verbal attacks of the missionaries. According to Freuchen, they insulted the people and their beliefs, always striving for greater control over the Inuit's actions and behavior. Even so, he was shocked by the callous treatment of Navarana.

Freuchen took great relish in detailing the missionaries' own moral failings, such as when they tried to lure local girls into various sexual encounters, including once with Navarana when Freuchen was away—all while berating these people for remaining outside the church. He was frequently ordered away from the mission and seldom invited the missionaries to visit at Thule

Station. Rasmussen rarely mentions either the missions or the missionaries, apart from his bland and unrevealing comments that the Inuit needed somehow to be eased into the modern world before the modern world unceremoniously swamped them. The great irony is that Rasmussen was rushing to preserve the timeless oral traditions of an ancient culture while accepting that these traditions were threatened by the twin powers of colonialism and the church.

WHEN THE *SØKONGEN* sailed into Nuuk on August 24, the families of the Thule Inuit were also becoming sick with the flu. Many were rushed to the hospital, where they spent weeks recuperating. On September 6, the hunter Iggiannguaq died, his wife helplessly holding his hand, crying and stroking his head. When after this death Rasmussen asked the other Inuit if they wanted to return, because of the ill-omened start to the grand expedition, they proclaimed that their greatest fear was that they wouldn't be well enough to go on the journey—they really wanted to see their "cousins" in Canada, a semi-mythic people known as Akilinermiut, "those who dwell on the land beyond the Great Sea." One day later, the overburdened *Søkongen*, supplies stacked dangerously high on its deck, launched west across ice-choked Baffin Bay into Davis Strait for a late-season crossing. The boat was crammed with people and about seventy dogs lolled about the deck, fighting and chasing each other, as the ship wound its way through the ice toward a land none of them had ever been before.

The Spanish flu continued to ravage the Inuit in Greenland. As Rasmussen and his compatriots were to discover, the epidemic had also had devastating effects on the Inuit in Canada and Alaska. So much death, and their long absence from their old life in Thule, coincided with the profound change in their own lives—the passing of their youth and the carefree days of adventure, when their whole lives were in front of them. Now a great loss was behind them, too. Freuchen had two motherless children, living worlds apart from each other; Rasmussen had three children and a wife he rarely saw in Copenhagen. Neither Rasmussen nor Freuchen would ever return to live in Thule, at one time home to them both.

To fight off depression and guilt and to keep grief at bay, Freuchen threw himself into work, while Rasmussen lamely and stoically mused that life must go on, even—perhaps especially—during an expedition. He planned very few all-night dancing parties in the fall of 1921. This was not how an adventure was supposed to start.

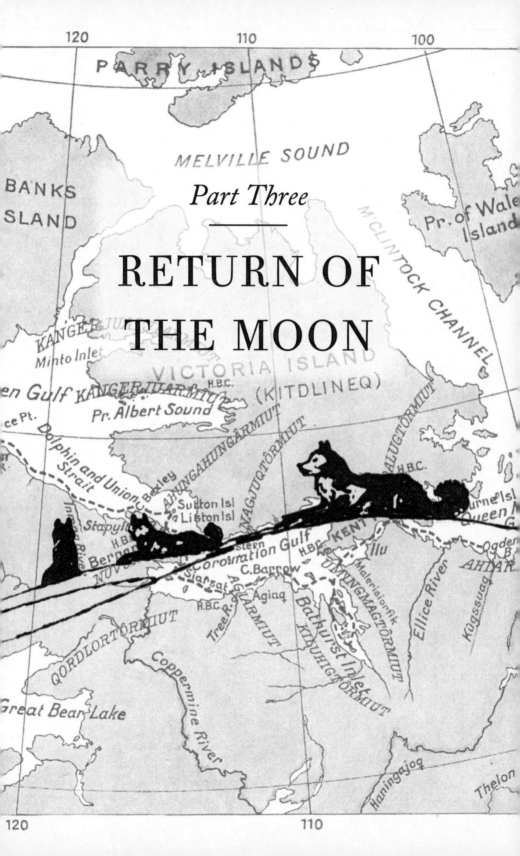

Part Three

—

RETURN OF
THE MOON

 **10**

THE LAND BEYOND
THE GREAT SEA

The Great Sea has set me
in motion
Set me adrift
And I move as a weed in
the river.
The arch of sky
And mightiness of storms
Encompass me,
And I am left
Trembling with joy.

—Uvavnuk, recorded and translated by
Knud Rasmussen in the Hudson Bay area,
Report of the Fifth Thule Expedition

THE SLED TRACKS were clear in the snow, the first tracks the visitors from Greenland had seen in the new land. The style of the runners was different from theirs—broader, and set closer together. The Greenlanders had stopped to thaw their cheeks and for Rasmussen to enjoy a puff of "the sweet sin," as he called tobacco, when a gunshot rang out. In the distance they saw a cluster of "black objects" moving on the ice. "I had often imagined the first meeting with the Eskimos of the American Continent," Rasmussen wrote, "and wondered what it would be like. With a calmness that surprised myself, I realized that it had come." He took out his spy glass and scanned the horizon, where he saw that a line of sleds had stopped to look at him and his team. Then one man dashed forward.

Rasmussen became excited and, with a shout and a crack of the whip, urged his dogs toward the people he imagined to be hunters. As he drew near, "tearing along at top speed," the people brandished their rifles. Freuchen shouted a warning, which Rasmussen predictably ignored. He leaped off his sled, removed his fur mitts, and raised his hands above his head. Freuchen and Nasaitordluarsuk, known as Bosun, followed Rasmussen's example, whereupon the hunters brought their rifles down and raised their hands. They all stood there momentarily, a few humans amid panting dogs on a vast, snowy plain, until one hunter stepped forward. "We are only plain common people," he said. Because of the pale color of the Greenlanders' coats and pants, at first the hunters had thought the newcomers were ghosts.

"We also are only plain common people," said Rasmussen.

Rasmussen marveled that "I had yelled at the dogs in the language of the Greenland Eskimo. And, from the expression on the stranger's face, in a flash I realized that he had understood what I said." Papik, the leader, was "a tall, well-built fellow, with face and hair covered with rime, and large, gleaming white teeth." Soon all the people were chatting amiably. "As soon as they saw we were friendly folk, as interesting to them as they were interesting to us, they went wild with delight," Rasmussen wrote. "There was a shouting and laughing and cracking of jokes."

The delighted hosts were called the Akilinermiut, whom Rasmussen had heard about in Greenland. They had been moving their village to its winter location. Rasmussen decided to set up camp in some nearby snowdrifts and have a feast to celebrate the encounter. "The meeting could hardly have been more effectively staged," Rasmussen recalled. "A whole caravan of them suddenly appearing out of the desert of ice, men, women, and children, dressed up in their fantastic costumes, like living illustrations of the Greenland stories of the famous 'Inland-Dwellers' . . . All was so unlike the fashions I had previously met with that I felt myself transported to another age; an age of legends of the past."

THE CROSSING FROM Greenland had not been easy. The ship's destination was the coast of Hudson Bay, north of Southampton Island. Storms, thick ice and fog had impeded the expedition's progress across Davis Strait and through Hudson Strait. "The ice one finds around Greenland is treacherous and never to be relied upon," Rasmussen wrote. "It grips the traveller, holds him, carries him about and mashes him. It is ever on the move, ever changing. But here in Hudson Bay we encountered for the first time in our lives ice that froze and remained where it froze, some of it gray and rotten and lifeless." Their ship, *Søkongen*, even under Captain Peder Pedersen's expert guidance, barely covered a few miles each day. "The wind howled and the days became increasingly wretched," and their plans changed. Originally, Freuchen and a companion were to be dropped off in Hudson Strait to head north and meet up with the rest of the party the next summer, but the "jungle of ice" would not let them near land. Eventually, however, through the haze, a low range of mountains appeared. Rasmussen cheerfully described the scene as "a smiling valley opening seaward upon a shelving beach, and landward sheltered by a great crescent of guardian hills." It proved to be a small, uninhabited island, now called Danish Island, just off the mainland and Vansittart Island.

Finding a harbor, the *Søkongen* landed the expedition's equipment and seventy-five now-scrawny dogs. The thirsty animals rushed to a pond and drank until their bellies bulged, then sniffed the new land on legs still wobbly from disuse on the voyage. From the top of a nearby hill, the explorers had a welcome view of the surrounding coast and fjords: walrus lounged on the ice nearby and caribou grazed in the distance. It was "a land truly hospitable in its promise of game." Freuchen and the two scientists, Birket-Smith and Mathiassen, began working on the winter house while Rasmussen and some of his Inuit companions ventured out to explore. Rasmussen quickly hunted a dozen caribou and many other animals and began storing meat for the winter. He continued his dogsled journeys, exploring the land around their new home.

Freuchen and the two scientists learned how to work together, with Freuchen teaching them how to dogsled and generally how to survive in Arctic conditions. At first Birket-Smith and Mathiassen were disgusted with the filthy conditions of camp life. "It is not easy," Freuchen wrote, "for students who come from the university to be with guys like me. I scared them in part with my actions. In particular, we were amused by the horror that was painted on Therkel Mathiassen's face when he saw that I let one of my dogs lick the pan clean after our meal. As if he'd seen me practicing murder, he whispered in the greatest excitement to Birket-Smith: 'He lets the dog lick the pan!'" But the scientists were soon inured to the reality of life in the Arctic and they all got along well during their time at "the Bellows," as they called their camp, on account of the wind.

On December 4, 1921, one month after arriving in the new land, Rasmussen, Freuchen and Bosun encountered the first group of local Inuit. Their dialect was slightly different from that of the Greenlanders, but Rasmussen had no problem understanding them. Freuchen and the other members of the expedition,

lacking Rasmussen's facility with the language, had more difficulty, but soon they too could pick out the rhythms and idioms
of the local dialect. Rasmussen learned that in the vicinity of the
Bellows there were many bands of Inuit. He also learned of a
nearby Hudson's Bay Company post at Repulse Bay, so he and
his entourage set off to introduce themselves at the post and inquire about the possibility of mail delivery in the spring. Captain
George Washington Cleveland—known locally as Sakoatarnak,
the harpooner—was a legendary figure in the region. Cleveland
was the only white person to live alone at the post, which was
a gathering place for Inuit traders. American by birth, he had
lived in the area for more than two decades, first as a whaler and
eventually as the Hudson's Bay Company representative. When
Rasmussen arrived at the post, he produced a letter from the
company's head office in London. Cleveland waved it away: "I
don't care to read it," he said. "I know good men by sight." Rasmussen later learned that Cleveland was illiterate.

The old whaler had a warm relationship with alcohol, despite Prohibition—he was allotted only six bottles per year, for
"medicinal purposes"—so he was happy to receive some Danish
aquavit. "Liquor is my favourite drink—any kind and any brand,"
he claimed. Rasmussen's donation to the medicine chest ensured
a warm welcome on this and many other occasions during the
next year and a half. Over a meal of caribou, canned fruit and
aquavit, they solidified their friendship. Then followed a late-
night dance party. Cleveland was garrulous and helpful, but not
all his claims and stories were to be trusted. Nevertheless, Rasmussen obtained the information he needed to plan the next two
years of exploration, including tips about which groups lived in
which regions and a strategy for visiting them all. He also learned
something unexpected: that there were two distinct groups of Inuit in Canada, one concentrated around Baffin Island and along
the Northwest Passage, who lived much like their Greenlandic

cousins, in a culture based on marine mammal hunting, and another smaller group that kept more to the interior and lived on land mammal hunting. The expedition would have to cover as much territory as possible in the next two years to become familiar with both these groups.

While Rasmussen and Bosun returned to Danish Island to see how the others were getting along, Freuchen sledded south alone to visit the Hudson's Bay Company ship *Fort Chesterfield*, commanded by Captain Jean Berthie, which was frozen in farther south in Wager Bay. Rasmussen later met Berthie on several occasions—as everyone in the sparsely populated region was eager to meet new people—and described him as having "all the good qualities of the French Canadian." Berthie was also "thoroughly familiar with all forms of travel in the Arctic, and speaks Eskimo fluently." His crew were young Newfoundlanders, full of "cheerful hospitality." Freuchen and Berthie agreed to meet at Captain Cleveland's station for Christmas, along with the crew.

On his way back to Danish Island, Rasmussen encountered more sled tracks. Not being able to resist seeing where they went, he urged his dogs on. He soon found an old woman, Takornaoq, ice fishing for trout on a large lake. She brought Rasmussen and Bosun to her small village of three snow huts. One of the notable residents was an old man named Inernerunassuaq, an angakoq from farther north, near the North Magnetic Pole, who told them many tales that evening by the light of seal-oil lamps.

Just before serving a meal to her visitors, Takornaoq, overcome, seated herself between Rasmussen and Bosun and sang an impromptu song in their honor:

> *Aya iya, aya ya-iya,*
> *The lands about my dwelling*
> *Are grown fairer this day*
> *Since it was given me to see*

The face of strangers never seen.
All is fairer,

All is fairer,
And life is thankfulness itself.
Aya, these guests of mine
Bring greatness to my house,
Aya iya, aya ya-iya.

After they had eaten, Rasmussen continued to ask many questions. Now Takornaoq told him stories, including one that illustrated the terrible fragility of life in those regions. "I once met a woman who saved her own life by eating her husband and her children," she said softly. One winter, she told Rasmussen, she and her husband were traveling by dogsled when they "came to a spot where strange sounds hung in the air." The words slowly became clear: "I am one who can no longer live among humankind, for I have eaten my own kin." Searching for the source of the lament, they found a small snow shelter, and nearby a human head. They crawled into the shelter and saw a near-skeletal woman muttering about her deeds. She had eaten her husband and children. "You had the will to live and so you are still alive," they claimed and nursed her back to strength before taking her away, to the place where her brother lived. "She is still alive to this day," Takornaoq recalled, "and married to a great hunter, named Igtussarssua, and she is his favorite wife, though he had one before. But that is the most terrible thing I have known in all my life."

Rasmussen stayed with them for several days before returning to Danish Island, full of hope that these people would not only provide a wealth of ethnographic material, "the first intimate picture of a little known people, but also . . . produce evidence of the origin and migrations of all the Eskimo Tribes. The key to these mysteries would be found in hitherto unexplored ruins of former civilizations on the shores adjacent to the Barren Grounds, and in the present-day customs of isolated aborigines who were themselves strangers alike to the white man and to the Greenland Eskimos I knew so well." The Barren Grounds, also known as the Barren Lands, was the name given to the region between east Hudson Bay and the Arctic coast, "among the most isolated and inaccessible portions of the globe."

At first the Inuit living near Danish Island were afraid of the Danish and Greenlandic travelers, but word soon spread of Rasmussen's hospitality and charisma. The Inuit learned to regard the small collection of huts on Danish Island as a home away from home, coming and going as they pleased, which is exactly as Rasmussen wished. Only in this way, by building confidence and mutual respect, would he gain the advantage of studying their history and culture. Within a few months he was, according to Freuchen, "already their dearest friend, and wormed every secret out of them." In addition to learning about their material culture—their houses, clothing, weapons and food preparation techniques and tools—Rasmussen wanted especially to know about their religious practices, their songs, dances, stories and ceremonies.

THROUGHOUT JANUARY AND February 1922, Rasmussen began to organize the expedition into teams for the summer fieldwork. Mathiassen and Birket-Smith would first sled south to visit Cleveland and obtain more detailed information about the tribes in the vicinity of the post. Then Birket-Smith, with Jacob Olsen as an interpreter, would continue south to Chesterfield Inlet and proceed inland to investigate the Inuit who lived near other non-Inuit native peoples. Rasmussen was keen to head inland to study "people who were even more interesting"—those who eschewed marine mammal hunting and lived in the Barren

Lands. Mathiassen would return to Danish Island and head north with Freuchen to map the shores of Baffin Island (called "Baffinland" by the expedition) and to meet the people of that region. Their journey would take them to Igloolik, where they would part company: Freuchen would chart the unexplored portions of Baffin Island and Mathiassen would chart Admiralty Inlet, before meeting again at Igloolik for the return journey. Later, Mathiassen was to begin excavating the nearby ruins at Repulse Bay and Southampton Island—the remains of what would come to be called the Thule culture.

But the winter was not all taken up with planning and preparation. Rasmussen went on many hunting expeditions, although sometimes it was so cold that "every time we picked up our guns with the naked hand the cold steel took the skin off." On one such journey near the end of January, after a hard day on the trail when they "wished for nothing better than to find a shelter without having to build it ourselves," he and his two Inuit companions were surprised to see a huge sled with six men and a team of fifteen dogs coming toward them. A small man with a frosted beard leaped off the sled as it drew alongside, held out his hand "in the whiteman's fashion" and gestured behind him to a cluster of snow huts that Rasmussen hadn't seen. "*Qujangnamik!*— Thanks to the coming guests!" he yelled. He introduced himself as Aua, an angakoq, and proved to be a superior host as well as a valuable source of local spiritual lore.

Aua brought them to the shore of a large lake, where a small group of Inuit emerged from their snow houses to greet them. About sixteen people lived there, in multiple dwellings and storerooms connected by tunnels. The entire complex was lit by blubber lamps, and the floors were strewn with thick caribou hides. It was the largest housing complex Rasmussen had ever seen in the north, and he was delighted to be introduced to the residents, to sip tea and relax, feasting on a roasted hare.

They agreed to go walrus hunting together, an event that took
two days of organizing and packing. The provisions were stacked
outside in a chaotic mound that looked much like the piled-up
possessions of any "suburban family waiting on the pavement for
the furniture van."

The sleds were loaded and the dogs panting and eager again
to "give tongue," as Rasmussen was fond of writing. But before
they set off, he had the rare pleasure of seeing an intimate domestic ceremony: a prayer for a newborn infant's first journey
into the world, to give it good fortune on life's greater journey.
Aua leaned over the swaddled baby and sang quietly:

> *I rise up from rest,*
> *Moving swiftly as the raven's wing*
> *I rise up to meet the day—*
> *Wa-wa*
> *My face is turned from the dark of night*
> *My gaze toward the dawn,*
> *Toward the whitening dawn.*

Soon they had arrived at a good campsite and set to work cutting snow into blocks and building a new cluster of snow houses
against an outcrop. Once again, these were large dwellings. The
largest hut could sleep twenty people with ease and was linked by
tunnels to adjoining rooms. The interior was made homey with
the use of plentiful furs and skins, while numerous oil lamps provided warmth and light. Here Rasmussen remained with Aua for
several weeks, until mid-February, hunting walrus, feasting and
singing. The hunting was good and the food was plentiful. "A
well-stocked larder sets one's mind at rest, and," Rasmussen observed rather loftily, "one feels more at liberty to consider higher
things." With the lamps casting mysterious shadows in the evenings, their stomachs full "and the place so warm that one could

go about half naked and enjoy it," night after night the people settled in to hear Aua's stories of the supernatural and his responsibilities as an angakoq. "Men and beasts are much alike," he said. "And so it was that our fathers believed that men could be animals for a time, then men again." He told the story of a polar bear that hunted walruses like a man, creeping across the ice to their air hole and then leaping up to crush the beasts with a giant ice block.

"With eloquent gestures and a voice that rose and fell in accord with the tenor of his theme," Aua spoke of the Mistress of the Sea, a creature who dwelt on the bottom of the ocean. How she began as a girl who had been kidnapped by a petrel that was disguised as a handsome young man. How she had been rescued by her father and then abandoned when the powers of the petrel-man raised a mighty storm. Her father, seeing her clinging to the side of the boat, chopped off her fingers and wrists, which became the seals and the walruses. How she sank below the waves and now ruled the sea and its myriad creatures. Aua intoned that the girl's father lived nearby and was responsible for punishing those who had sinned on earth until they were ready for the afterlife.

Aua spoke quietly to Rasmussen of the two regions of the afterlife: the Uvdlormiut, a place near the dawn where lived the People of the Day, those who were drowned or murdered. And the Qimiujarmiut, where lived the People of the Narrow Land— an island under the sea populated by those who died of sickness. In both places, game was plentiful and life was full of laughter. The souls of the dead played kickball with a walrus skull, and their singing was the source of the northern lights. Aua also told Rasmussen about the rites of an angakoq, and the ceremony to prepare an angakoq for a visit to these two realms of the afterlife. And how, in times of famine, an angakoq would visit the Mistress of the Sea to beseech her to release more animals for hunting. Rasmussen, entranced, recorded all he could; but the most surprising thing to him was that much of what Aua told him was familiar. He had heard it from angakoqs in Greenland. These were obviously closely related people.

ALTHOUGH HE WAS occupied primarily with legends and beliefs, Rasmussen had observed some similarities and differences in material culture between the Inuit of Greenland and those of central northern Canada. These included slight variations in the construction of snow shovels, snow huts and harpoons. The sleds were also longer, narrower and heavier than those commonly used in Greenland. But it was the Canadian Inuit method of making sled runners that stood out. Because of the dry climate, the snow along the coast of Hudson Bay was "dry and powdery," making the traditional Greenlandic sleds slow and sluggish. It was like driving through sand, the runners screeching and whining with the friction. Under these conditions, even light loads were "troublesome to move" and wore out the dogs. The Inuit here had adapted to this by doing what Rasmussen called "ice shoeing." In Canada, the Inuit made the icy runners not from ice-encrusted hides but from frozen mud. The mud was dug up in the summer specifically for this purpose and applied in a two-inch-thick paste to the runners. When it froze it was smoothed with a knife and then covered with water and saliva squirted from people's mouths. During travel, the ice on the runners wore off several times a day. If the drivers' mouths were too dry to spit, they urinated on the runners' mud. If a runner was damaged by hitting a stone, repairs were done by applying a piece of chewed meat to the runner. "With a good ice shoeing and reasonably level ground," Rasmussen noted, "even heavy loads will run as smoothly as in a slide, without fatiguing the teams . . . the sledges run almost by themselves, with just a momentary pull every now and again."

Because they had missed the season for digging up mud, Rasmussen and Freuchen came up with the ingenious idea of using frozen rye-flour paste as an alternative until they could obtain mud in the spring. They later made pancakes out of the paste. Rasmussen, who had bowed to propriety in his quest for professional credibility, claimed in his account of the journey, *Across Arctic America*, that the pancakes were fed to the dogs. Freuchen was more revealing: "As I said before," he remarked, "we were rather careless of what we smeared on it, and I gladly dispensed with my share of the pancakes."

By mid-February, Rasmussen knew he was running out of time if he wanted to reach the inland caribou hunters. He and his crew returned to the Bellows through a blizzard "with bent backs and bowed heads; we had literally to creep along, following the well-worn sledge track with our noses almost to the ground." After a brief reunion with the other expedition members, they set off on their respective journeys, according to Rasmussen's plan. They had about eight months of work to do. The two Danish scientists were now well trained in Arctic travel—they were nowhere near as proficient as Rasmussen, Freuchen and the Inuit assistants, but they had enough skills not to hold anyone back and were unlikely to perish from bad decision making.

Rasmussen's team consisted of three sleds, three men, two women and twenty-four dogs. With the sleds weighing over one hundred pounds each without riders, the dogs were happy to have ice shoes on the runners as they shot east and south along the frozen coast of Hudson Bay. They were headed toward Chesterfield Inlet, following Birket-Smith and Helge Bangsted, who had gone ahead. The team rested at Cleveland's Hudson's Bay Company post at Repulse Bay for a few days and then pushed on, stopping only briefly when the travelers encountered hunters or small clusters of snow huts, or the abandoned stone ruins of older encampments. Several days out, they noticed a lone traveler sledding toward them from the south. It was Constable Packett, of the Royal Canadian Mounted Police, traveling from the police headquarters at Chesterfield Inlet to meet Rasmussen and write a report. Packett spent his winters alone, dogsledding thousands of miles and sheltering in snow huts. He told Rasmussen that his main work was to bring order to the whalers who sometimes wintered along the coast—they could be unruly and "required a good deal of looking after." As part of the Canadian government's initiative to bring a more universal application of law and order to the Arctic region, Packett occasionally had to investigate murders committed by Inuit as well. In all other aspects, the Inuit were left to regulate themselves. Rasmussen agreed to submit a report to police headquarters, such as it was, at Chesterfield Inlet before he headed inland. "I confess to being somewhat impressed by the Canadian Mounted Police as undaunted travellers," he wrote.

By early April, when they passed the ship *Fort Chesterfield* iced-in north of Wager Bay, the sun was lighting the sky for half of each day and warming the snow. Rasmussen called for a few days' rest, not only to visit the crew but also because a band of Netsilik Inuit were camped around the ship. One of the Netsilik elders, Manilaq, was "an excellent story-teller," but Rasmussen knew he must hurry to get inland before the warmth of spring made sled travel to the interior difficult. He made plans to meet Manilaq later, to share stories, but it was not to be. Manilaq committed suicide soon afterward, "in the presence of his family, preferring to move to the eternal hunting grounds rather than live on growing feebler under the burden of days."

Rasmussen frequently wrote about the cultural custom of suicide, and other seemingly harsh and unsavory traditions, in Inuit communities in Greenland and North America. For all his romantic portrayals of Inuit life—the freedom, mystery, celebrations and fine oral traditions of poetry and story—Rasmussen was unsentimental in recording the less-than-ideal aspects of life in the harsh land. Suicide was a necessary social adaptation to an unforgiving world, and individuals were responsible for killing themselves when they were too old to keep up with the efforts that survival demanded and became a burden to others. Usually communities did not have excess food, and life was too precarious for families to maintain dependents other than their own children. Rasmussen wrote in detail about the death of an old angakoq many years earlier in Greenland:

"Sagdloq is growing old," he said to me. "Sagdloq is losing his power. His wife will die."

This was Sagdloq's last great inspiration; his wife died when the summer came. Shortly after her burial, people began to report that Saqdloq would not leave his tent. No one could get him to take food, and he refused to speak. I went down then to see him. He was sitting in a heap on the stone sleeping-place, and had already grown strangely yellow in the face. His excoriated eyelids were bleeding.

When I went in, he signed to me, with a movement of his hand, to sit down; and, interrupted by constant fits of coughing, he explained himself: "You are a stranger, to you I am glad to speak; I act as I am doing because life is no longer good for me. I am too old to be alone. She who looked after my clothes and prepared my food for so many years is dead. For many years I have lived with her, and it is best that I follow her."

I went softly away; I did not like to intrude upon him. And I did not visit him again.

The villagers came and brought him food, which they left in his tent. But he was never heard to speak after that. Old Sagdloq literally starved himself to death; all the gifts of meat that his countrymen had brought lay heaped up by his body.

In mid-April, Rasmussen was welcomed into the home of a family of five Inuit who lived in three roomy, connected snow huts. Generous as usual, the people offered to feed Rasmussen, his companions and their dogs, and soon they were "firm friends." Rasmussen wondered "where else in the world could one come tumbling into people's houses without ceremony, merely saying that one comes from a country that they do not know, and forthwith begin to question them on matters which are generally considered sacred—all without the least offence?" Even though they were only a day's travel from Chesterfield Inlet, where they would turn inland, Rasmussen decided to stay with his hosts for eight days—the walrus hunting was excellent and the patriarch Inugpassugssuk was a loquacious and forthcoming narrator. Of course, Rasmussen should have realized that it was his own charm, familiarity with their customs and fluency in their language that eased his way in their world; no one else could have done it. No one else did do it.

Chesterfield Inlet was a city in comparison with any community they had visited since leaving Greenland. It consisted of a handful of white-painted wooden buildings, including Hudson's Bay Company storehouses, the barracks of the Royal Canadian Mounted Police, "in lordly isolation on the farther side of a frozen creek," and astonishingly, a small Roman Catholic church built of wood. Many snow huts filled the spaces between the buildings, "the open entrances of which gave the whole the appearance of a rabbit warren." When the visitors arrived, the church bell was ringing and a handful of people were shuffling across the snowy clearing toward the "civilized and city-like" building. A photograph of the community taken by Rasmussen exudes desolation, but to him and his companions it was very welcoming.

He introduced himself to the non-Inuit residents at the Hudson's Bay Company post, to the police and to the three Jesuit priests, who were "highly cultured and most interesting to talk to." But he declined an invitation to stay at the home of the station manager. Wanting to maintain close contact with the Inuit, he continued to live "Eskimo fashion on the stores of walrus meat" so that he would always be perceived as being part of the Inuit community "in their free and easy fashion" rather than a cultural outsider. It was essential, he believed, to maintain this distinction in order to be accepted and therefore entrusted with their cultural secrets.

On May 3, he and his companions harnessed the dogs and set off along the north shore of Chesterfield Inlet en route to Baker Lake, hoping to meet the remote inland Inuit, who lived entirely without access to marine mammals for food. The sun was warm, and as the snow was moist and soft with the temperature above freezing, Rasmussen removed the ice shoeing from the runners. They pushed on quickly through the fast-corroding snow, drinking from freshly melted ponds. On May 12, they reached Baker Lake and were reunited with Birket-Smith, who had been waiting "impatiently" for Rasmussen to arrive. They did not linger at Baker Lake because the people who lived there were in frequent contact with whalers, traders and missionaries, and thus "much of their original character had been lost." The explorers pushed on into the unknown interior. It was now so warm during the many hours of daylight that they traveled at night to keep the heavy sleds from bogging down in slush.

On May 18, they reached a region about 250 miles west of Baker Lake where "isolated masses of rock [rose] up here and there amid the innumerable lakes and streams." Ridges of rocky hills undulated and shrank into a great, swampy plain that was "tinged with beauty" in the lingering sunset. Rasmussen skied ahead of the sleds, and from the vantage of a slight rise he saw, not far away, a village on the shore of a small lake. They were in the land of people generally known as the Caribou Inuit, the inland Inuit who had no history of the marine mammal hunting that so clearly defined the Inuit cultures of Greenland and Hudson Bay.

The villagers ran about in confusion when they saw Rasmussen's band on the rise. By the time he reached the settlement, all the women and children had vanished and two men sat on blocks of snow waiting for him. The Caribou Inuit were frequently in conflict with the coastal Inuit and southern Indian groups, so the arrival of strangers with sleds might easily signal a war party. "For centuries past," Rasmussen wrote, "the Eskimos and the Indians had been at feud, and the atrocities on both sides were not yet forgotten."

But he knew the preferred greeting in such situations. He yelled out in Greenlandic: "*Ilorrainik tikitunga!*" which meant "I come from the right side!" The inland Inuit understood the language perfectly. The two men leaped up with grins on their faces and ran up to Rasmussen; the tent flaps flew open, and the women and children rushed out. It had been a severe winter, during which several people and many dogs had starved to death. They were now waiting for the spring caribou migration and had sent off runners to the nearby settlements along the Kazan River. Rasmussen's crew made pancakes and tea for the entire village, and the Inuit started preparing a celebratory meal while Rasmussen chatted with them. He discovered, to his great interest, that some of them had never before seen a white person. Before the afternoon was over, runners arrived, shouting, "The caribou are coming!" and the village went into action with "extravagant rejoicing." Soon the land was "so thick with game" that it made travel by dogsled difficult.

As they pushed farther inland, Rasmussen and Birket-Smith met other bands that were busy with the caribou hunt, and they were invited to "an extravagant banquet" of boiled caribou by

Igjugarjuk, the leader of the head tribe of the Padlermiut, or Willow-Folk. Rasmussen was again astonished at how much meat could be consumed at one sitting by people accustomed to the vagaries of an erratic food supply. As they relaxed after the "heavy meal," he broke out some tobacco to share. At first he was disheartened by what seemed to be the "worst kind of tin-pot store and canned-provision culture"—a result of trade with the Hudson's Bay Company. The Padlermiut had a gramophone that played songs sung by the great opera tenor Enrico Caruso, leading Rasmussen, who usually traveled with a gramophone in Greenland, to remark that he had arrived here "about a hundred years too late." As he mingled and chatted, though, a young man came up to him and asked if seals had horns, like caribou. At this, Rasmussen was so pleased that he "forgot [his] disappointment altogether." These people may have had metal pots and guns, but they were culturally distinct and very regional in their worldview: exactly what Rasmussen sought in his exploration of Inuit folklore and legends.

As the snow melted with the late spring sun hot and high overhead, hares, birds, lemmings and marmots emerged and crept about in the tall grass. Caribou were visible everywhere, and wolves and foxes were birthing their cubs. Gulls and terns and loons covered the lakes. Igjugarjuk said, "A youth is dead and gone up into the sky. And the Great Spirit colors earth and sky with a joyful red to receive his soul." At the end of June, only patches of the snow lay over the ground, and sled and ski travel was only possible through the slush and along frozen lake shores. The local people preferred travel by canoe at this time of year; they had never seen skis and delighted in experimenting with them in the snowdrifts still remaining at the summer solstice.

Rasmussen asked questions of all the old people, wanting to hear their stories and discovering that many of these stories were already familiar. One was especially intriguing—a story about conflict with "red Indians" from the south, who would sneak up and attack the unsuspecting Inuit villages. Rasmussen had heard and recorded nearly word for word the same tale in Greenland—but Greenland has no other native peoples, and he had always wondered about the story's origins. Now he knew that it must have come from people who had migrated from North America at some time in the distant past and had brought their stories with them.

Many other stories Rasmussen heard here were nearly identical to those he had heard and collected in Greenland. Indeed, when he began to tell his stories, he found that his Canadian listeners had already heard them before and were surprised that an outsider should know their stories and legends. This was a powerful discovery, bolstering Rasmussen's theory of a pan-Arctic culture that had migrated at some distant time from west to east. But he now began to think that perhaps the origin of the culture lay not in Asia but somewhere along the rivers and lakes of the northern Canadian mainland, and that the people had migrated from the interior to the coasts.

The inland Inuit had no stone houses, unlike the people of Greenland and the coast of Hudson Bay, and Rasmussen and Birket-Smith during the summer expedition found no evidence they had ever been built here. Also, because the Inuit here had no access to marine mammals, they had no blubber for lamps and their snow houses were unheated in the winter. They lived a harder life than people along the coast, leading Rasmussen to pronounce them "the hardiest people in the world." He and Birket-Smith ascribed the differences in these people's material and social culture to their distance from the coast, as well as noting the similarities in various Inuit cultures. Out of fifty-two stories Rasmussen recorded here, thirty were identical to Greenlandic stories, despite the many centuries that must have elapsed since the time of the Inuit migration. "An unquestionable connection exists between the Greenlanders and their Canadian kinsfolk in the matter of story and legend," he wrote. "Many of these stories show a forceful simplicity, a touch of epic strength, and a poetic sense."

Of those stories that were unique to the region, Rasmussen observed that metaphors from the wild and tales concerning animals were used to reflect on human life. Some of the memorable titles include "The Owl That Wooed a Snow Bunting," "The Raven and the Loon," and "The Owl and the Marmot." The songs were fascinating, too, with several being unique to the region.

Kivkarjuk's Song

I am but a little woman
Very willing to toil,
Very willing and happy
To work and slave . . .
And in my eagerness
To be of use,
I pluck the furry buds of willow
Buds like beard of wolf.

I love to go walking far and far away,
And my soles are worn through
As I pluck the buds of willow,
That are furry like the great wolf's beard . . .

Akjartoq's Song

I draw a deep breath,
But my breath comes heavily
As I call forth the song . . .

There are ill rumors abroad,
Of some who starve in the far places,
And can find no meat.

I call forth the song
From above,
Hayaya—haya.

And now I forget
How hard it was to breathe,
Remembering old times,
When I had strength
To cut and flay great beasts.
Three great beasts could I cut up
While the sun slowly went his way
Across the sky.

Rasmussen traveled across the tundra to the west of northern Hudson Bay throughout the summer, meeting as many people as he could, until he reluctantly began the long journey east to the coast. Sometimes he met up with Birket-Smith and Helge Bangsted, who were now doing botanical collecting, but often he traveled only with his two Greenlandic Inuit companions and a variety of local Inuit guides. Hauling their dogsleds through the slush and grasses and across raging rivers swollen with melt-water, they shot caribou and feasted on meat roasted on flat rocks over large fires in the near-perpetual light. It was an exhausting journey, especially for the dogs, dragging the heavy sleds over less-than-ideal terrain, but Rasmussen thrived. "The weather was fine," he wrote after one tiring jaunt over the tundra, "and as sleep is not so essential in summer, we were soon on our way once more." It was all a great adventure to him, even those times when he and his companions were trapped on the wrong side of a flooded river and struggled to get the sleds across while ice smashed into them; or when one of the canoes, holding valuable equipment, washed away and they spent over two hours chasing it downstream, grappling with the lead lines to haul it ashore, leaving their hands bloody while they shivered with exhaustion; or when they "had to cross a lake on a block of ice . . . using our skis as paddles."

They returned to Chesterfield Inlet on July 31. Rasmussen hardly recognized it. When he had passed through months earlier, the village was firmly in the grip of winter, "one's nostrils froze in the icy blast and the blood fairly hardened in one's cheeks"; now it was warm, and instead of seeing fur-clad people in snow huts, he saw the Inuit living in large white canvas tents and wearing cheap, factory-made clothes, which in his opinion were ugly and ill-suited to them. He was also surprised that none of the Inuit hunted the numerous seals and walruses that had congregated just offshore; they were inland Inuit, who had made their way to the coast to be near the Hudson's Bay Company post, and they had neither the skills nor the knowledge to hunt these animals. Rasmussen was amazed at the power of culture and custom, so strong that it prevented hunters of land mammals from taking advantage of the abundance of marine mammals.

Two weeks later, Birket-Smith and Bangsted rejoined him in Chesterfield Inlet. The men set off together in a schooner heading north to Repulse Bay, where they planned to meet Freuchen. There, Cleveland informed them that although Freuchen and Mathiassen had returned to the Bellows from their northern excursion, migratory ice had prevented Freuchen from bringing a boat south to meet them. A blast of winter weather kept them at Repulse Bay until September 1, when they were fortunate to meet the Inuit whaler and trader John Ell, who spoke English fluently. Ell owned two boats and several sleds and dog teams and offered them passage to Danish Island. What astonished Rasmussen was the man's easy fluency in two cultures, much like his own—Ell was also a distinguished angakoq, renowned for his magic powers. The world was indeed changing, and cultures were no longer distinct.

RASMUSSEN AND HIS entourage arrived at Danish Island on September 18 to find the Bellows empty. But their disappointment was temporary; they found Freuchen and several Greenlanders out hunting walrus, "and our reunion was as joyous as any meeting in the Arctic is likely to be between companions long separated." It was time to compare notes and make plans for the next phase of the expedition. Rasmussen spent the fall sledding around the region, meeting with people he had missed before or who had arrived recently, searching for more stories and legends. He made several visits to the angakoq Aua, still the source of a vast collection of stories. The information about many of the local religious beliefs, taboos and festival rituals that Rasmussen wrote about, and much of his information about angakut in general—their skills, duties and spiritual adventures—came from his meetings with Aua.

One of their most revealing discussions shows just how thoroughly Rasmussen could be taken into a community, how much he was trusted and respected. Aua explained to him why the Inuit remained respectful of so many ancient customs and taboos, why their behavior was so frequently governed by rules that had no apparent practical foundation and seemed annoying and arbitrary. He took Rasmussen to see Natseq, his very ill and elderly sister. "Why should we human beings suffer pain and sickness?"

he said. "All fear it, all would avoid it if they could. Here is this old sister of mine, she has done no wrong that we can see, but lived her many years and given birth to good strong children, yet now she must suffer pain at the ending of her days? Why? Why?" Rasmussen listened respectfully, and Aua continued his long philosophical discourse: "You see, even you cannot answer when we ask you why life is as it is. Our customs come from life and are directed towards life; we cannot explain, we do not believe in this or that; but the answer lies in what I have just shown you." He then chanted:

> *We fear!*
> *We fear the elements with which we have to fight in their fury to*
> *　　wrest out food from land and sea.*
> *We fear cold and famine in our snow huts.*
> *We fear the sickness that is daily to be seen amongst us. Not death,*
> *　　but the suffering.*
> *We fear the souls of the dead, of human and animal alike.*
> *We fear the spirits of earth and air.*

Aua conceded that they did not know why they obeyed all the old customs and rules, except that these traditions were "built upon the knowledge and experience of generations." Perhaps clinging to them helped the people to live in peace. "For all our angakoqs and their knowledge of hidden things," Aua said, "we yet know so little that we fear everything else. We fear the things we see about us, and the things we know from the stories and myths of our forefathers. Therefore we hold by our customs." In this way, in discussion and debate, Rasmussen passed the final months of 1922.

The members of the Fifth Thule Expedition celebrated Christmas by decking the Bellows with Danish flags and hanging cords of homemade ribbons from the ceiling. They cleaned their cabins, brought out a tablecloth, sang Danish songs and ate boiled trout and caribou. The gramophone scratched out Danish carols as they reread old letters from loved ones, letters now many months old. Outside, the northern lights swirled under the starry dome of winter.

11

THE GREAT
SLED JOURNEY

Once upon a time two men thought they would like to travel round
the world, that they might be able to tell others what it was like.

The two who were anxious to set out on their travels had
just taken wives and had as yet no children. They cut themselves
drinking-cups from musk-ox horns, each of them one, cut from
the same head, and then they set out, each in his own direction, to
meet again someday. They set off with sledges and camped when
the summer came. It took them a long time to get round the world;
they had children, they grew old, and the children themselves
grew old; at length the parents were so old that they could not
walk alone, and the children guided them. One day, both parties
eyed in the far distance another group moving toward them very
slowly. It was the two couples who finally met. Very slowly they
walked up to meet each other, and they recognized each other's
voices. They had been so long on their journey that their cups
made of musk-ox horn, with which they scooped water from the
river, were now so worn that only the handles were left.

They greeted each other and sat down.

"The world is big."

"Yes even bigger than we thought when we parted."

—Collected by Knud Rasmussen,
Eskimo Folk Tales

IN JANUARY 1923, while he completed his final ethnographic interviews and supervised the packing of thousands of artifacts for shipment to Denmark, Rasmussen sent Freuchen on an expedition to map the uncharted coastline of western Baffin Island. The bearded Danish adventurer set out from the Bellows with Bangsted and the hunter Akrioq. Although the temperature hovered around −76° Fahrenheit (−60° Celsius) and "the north wind burned into" their faces, the now-experienced travelers did not expect the journey to be particularly difficult or challenging. Inuit stories from Greenland to Hudson Bay, however, were filled with accounts of untimely death, disaster, accidents and maiming, among even the most seasoned and capable of people, so trouble should not have come as a surprise.

On previous expeditions, both Rasmussen and Freuchen had been injured or become debilitated for periods of time, as had their Inuit companions. The group dealt with the problem in various ways, sometimes offering to remain in one place until all its members had recovered, as they did during the First Thule Expedition a decade earlier. But Rasmussen, now middle aged, was no longer a carefree wanderer seeking adventure and fame. Now he was on a schedule, and he had ambitious dreams and expectations for this expedition, and little patience for anything that would threaten its successful outcome. In Thule, he could take risks; it was so remote that nothing he did would ever get back to Denmark and affect his life. But now there were witnesses, and his reputation was at stake. He had become more mindful of public perception following the deaths that had occurred during the Second Thule Expedition.

On his journey west with Bangsted and Akrioq, Freuchen ran into serious difficulty and nearly froze to death. When he was brought back to the Bellows, Rasmussen was angry with Freuchen and blamed him for being irresponsible. In his account of the accident, Rasmussen merely stated that "Freuchen was quickly brought back with a bad case of frostbite which made him temporarily an invalid." The true story wasn't told until many years later, after Rasmussen's death, and it is much more interesting.

AFTER A WEEK of hard travel through a blizzard, with the dogs struggling through soft snow under loads that were too heavy for the conditions, the three men decided to offload some weight from the sleds and cache it. Now pulling lighter loads, the dogs surged forward and soon the snow became firmer. Freuchen decided he would return and bring up the cached supplies while Bangsted and Akrioq built a snow hut and rested. If he traveled all night he could be back before "morning," which was mostly a theoretical concept in the middle of an Arctic winter. He harnessed the dogs, "who were none too pleased at backtracking when they expected to be sleeping," and dashed back through the gloom. On reaching the depot he loaded the crates, but soon another storm blew in. With the wind "howling like a fiend," the drifting snow was "alive under [his] feet," obliterating his sled tracks and making his return a game of chance.

Freuchen became disoriented as the storm increased in ferocity. He kept stopping to check snow conditions, planning to build a snow hut to wait out the storm when the conditions were right. But there was never the right kind of snow. The dogs became exhausted, but he drove them on. Finally, he decided to leave the sled and its heavy load behind and push through the blowing snow on foot, with the dogs on ropes. This plan had to be abandoned when Freuchen found that he had to turn his back to the wind just to take a breath, and he returned to the sled exhausted. He struggled to a nearby rock outcropping that offered a slight wind block and hollowed out a spot. There he and the dogs crawled under the sled and huddled for warmth. He again tried to cut some snow blocks, "but the snow was as hard as ice" and he gave up.

Freuchen stumbled around in circles for hours, trying to keep warm, until exhaustion finally overtook him. When he became "nauseated" from lack of sleep, he dug a shallow "grave" under the sled, crawled in with his sleeping bag and fell asleep. When he awoke, the storm was still raging and he had no feeling in his left foot. He tried to crawl out, so as to run around and increase circulation but discovered that he was frozen to the ground, unable to move. He dozed again and awoke even colder. If he didn't get up and move he would "freeze stiff as a poker." Although it was now morning, the day remained completely dark and bitterly cold. Freuchen tried scraping his way out of his prison in a desperate burst of thrashing, to no avail. He was stuck, frozen in place "like a fox in a trap," and for hours he clawed at the ground and the sled, while the blizzard whipped snow around in the darkness. Finally managing to free himself, he leaped up, only to crash down again. His entire left foot and lower left leg were frozen solid; it was "impossible to bend the joints."

Freuchen crawled to the dogs and with great difficulty, harnessed them and cracked the whip to urge them on. Roused from their lethargy, the dogs dragged him for hours in the direction in which he hoped his friends had made their camp, and he crawled painfully for the last few hours when he couldn't hold the line any longer. When they heard him approaching, the others rushed him inside their snow hut. They cut open his kamik and found his foot in bad shape. As it began to thaw, the pain grew worse. Soon his foot "was puffed up like a football" and his toes "had disappeared completely in the balloon of blue skin." Infection had begun in one big toe. He, Bangsted and Akrioq abandoned their journey and began sledding back to the Bellows, with Freuchen trying to keep his foot cold so that it wouldn't hurt. "It was a bad week," he recalled.

When they reached the Bellows, Freuchen was placed in a bed. As he lay there, the stench of gangrene clogged the atmosphere. He could only watch as the others worked and an angakoq muttered spells and sang "pain-killing songs" over his swollen foot. Finally the "flesh fell away until the bones protruded," and Freuchen "felt that the old man with the scythe was close after me." Knowing he had no choice but to act before the infection spread, Freuchen held a nail pincer over his left big toe and hammered down, severing the foul appendage. He passed out from the pain.

Rasmussen himself had endured a similar situation when he had been caught in a blizzard and had forgotten to bring along his snow knife. For him, however, the tragic ending never seemed to materialize: he might fall into freezing waters, but he would be pulled out before he drowned; he might nearly starve, but he would find food before he became too weak to hunt; he might get caught in a blizzard and spend a day exposed and freezing, but he would not get serious frostbite. As Freuchen wrote, "somehow whenever Knud travelled he always escaped the ultimate disaster and the more hardships there were the more Knud enjoyed life." Although Rasmussen was angry with Freuchen for doing something that he considered only an inexperienced explorer would do, he offered to delay his great sled trip. Freuchen was an independent man and waved off the offer, confident that he would heal later.

ON MARCH 10, 1923, after eighteen months of exploring the vast region west of Hudson Bay, it was time for this company of adventurers to split up. Birket-Smith and Olsen traveled south to Fort Churchill and then on to Winnipeg. Mathiassen headed north to Igloolik and Pond Inlet, boarded a Hudson's

Bay Company ship to St. John's, Newfoundland, and then sailed
to New York. Freuchen's injury resulted in a change of plans: the
expedition had to abandon the final mapping of Baffin Island, so
his new job was to stay and oversee the packing and shipping of
the expedition's thousands of collected artifacts and decommis-
sion the Bellows.* The ethnological items being shipped included
Inuit fishing and hunting gear, household implements, amulets,
masks, clothing, miscellaneous tools and many other examples
of local physical culture. Bangsted and two of the couples from
Thule—Akrioq, Arnanguaq, Bosun and his young wife—would
remain with Freuchen at the Bellows for another year, not returning to Greenland until January 1924.

Although Freuchen eventually sailed to Greenland, he would
never return to Thule. Peder Pedersen, the captain of the *Søkongen*, was told not to bring Freuchen to Thule but to drop him and
Bangsted off farther south; the Thule Inuit families would have
to make their own way north. In a letter to Hans Nielsen, the
new station manager at Thule, Marius Nyeboe wrote from Copenhagen in May 1923 that if Freuchen made his way north to
Thule, he should not be made too welcome; he was to be treated
as a "guest" at the station. If he stayed too long, he might again
start to think of it as his home. In the winter of 1923, Rasmussen, Nyeboe and Nielsen knew that Freuchen wasn't supposed to
return to Thule, but Freuchen did not.

But Thule was Freuchen's home; having lived there for over a
decade, he had no other. Why did Rasmussen agree to have his

---

*In the summer of 1923, while Freuchen was in Chesterfield Inlet arranging
for the artifacts and his mail to be sent to Greenland, a doctor operated on
his injured foot. The operation was only a partial success, and his foot never
entirely healed, eventually having to be amputated. Freuchen also found
time to father a child with an Inuk woman from western Hudson Bay; his
grandson, Peter Freuchen Ittinuar, was Canada's first Inuit member of Par-
liament in the 1980s.

friend cut off from his home and employment? Did he now see Freuchen as a liability? He certainly was not part of the establishment, nor was he an academic. Mathiassen and Birket-Smith, while acknowledging his work ethic and general good nature, were unimpressed with his unscientific approach to the work. Since the Second Thule Expedition, Rasmussen had noted problems with Freuchen's management of Thule Station, but he had never broached the subject with his old friend. Freuchen had a big heart and frequently gave the station's supplies to the sick and the poor. He was also a poor record keeper; his inventories were untrustworthy, and frequently the lines were blurred between Freuchen's inventory and that of the store. Complicating matters was the fact that Rasmussen was little help because of his poor math skills and general lack of interest in this aspect of the business. Nyeboe wanted better records so he could gain a sense of how much money Thule Station was making. Added to this was Freuchen's lack of diplomacy in dealing with the missionaries—they frequently complained about him.

But the real problem with Freuchen at Thule, so far as Rasmussen was concerned, was that Freuchen could "no longer tolerate the loneliness." Certainly he was part of the local community, but he was also an outsider, and his life depended on living according to the locals' traditions. Life at Thule Station was not always a celebration—especially during the war years, when the post was so isolated. In Copenhagen in 1920, Rasmussen and Nyeboe had told Freuchen that he would need to be replaced as manager of Thule Station because his debilitating bout with the flu had rendered him unable to work in Greenland any longer. Rasmussen, however, had asked Freuchen to join him on the Fifth Thule Expedition when he saw that Freuchen had mostly recovered from the illness. Freuchen was indispensable as an Arctic explorer. He was a good-natured and indomitable travel companion, and he knew the language and customs of the Inuit.

Rasmussen wrote that he was prepared to recommend to the committee that Freuchen be asked to resign if his friend had not been capable of joining the Fifth Thule Expedition. He suspected that with Navarana dead, Thule Station would no longer be a good place for Freuchen. He knew it was time for Freuchen to move on, to leave the past behind, but he didn't want to be the one to tell him. He was instead quite happy to set off on his epic dogsled adventure following the route of the Northwest Passage and leave these problems behind.

MARCH 10, 1923, was the start of the longest dogsled expedition in polar history. On the morning of his departure, Rasmussen had with him only two trusted companions, Miteq and Arnarulunguaq, who had accompanied the expedition from Greenland. Miteq was a young hunter and a superior dog driver whom Rasmussen admitted he had known "from the time when [Miteq] lay screaming lustily in his mother's amaut [parka]." Arnarulunguaq, Miteq's cousin, was the young woman who had lost her husband just before the expedition left Greenland. She was a skilled seamstress and cook, and a master snow-hut builder. The two Inuit were experienced and cheerful companions, eager for adventure and imbued with the indispensable quality Rasmussen possessed in abundance and always looked for in others—adaptability to changing circumstances. Once they left the Bellows, the travelers would have no direct means of communication with anyone at home until they reached a telegraph station in Alaska one year later.

The three companions shared two six-yard-long narrow sleds of the style prevalent west of Hudson Bay, each pulled by twelve robust dogs. The sleds were each piled with about 1,000 pounds of equipment, including sleeping bags, summer tents, pots and other cooking tools, hunting weapons (including a year's supply of ammunition) and kerosene. They also carried luxuries such as tea, coffee, sugar, flour and other trade goods to ease their welcome into new communities or to exchange for goods that would be added to the ethnographic collections. And, for Rasmussen, there was the indispensable tobacco. The bulk of the weight consisted of food for the dogs, vast quantities of frozen meat and fish.

Tingling with anticipation of the journey, Rasmussen urged his dog team as they surged forward, northwest, toward new adventures in a new land with new people. They sledded across Rae Isthmus toward Simpson Peninsula and King William Island (King William's Land), heading toward the small harbor where Roald Amundsen's ship *Gjøa* had stayed nearly two decades earlier.

On March 28, finding themselves in "a tearing blizzard" on the shore of Committee Bay, at the southern tip of the Gulf of Boothia, they were building a snow hut as shelter from the storm when two figures materialized out of the snow. Although the strangers carried long knives and harpoons, Rasmussen jogged toward them. He shouted: "You may lay aside your weapons; we are peaceable folk who have come from afar to visit your land."

The strangers stopped, astonished to meet others in the storm, and called the traditional reply: "We are just quite ordinary people, and you need fear no harm from us. Our huts are near; our weapons are not meant to do you hurt; but it is well to have weapons here when meeting strangers." Rasmussen decided to follow the men back to their huts, a three-hour slog through the worsening blizzard. Not long after, they were drinking tea and smoking inside the warmth of the hut and "we soon made friends with them." The two men, "remarkably well built and handsome," were with their families traveling south with fox furs to trade for new guns, theirs having been lost while crossing a river the previous summer.

The two groups of travelers stayed together for about a week, sharing meals and stories. The Canadian Inuit were intrigued that a white man spoke their language so perfectly, and even more intrigued to meet their Greenlandic cousins, come from so far away to the east. They laughed on discovering that they shared many of the same stories and legends. One of the men, Orpingalik, an angakoq, agreed to share magic songs with Rasmussen. Always humming and singing, Orpingalik was "a poet, with a fertile imagination and sensitive mind." His numerous songs, his "comrades in loneliness," were mostly hunting chants, to bring good fortune or placate the animal spirits. Rasmussen claimed these songs were difficult to translate, yet he did a fine job, particularly in the song called "My Breath," about a time when Orpingalik was ill:

> *I will sing a song,*
> *A little song about myself*
> *I have lain sick since the autumn*
> *And now I am weak as a child,*
> *Unaya—unaya.*

> *Sad at heart I wish*
> *My woman away in the house of another*
> *In the house of a man*
> *Who may be her refuge,*
> *Firm and sure as the strong winter ice.*

> *Sad at heart I wish her away*
> *In the house of a stronger protector*
> *Now that I myself lack strength*
> *Even to rise from where I lie.*
> *Unaya—unaya.*

Who knows his fate?
Here I lie, weak and unable to rise,
And only my memories are strong.

Before the two groups went their separate ways, Rasmussen traded some sugar, tea, tobacco and a small knife for the contents of a cache containing frozen sea trout, a seal and a caribou. This was a land of plenty, and the periodic starvation experienced in other regions of the Canadian Arctic, particularly west of the Boothia Peninsula, was apparently unknown here. Rasmussen visited many other family groups in the region until May, when he, Miteq and Arnarulunguaq were again on the move, heading north and west toward the vicinity of the North Magnetic Pole, searching for bands they hadn't yet met and learning from them the likely locations of others. Whenever they picked up the scent of new people, the dogs grew excited and rushed forward. Occasionally, Miteq would head off on separate missions to hunt or trade.

As summer began, the three Greenlanders pushed on under the midnight sun to King William Island, "plunging into the icy mess . . . the snow broth seething about the runners, and we drove through it singing." The once-snowy world came to life. "Geese, duck and waders were gathered in thousands on the lakes and marshy ground, red patches of saxifrax glowed among the rocks, the first flowers to greet the light and warmth of the sun." Long-distance dogsledding was nearly impossible in the summer, so Rasmussen spent the warm season in this region, exploring old ruins, meeting people and generally enjoying the short summer. The profusion of life amazed him: "Over the sappy-green meadows there was the song of thousands of birds, one continuous tremulous tone of joy and life . . . The swamps were full of wading birds building their nests and laying their eggs, and all these voices joined into one great chorus that once again the earth lived.

On a sunny day like this there is no feeling of being in the world's most rigorous regions."

King William Island, about 5,000 square miles in size, was populated by only several hundred Inuit: it was "shut off from the rest of the world by ice-filled seas and trackless wastes of vast extent." Its residents, the Netsilingmiut, "people of the seal," lived inland from mid-July to mid-December, hunting caribou and salmon fishing before scattering to the coast for the other half of the year to hunt seal on the ice.

Here, in the vicinity of the North Magnetic Pole, Rasmussen was intrigued by the prevalence of amulets with special powers, particularly those used to ward off spirits and to bring luck or fertility. Although amulets were a common cultural artifact in all the Inuit communities Rasmussen visited, they were far more common among the Netsilingmiut. He wanted a collection of them, as well as an understanding of their importance and purpose. As "amulet hunting is rather a delicate business," he relied on his charisma and the many techniques that had always worked for him before, but he had to be especially careful to make his inquiries and collections "in such a manner that I should not be held accountable afterwards for any evil that might befall those who had parted with their treasures."

Rasmussen composed a speech wherein he claimed that the power of the amulets did not apply to him because he was a stranger from across the sea. Speaking with authority about the Netsilingmiut's customs, he invoked the names of famous angakoqs from other tribes to bolster his opinion. Then he emphasized that he was not purchasing the amulet's power, only the article itself. Nevertheless, acquiring amulets involved extra distribution of goods and the hosting of additional meals. This slowed their journey, as the region was home to many bands. "After all," he remarked, "human kind is much alike all over the globe, and one of the best ways of getting to know your neighbour is to dine with him." The gifts he offered were thimbles, nails, matches and small knives that were of "inestimable value to those beyond the verge of civilization"—a round trip from here to the nearest Hudson's Bay Company trading post could take half a year.

In this manner, Rasmussen acquired several hundred amulets, many of them "pitiful little odds and ends, half mouldy, evil smelling, by no means calculated to impress the casual observer with any idea of magic power." Amulets of animal parts conveyed particular attributes: a foot of a loon for skill in paddling a kayak, the head and claw of a raven for a good share of meat from the hunt, and caribou teeth for luck in caribou hunting. Women and girls wore amulets to gain protection for the future of their children. Rasmussen, considered a powerful angakoq in his own right, once had to contribute locks of his hair, shorn with a hunting knife by the respected angakoq Niaqunguaq. For a man who was fond of his appearance and who trimmed his hair neatly and regularly, this was a considerable sacrifice. "By the time he had done with me, I am afraid my appearance was hardly what my hairdresser at home would consider that of a gentleman," he remarked.

By the end of August, Rasmussen had met and entertained so many people that he had run out of items to trade. Miteq had set off at the end of May for the Hudson's Bay Company post on the Kent Peninsula to ship the artifact collections to Denmark and return with supplies, but he was taking longer than Rasmussen had hoped. "Living as we did, chiefly on raw meat, and going about with an aftertaste of suet or blubber in one's mouth, it was hard to be deprived of one's pipe at the end of the day." Rasmussen and Arnarulunguaq were joined intermittently by small bands who helped them by hunting for food while the visitors prowled among the ruins.

The people there were "tall and strongly built," despite having to endure "an almost uninterrupted struggle for bare existence." Just as in the Thule region of northern Greenland, "periods of

dearth and actual starvation are not infrequent." Female babies
were frequently killed at birth unless they had been promised in
marriage already, reflecting a need to keep the population from
growing beyond the carrying capacity of the land. Suicide among
the elderly was common, and cannibalism was not infrequent.
Rasmussen interviewed one man who claimed that "many people
have eaten human flesh. But never from any desire for it, only
to save their own lives, and that after so much suffering that in
many cases they were not fully sensible of what they did." There
were many tales of those who had killed and eaten even their
own wives, claiming that the spirits had told them to do so. But,
as one angakoq told Rasmussen, "we who have endured such
things ourselves, we do not judge others who have acted in this
way though we may find it hard, when fed and content ourselves,
to understand how they could do such things . . . We only know
that every one of us has the same desire to live."

THE FIRST SNOW of the year fell on August 25. Soon afterward
a canoe was seen coming across the lake, and Arnarulunguaq
rushed to the shore to see who the paddler was. The figure was
Miteq, returning from the Hudson's Bay Company store on the
Kent Peninsula. The first words out of Miteq's mouth as he and
Rasmussen embraced were, "No ammunition, no tobacco, no tea,
coffee, sugar or flour. But . . . we are alive ourselves, and it might
easily have been otherwise." He had endured a harrowing journey
in which he and his companions were forced to flee from another
Inuit band that they suspected were hiding to ambush them, only
to find that the Hudson's Bay Company outpost at Kent Peninsula had had an unusually good season for fox pelts and had sold
out of most items Rasmussen needed, including ammunition
and matches. Without more ammunition, keeping the dogs fed

would be a problem: only about seventy-five cartridges remained; and without matches, lighting the lamps would become much more of a chore.

By mid-September nearly one hundred people had gathered around the camp on King William Island in preparation for the annual caribou-migration hunt. Excited shouts brought everyone out of their tents to observe a spectacle that Rasmussen described as "a great body of cavalry on the move, the herd advancing in a line of 50 to 100 abreast, in steady formation." The camp burst into action, the hunters grabbing their rifles and rushing to conceal themselves behind rocks and hummocks. The great herd plodded toward the coast until the thunderous explosion of rifle fire split the air. "They stood as if paralyzed for a moment, and they gazed about helplessly in search of the invisible foe," giving the hunters time to reload and fire another volley. With shot after shot cracking the air, about fifty animals dropped, until finally the herd splintered into smaller groups and ran inland. Rasmussen and Miteq did not shoot any caribou, preferring to save their ammunition—firing at long range wasted a lot of ammunition. They later went hunting on their own and killed seven caribou, the finest and the fattest they could find.

On September 21, with snow now covering the ground, the camp was shaken from its torpor by cheering and a "great cry of wonder," which Rasmussen thought might be greeting another caribou herd but turned out to be something more unusual. He thought he was dreaming when he saw a ship, under full sail, winding its way through the ice-choked bay. The Inuit stood with mouths agape, for they had never seen such a thing. It was "the Great Event of all their lives." The last ship to visit the region had been Roald Amundsen's *Gjøa*, a generation earlier, and this one appeared to the onlookers to be "swimming on the water like some great bird, yes, and with sails spreading out above like huge white wings!"

Rasmussen tied his skis together to make a flagpole and hoisted two flags, the Danish and the British, from its tip—and waited. Soon a motorboat was lowered from the ship and "came sputtering" ashore. Two men scrambled up the stony beach and introduced themselves, a Swede and a Dane working for the Hudson's Bay Company. They were, incredibly, just now setting up a new post on the island. Ten minutes later, Rasmussen was on board the ship "with my teeth deep in an orange," savoring the smell of hot coffee brewing. The traders also treated Rasmussen to a feast, including luxuries such as bread, cheese, butter and, most important, a new supply of tobacco. Soon he sat "puffing great clouds of smoke."

Within a week, it was traveling season again and Rasmussen was anxious to get moving—there was new terrain to explore and new people to meet. He, Miteq and Arnarulunguaq, preparing to leave for the west, had built two new sleds with iron runners. The Hudson Bay style of sled—long and narrow, with peat-and-ice runners—would be of little use in this climate of sloppy ice mush.

When they had finished packing for the next leg of the journey but were waiting for the weather to improve, Rasmussen decided to investigate some stories about the lost Franklin expedition of half a century earlier. Many local people remembered those times and told stories of the white men who had come in search of Sir John Franklin: John Richardson, John Rae and George Back. Rasmussen and one of the newly arrived traders sailed up the east coast of the Adelaide Peninsula looking for a spot that had been described by a number of Inuit elders. Exactly where they had been told to search, Rasmussen found a collection of human bones, tattered clothing and old boots. They covered the remains with a cairn of stones and held a memorial ceremony, flying the Danish and British flags at half-mast. "Here on this lonely spit of land," Rasmussen wrote, "weary men had toiled along the last stage of their mortal journey. Their tracks are not effaced, as long as others live to follow and carry them farther; their work lives as long as any region of the globe remains for men to find and conquer."

Finally the day came to leave King William Island and head west across a land newly covered in snow that was "a glittering carpet of innumerable tiny crystals; and across it moved the caribou in their hundreds." It must have been strange for Miteq and Arnarulunguaq, years after leaving home, to be heading even farther away. Fortunately, they were accepted without question in the communities they visited. Rasmussen didn't record any misgivings they may have had, but he was fond of describing the Inuit as a wandering people, always in search of new and hidden things.

Rasmussen didn't seem to be in a hurry, though he surely must have given the occasional thought to his wife and children in Denmark, but he never mentioned them in any account of his travels. His editor, Tom Kristensen, once remarked that he had tried to convince Rasmussen to mention Dagmar but he refused; Rasmussen never made himself or his family life the focus of his stories. Letters to and from Denmark were infrequent and rare, and not possible at all from this remote stretch of Arctic coast; it might take more than half a year if he entrusted a letter to the Hudson's Bay Company. One letter he sent from Chesterfield Inlet before he departed on this leg of his epic journey had called on Nyeboe and his Thule Committee to send a field photographer—ideally Leo Hansen, the photographer who had filmed the expedition at the start of their journey years earlier—to meet him somewhere near the western end of the Northwest Passage. He "felt that motion pictures would be a valuable addition to the other material we were collecting."

The culture of the people they had met on their journey so far had been very much the same, as was the food and the climate. The farther west they traveled, however, the more the Inuit's material culture became influenced by the goods provided by the Hudson's Bay Company trading stations and American whalers. Rasmussen wasn't impressed. "I thanked my lucky stars that I had visited King William's Land at least before the trading stations had got hold of it; while there was still some native life and folklore left to explore." He could tell when they were nearing a trading post, as he saw the evidence on display in the villages: wool blankets instead of caribou hides, ironware instead of carved and polished driftwood or stone, aluminum and tin instead of soapstone. In one hut he was astonished at the greeting he received. "On the sleeping place sat a young woman, crosslegged, her magnificent caribou furs partly covered and utterly effaced by a horrible print apron. Her hands were covered with cheap-jack rings, a cheap cigarette was held between two fingers, and she breathed out smoke from her nostrils as she leaned back with the languid insolence of a film star and greeted us with a careless 'how do you do.'"

On the morning of November 14, the sleds drew to a halt outside a small trading post at the mouth of Arctic Sound and several men came out to greet the Greenlanders. One was Leo Hansen, who told of his adventures in reaching the outpost. He had taken a steamship from Copenhagen to New York, traveled north into Canada and west to Vancouver by train. Then he had boarded a Hudson's Bay Company steamship north to Point Barrow, Alaska, and on to Herschel Island in Mackenzie Bay, and finally he journeyed east through Coronation Gulf to the Kent Peninsula in the tiny schooner that serviced the handful of small trading posts in the western part of the Northwest Passage. Hansen had brought all his equipment and was eager to start filming. Rasmussen, too, wanted to get some film down soon, as the days were nearly completely dark and they had only about two weeks before the total darkness of December set in, which would make filming very difficult.

On November 22, they arrived in Malerisiorfik, a community at the northern part of Bathurst Inlet. Rasmussen particularly enjoyed Bathurst Inlet, a great fjord that reminded him of Greenland, just "somehow colder and harsher." This new terrain and its people were a welcome respite from the "monotonous" lowlands of the east. Rasmussen chose to film the residents, the Umingmagtormiut (Musk Ox People), because no ethnographer had ever visited them, and as it was the start of the seal season, traditional seal hunting would make for a good documentary film. When the Greenlanders' sleds slid up to the small community of snow huts, even though a blizzard was raging, all the men rushed out to greet them and help them construct a shelter, and the women eagerly brought Arnarulunguaq inside. The visitors stayed in the vicinity for over two months, until the end of January.

The Umingmagtormiut paid special attention to their clothing, particularly its cleanliness and design, and they had a different set of clothing for special occasions. They were gregarious, highly social and shrewd traders, possibly owing to their relative nearness to the Hudson's Bay Company posts. Although "they seemed to place no value at all upon their time" and Rasmussen dispensed only a few presents during many days of interviewing and questioning, they were loath to part with material items without receiving a huge payment. In addition to noting these cultural attributes, Rasmussen was pleased that "they are the most poetically gifted of all the tribes I met with, and their songs are not restricted to epic and narrative forms, hunting achievements and the like, but include also more lyrical elements in which feeling and atmosphere predominate." He went on several excursions to meet the residents of nearby communities in order to interview them, doling out tobacco and coffee both in celebration and to get them to talk.

After hearing a particularly perplexing story about a fox with magical powers, Rasmussen asked about the meaning of the story. "Hm, well," Netsit, the storyteller, pondered. "We don't really trouble ourselves so much about the meaning of a story, as long as it is amusing. It is only the white men who must always have reasons and meanings in everything. And that is why our elders always say we should treat white men as children who always want their own way. If they don't get it, they make no end of a fuss."

Not long afterward, Netsit brought Rasmussen to his home village, at the south end of Bathurst Inlet. It was a large village of perhaps thirty snow huts set in a great natural amphitheater. A giant dancing house dominated the center of the village, and Rasmussen found the community to be "quite a metropolis after what we have been accustomed to for months past." The most unusual aspect of the settlement was the black stovepipes that stuck out of the white domes of the houses, looking like spears dropped from the sky. *Ugly*, was Rasmussen's first thought; but, on reconsideration, "a welcome sight to the half-frozen traveller for all that."

Soon, "tumbling out of their burrows," came an unruly mob that engulfed Rasmussen. Some grabbed at his sled and others plucked at his clothes, while one man snatched his pipe from his mouth. Some of the women came up and begged for seal blubber. These were the people rumored to have killed two white men a few years earlier, and among the other tribes they had a reputation for aggressiveness, so Rasmussen had had some trepidation about visiting them alone. (Miteq, Arnarulunguaq and Leo Hansen would not join him until a few days later.) Netsit, meanwhile, had vanished, visiting his kin. Rasmussen realized that "it was essential to show them a bold front, if I wished to keep them in hand." Led by his seemingly unerring social and cultural instincts, Rasmussen announced: "I have come to you alone, though ill things are said of you in other parts." Rasmussen had heard about the 1913 killing of two men he names as Radford and Street. "It is not many years since two white men were killed here; and the Police do not speak well of you to travellers. But I am not afraid of meeting you alone, as you can see." Playing to their pride as hosts had the desired effect: soon his equipment was left alone, and no one grabbed at him.

"It was not our fault!" one man protested. "It was the white men who began the quarrel. We are peaceable enough, only somewhat given to fun, fond of singing and laughter, and with no evil thought as long as we are not afraid. You are our friend and need no fear no harm." One of the murdered white men, who apparently had been "excitable," had thrashed an Inuk man who refused to obey him. Rasmussen's conclusion was that the man had "thus doubtless brought the disaster upon himself." Although the police had described the people of Netsit's village as "born thieves, terrible liars and altogether unreliable," Rasmussen found them to be "kindly, helpful and affectionate." Radford felt that he was entitled to thrash a man who refused to do his bidding, but in the local culture attacking a free man who refused to be ordered about was grounds for severe reprisal.

"WHO ARE YOU?" asked one of the elders, curious that Rasmussen was fluent in their language, albeit with an accent. "Are you a trader come to buy foxes?"

"I have come to look at you," Rasmussen responded, "and see what you are like inside."

Once the laughter died down, the elder replied: "Hm. Well, you will find all manner of folk here. Some of them are quite nice to look at, but most are ugly, and you will find little pleasure in looking at their faces."

In order to keep the more inquisitive people from taking advantage, Rasmussen affected a stern demeanor. This worked for a while. However, after he had visited many people in their houses, a woman came up to him as he was tending to his dogs. She placed a hand on his shoulder, looked him in the eye, and said: "Tell me, stranger; are you the sort of man who has never a smile for a woman?" As Rasmussen tells it, "I laughed aloud . . . And with that the ice was broken."

That evening, they celebrated his arrival in the ceremonial house. Large enough to contain sixty people, it was lit by a series of blubber lamps placed in niches. Light and shadows played on the gathered assembly, adorned in costumes of fur and feathers. A drummer stood in the center while singers clustered around him, the throng celebrating all night with "hops and leaps and writhings of the body." Rasmussen, too, danced all night, but he also paid attention to the songs and stories he heard. He recorded many of them during his three-week stay in the community. "These songs of theirs," he wrote, with his general audience in mind, "their harmless fun, and a wistful sense of beauty, of loneliness, all struggling for expression, showed them as children in the wide strange world; at least as human beings like ourselves."

These spirit songs were meant, Rasmussen reminded readers, to be repeated chantlike to the rhythm of the drum:

> *Spirit from the Air,*
> *Come, come swiftly hither,*
> *The wizard here*
> *Is calling thee.*

> *Come and bite ill-luck to death,*
> *Spirit from the Air*
> *Come, come swiftly here.*

I rise,
Rise up amidst the spirits,
Wizards help me,
Lift me up amid the spirits.

Child, O Child, great Child,
Rise up and come hither
Child, Child,
Great Child. Little one,
Rise up among us!

I will visit
Unknown woman,
Search out hidden things
behind the man.
Let the boot-thong hang loose –
Seek under man
And under woman!
Smooth out the wrinkled cheeks,
Smooth wrinkles out.

I walked on the ice of the sea,
Seal were blowing at the blowholes –
Wondering I heard
The song of the sea
And the great sighing of the new-formed ice.
Go, then, go!
Strength of soul brings health
To the place of feasting.

In mid-January 1924, Rasmussen, Miteq, Arnarulunguaq and Leo Hansen returned to Malerisiorfik to retrieve some of the equipment they had left there before continuing west. They had about 1,400 miles of Arctic coast to travel before reaching the next region where Rasmussen wanted to meet and interview people— the "semi-civilized Eskimos of the Mackenzie Delta," Alaska and the Bering Strait. The section that he wanted to pass through quickly, roughly from Bathurst Inlet to Baillie Island, had been thoroughly documented by the ethnographer Diamond Jenness on Vilhjalmur Stefansson's Canadian Arctic Expedition between 1913 and 1918. As Jenness had already interviewed many of the region's people and recorded some of their oral culture in his book *The Life of the Copper Eskimos*, Rasmussen felt he should concentrate on the people no one had yet visited. He had already formed many conclusions about the universality of Inuit culture throughout the polar region based on what he had seen and heard so far on his journey, but he still wanted to visit the western regions— something new or interesting might yet be found.

Leo Hansen would travel with Rasmussen, Arnarulunguaq and Miteq for this final stage of the journey. Two massive sleds were readied for the long trek: Rasmussen and Arnarulunguaq would take the smaller, 200-pound sled with six dogs, while Miteq and Hansen would travel on the 250-pound sled, including all the photography equipment, with ten dogs. With the runners shod in ice they made good time, pushing through temperatures as cold as −44° Fahrenheit (−42° Celsius). Passing Cape Barrow on January 21, they continued along the coast to the Hudson's Bay Company post at Tree River, before heading across the ice of Coronation Gulf and past Amundsen Gulf. They pushed hard when there were no people to visit, covering between thirty and forty miles per day. The dogs trotted to maintain this speed and Rasmussen and the others had to jog to keep up with the sleds, "which was perspiring work, but gave one splendid rest at night."

As they neared the Mackenzie Delta, they discovered they had entered "the land of the Almighty Dollar," where everything had a price. At first Rasmussen was wistful and remembered how friendly and helpful the "uncivilized" tribes had been, offering hospitality and assistance without any thought of payment. Here, where the culture was influenced by American whalers and the increasing numbers of trading posts, "if I wanted folk tales, I found myself confronted with salesmanship . . . I felt hopelessly out of my element in all this. Legend and myth and ancient traditions were things they had left far behind." But after many weeks of travel through the region, Rasmussen changed his mind somewhat. "The Eskimos here had to compete with the white men, and if they were to make ends meet, it is necessary to ask a fair payment for services rendered. We were strangers, merely passing through the country, and had to pay our way." Many Inuit hunters made considerable money in selling furs to competing traders and were "highly paid and independent in proportion." With this newfound wealth, some purchased flat-bottomed schooners (sometimes with motors), others bought cameras and treadle sewing machines, and one man even had a typewriter—although to what use this hunter would put a typewriter, Rasmussen couldn't fathom.

Rasmussen was surprised to find the language spoken in the Mackenzie Delta region nearly identical to that spoken in Greenland, and the culture here based on sea mammals even more than it was in the east. Umiaks and kayaks, both for travel and for hunting whales and seals, were common. Snow houses gave way to log and peat huts, and again were more similar to habitations in Greenland than what the travelers had encountered so far. In one dwelling, they were all enjoying a meal of whale blubber that had become mildewed. They found the meat "uncommonly tasty" and Rasmussen was reminded of the Greenlandic saying: "Mildew cleans the bowels." The host chuckled, for they had the same saying, and then he said: "Laziness often makes things 'good for you' in that way." The similarity in customs made Miteq and Arnarulunguaq feel homesick for the first time.

In mid-April, they arrived at Herschel Island and Rasmussen met a storyteller named Apagkak, "an unquestionably magnificent artist, the finest I have seen outside of East Greenland." He paid the man $50 for five days of work, noting that "art and bargaining do not go well together." But he gained numerous new stories for his repertoire, including "The Wise Raven," which was "a whole creation myth in itself" that bore "traces of Indian influence." At the Royal Canadian Mounted Police post on the island, Rasmussen found Inspector Wood to be "keen and capable." The inspector had developed good relations with various native peoples by keeping the peace between them, the traders, and the whalers. They stayed only five days before moving farther west.

The travelers crossed into Alaska on May 5, reaching Point Barrow on May 23. Here, finally, was a real town of about 250 natives and a few white men, the most northerly permanent settlement in North America. Point Barrow boasted stores, warehouses, a hospital, a school and a church. Rasmussen now felt that his journey was at an end, as far as ethnography was concerned, but this proved only partially true.

"Only a few kilometres out from land was the open sea, rocking the loose icefloes; the sea birds had gathered in dense flocks, and their cries could be heard right up over the land." Only the women and children remained in town at this time of year; the men lived in crude storm shelters on the ice edge, on the lookout for whales and seals. They hunted whales from umiaks between April and June. When a whale was harpooned, it was pulled to land, where the lookouts raised a cry to bring the women and children to carve it into smaller portions. Some of the portions were taken to the elders and the rest was stored in huge subterranean larders, where it would remain frozen throughout the summer.

Rasmussen noticed many unique aspects of these activities, including the taboos and mystical beliefs surrounding the hunt, speculating that the differences he observed existed because, much more so than seal or caribou, "the whale is dangerous to hunt." Because the whaling season involved remaining on or near the coast, hunting caribou had become a specialized endeavor done by seminomadic people who lived inland along the rivers and traded with their coastal brethren. As usual, Rasmussen found much similarity between the old stories, songs and beliefs here and in Greenland, but here there was greater emphasis on the souls of humans and animals being interrelated and on shape-shifting between the forms.

During the summer, Rasmussen continued his journey along the Alaskan coast. It became too dangerous to sled, so the expedition left most of its dogs at Icy Cape and continued south along the coast of the Chukchi Sea. They traveled in a giant umiak to Point Hope (Tikeraq), where they stayed as guests of the local missionary before continuing along the coast of Kotzebue Sound, mostly traveling in small boats but also frequently walking while carrying packs. They had kept four dogs, which were also heavily laden. Rasmussen continued to meet with the Inuit whenever possible, but his interest diminished. The cultures and traditions here had blended with outside influences for so long that the old songs, stories and ideas had been abandoned or had evolved. Many people here now lived in wooden houses and managed reindeer herds, or were at least partly in the orbit of the market economy. Many had become Christians, of various denominations, and refused to even discuss the old beliefs. Rasmussen was not disappointed at these changes; he still admired the people, but his ethnographic interest was quenched. Despite the fact that Alaska had about 14,000 Inuit residents, compared with Greenland's 13,000 and Canada's 5,000, ethnographically Rasmussen felt he had arrived a generation too late.

In early August, in Kotzebue, a small Inuit settlement on the western Alaska coast that had the unusual distinction of having electricity, Rasmussen was struck with a strange unrest. Kotzebue also held America's most northerly telegraph station. For the first time in more than three years he would be able to communicate directly with the outside world, with the other part of his life—his Danish life, his wife and children. Thoughts raced through his mind as he walked across town. "The moment it becomes possible to be informed of how things are at home, it is as if all the emotions that have been kept down suddenly awaken with accumulated force." It was not until the next day that he received a return telegram from Copenhagen informing him that his family was well and that all the comrades he had left at Hudson Bay had likewise made it home. Freuchen had arrived safely in Greenland that same month, and he would travel to Denmark on his own. The news of Rasmussen's pioneering successful trek soon made international headlines.

Rasmussen was so relieved to hear that his family and comrades were safe that he fell asleep for a full twenty-four hours, "to the great astonishment of those about me." The hardship over, most of the travel now would be by boat rather than dogsled. On August 31, the expedition arrived in Nome, the "sort-of capital of North-west Alaska . . . an ugly town, but a town that quickly won one's heart." Rasmussen took Miteq and Arnarulunguaq to the theater and then for a ride in a Ford truck—a sled without dogs. Miteq found the wood-planked streets and crowds of people to be merely interesting, whereas Arnarulunguaq "could hardly believe it was real." But when they were refused service in a local restaurant because of their ragged appearance, Rasmussen suddenly realized that he really had completed his great sled journey and that "we were now in regions where people are judged by their outward appearance." They went shopping for new clothes, rented hotel rooms, and "arranged our mode of life on modern lines."

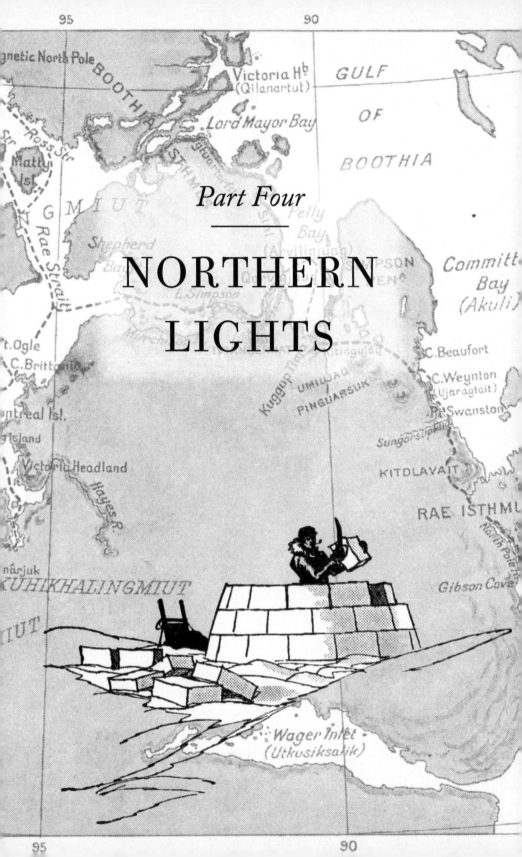

Part Four

—

NORTHERN

LIGHTS

12

RECORDS OF A
VANISHING WORLD

All true wisdom is only to be found far from the dwellings of men, in the great solitudes; and it can only be attained through suffering. Suffering and privation are the only things that can open the mind of man to that which is hidden from his fellows.

—Igjugarjuk, recorded and translated by
Knud Rasmussen, *Across Arctic America*

IN THE SPRING of 1923, Roald Amundsen brought two airplanes to Alaska in an attempt to fly across the Arctic Ocean to the North Pole. This first attempt at polar flight ended when the planes crashed, destroying their landing gear. But others would follow; the world was changing. In the previous three and one-half years, Rasmussen had traveled more than 20,000 miles and visited thousands of Inuit in three countries. He had done it by living off the land, in the local custom, and he had traveled by dogsled. He knew these traditions would not remain the ways of the Inuit forever, as he had already seen the changes wrought by modernization in much of the Alaskan population. These changes were not all for the worse, he felt; modern technology would surely make the lives of the people easier. But the situation saddened him a little. "From my heart," he wrote near the end of his journey, "I bless the fate that allowed me to be born at a time when Arctic exploration by dog sled was not yet a thing of the past."

His reminiscence was bittersweet—pleasures he hadn't tasted in years awaited him. Yet he also must have known that this was his final epic adventure. He was getting older at forty-five and had been nearly everywhere that Inuit lived. "To all these people, this is an ordinary day, a part of their everyday life; to me, an adventure in which I hardly dare believe." An airplane, even a primitive one, could cover in a day the distance a dogsled needed a season of hard labor to traverse. It was easier travel, but it wouldn't be an adventure, and you wouldn't meet anyone.

Before leaving the Arctic, Rasmussen had one final wish: to cross the Bering Strait and visit the East Cape of Russia's Chukchi Peninsula. He was curious about the small number of Inuit who lived in Russia. Were they the same people as those on the eastern side of the strait? What language did they speak? Were they marine hunters, or fishers? Rasmussen was very close to having visited every known Inuit group, and he had all but proven that they were culturally, linguistically and biologically related. But there were formalities to observe. In Nome, he went to the telegraph station and composed a brief message to the Russian authorities in the Central Office of the Soviet government, requesting a permit to enter Chukotka for research purposes. Usually Rasmussen did things as he pleased, and his international fame opened doors quickly for him, but in this case the speed was not forthcoming. The Bolshevik Revolution of 1919 had recently swept Russia, and relations with the United States were strained, owing to the recent conflict over Wrangel Island—only a few years earlier, Vilhjalmur Stefansson had planted the British flag on the island that Russians claimed as their own. Russian officials did not want to admit any potential spies. Rasmussen's request slowly wended its way through the byzantine bureaucracy in Moscow, and he grew impatient.

Every day for a week he wandered to the telegraph station, hoping for the permit to arrive, but to no avail. Finally, he became frustrated and worried that fall storms would make crossing the strait impossible. The Bering Strait between western Alaska and East Cape is not a wide stretch of water, only fifty-one miles across at its narrowest point, but it can be treacherous with erratic winds, strong currents and few safe harbors. As he so often did, Rasmussen decided to go ahead and see what happened. He ruled out crossing the strait in a traditional umiak, because the winds would be against him at that time of year. Going to the docks in Nome, he negotiated for a small schooner, *Teddy Bear*, to ferry him across. Setting out from Nome on September 8, the *Teddy Bear* endured a dangerous week battling storms before reaching a country of "desperate loneliness . . . a forbidding rocky coast with snowclad hills rising from the sea" and arrived at the settlement of Emmatown, near East Cape. One of the first people Rasmussen met was the trader Charley Carpendale, whose daughter Camilla had been taken by Amundsen to Norway for schooling a few years earlier as one of his famous "Eskimo girls." The other official was Allayef, a giant of a man in a fur cap who had "very friendly eyes but a hint of obstinacy about the mouth." Hauled to the police station, Rasmussen tried to explain that he wanted only to meet and interview people, not to engage in any form of illicit trade.

Allayef offered Rasmussen the opportunity to leave at once or to be taken inland to meet the governor. Rasmussen chose the latter because it would "at least prolong my stay in the country." His papers were confiscated, and Allayef brought him to a nearby village to find a guard to escort him farther inland. "It was at once evident," Rasmussen observed, "that these people were of a different type from the cheery, noisy Eskimos. These men looked serious, and from their expression, appeared to regard me as some dangerous criminal. . . . They were not unaccustomed to seeing people carried off never to return." The Chukchi were the northern Asian native peoples and had a different culture and language from the Inuit.

It was a day's journey by dogsled over swampy tundra to the governor's residence. Rasmussen was distressed to see his Chukchi guard use a barbed harpoon to prod his poor dogs into greater exertions. Inside the imposing governor's mansion, Rasmussen was surprised to meet friendly officials, people not at all in keeping with "what I had expected of the new Soviet type." They shared some Russian cigarettes and tried to make sense of Rasmussen's unusual request. He mobilized his considerable talents of persuasion to present his case—it would look bad if an internationally recognized scientific expedition were turned away from Russia after having received a favorable reception in other countries; it was surely only a matter of time before his request from the Danish consulate to Moscow would be approved anyway; in Canada and the United States, it was customary for travelers arriving from the Arctic to be exempt from the regular passport requirements; the expedition's purpose was purely scientific—but to no effect. Nevertheless, he was ushered into the dining room for a hot meal. He bowed at two smiling Russian girls, "finding time to notice their peculiar beauty," and ate in silence beneath a photograph of Lenin.

Given eighteen hours before he had to depart Siberia, he was free to interview as many people as he wished. Thousands of Chukchi and about 1,200 Inuit—the Yupiks—lived in the region. Although these two groups shared some similarities in their material culture, their languages were distinct and Rasmussen could understand nothing of the Chukchi language. He spoke mostly with the many traders bankrupted by the new Soviet regime, and only with a handful of the East Cape Inuit, barely enough to discern that they did indeed share the same language as other Inuit. He had reached as close to the source of Inuit cultural migration as possible.

It was in Chukotka, before being deported, that Rasmussen realized he had nowhere else to go. From a hilltop he stared east into the rising sun and imagined all the places and events of his monumental journey. "I see our sledge tracks in the white snow out over the edge of the earth's circumference," he wrote, "through the uttermost lands of men to the North. I see, as in a mirage, the thousand little native villages which gave sustenance to the journey. And I am filled with great joy."

In October, with the first snows dusting the land and a bracing wind coming off the water, Rasmussen, Arnarulunguaq, Miteq and Leo Hansen boarded the steamer *Victoria* in Nome, bound for Seattle. Ironically, as they began the slow journey home, things became ever more strange to Arnarulunguaq and Miteq. While the ship slowly wended its way south to the land of the white men, the two Inuit from Greenland experimented with appropriate southern clothing. A photo shows their new getup: Miteq exchanged his travel garments for a suit and leather shoes, and got a haircut; Arnarulunguaq looks distinctly uncomfortable in a dress with a white collar and leather high-heeled boots. She tried to master the skill of walking in heels but never did, expressing amusement as she waddled like a duck. She balked at wearing a hat but marveled at the comfort and softness of a pair of silk stockings (though she could not quite figure out what purpose they served). Rasmussen, also in suit and tie, looks perfectly at home, as usual.

On the voyage to Seattle, a party of distinguished American tourists and business travelers were delighted to be on the same ship as Rasmussen and invited him to join them for dinner at the "first sitting." The ship, however, had a rule that no "Eskimos" could eat at the first table; so Rasmussen politely told his hosts that he would join Arnarulunguaq and Miteq at the second table. The prominent people at the first table responded by declaring that they, too, would join the second table. So, reported the *New York Times*, in the end the second table "became the first, in a manner of speaking . . . a happy and gracious ending."

As the Greenlanders walked the gangplank off the ship in Seattle, crowds pressed in, snapping photographs, and a throng of journalists asked dozens of questions. Robert Flaherty's documentary film *Nanook of the North*, detailing a Hudson Bay Inuit family's struggle for survival in Arctic conditions, had been a massive hit two years earlier, and Rasmussen and his companions were celebrated as a real-life example of Arctic life and travel. Their story fed into the public appetite for knowledge of this remote and harsh region. "I have positive proof of the origin of the Eskimo race," Rasmussen enigmatically declared to the press, "but regret that I cannot make public my discoveries at present." But he did declare that all the tribes of people he had met, from Greenland to Russia, spoke a variation of a common language.

The three travelers were a great sensation, famous for completing the longest sled journey in history and the first through the entire Northwest Passage. And, in their hotel, the people of Seattle were amused at the Inuits' fascination with the elevator. Arnarulunguaq and Miteq rode the machine for hours, repeatedly pressing the buttons and exclaiming in surprise when the doors opened at various floors. When Arnarulunguaq looked out the window at all the skyscrapers, she mused: "It is strange that people never mimic the large animals like polar bears, but always the small animals like lemmings."

Rasmussen then led them on a cross-country train trip to Washington, DC. The scenery of the American countryside whipped past their windows as they now covered more distance in a few days than they would have in a season of hard travel in the

Arctic. At the station in Washington, they were met and cheered by crowds from the Danish American community. They stayed in more luxurious hotels and rode a variety of vehicles, or dogless sleds. Ushered into the White House to meet President Calvin Coolidge, Rasmussen was honored to shake the president's hand, though Arnarulunguaq and Miteq were more interested in the giant flag that hung behind the desk. Many more photographs were taken of the exotic "Eskimo" in southern attire; in some photos of Arnarulunguaq in furs, she looks far more comfortable and alive than in a cotton print dress.

After a few days the trio pressed on to New York City by train. One reporter noted that although they had never met, he recognized Rasmussen immediately and described him in glowing detail for the paper's readers as "a man of medium height, slender and sinewy, whose outdoor life and battles with the elements have developed muscle. His hair is straight and black as an Indian's and his skin is bronzed by wind and sun. From under shaggy brows his eyes gaze forth with a steady clearness. They are greenish-gray-blue—and look as though they had taken to themselves the tones hidden in the depths of frozen water."

As Rasmussen toured Miteq and Arnarulunguaq through the busy cityscape, their eyes were wide with wonder. They braved the terrors of New York traffic, crossed the busy streets clinging to each other as they stared in awe, and trusted Rasmussen to lead them safely through the unimaginable chaos and congestion of people, things and sounds. Stopping to eat at a restaurant, Rasmussen told the waiter not to place vegetables before them as they had never eaten them before. When plates of oysters and steak arrived, "their eyes lit up and their faces were wreathed in smiles. . . . their table manners were excellent," wrote the reporter who was accompanying them on their city tour. Arnarulunguaq delighted in squirting lemon juice on the oysters, puckering her mouth at the unknown flavor.

Rasmussen himself behaved nonchalantly, "as if he had not been away from our so-called civilization at all. He felt as much at home in New York as if he had spent three years here and not at the Pole. He was marvellously adaptable." He attended dozens of meetings, presentations, luncheons and dinners—at the Carnegie Institution, the Museum of Natural History, the National Research Council, the Coast Guard, the National Geographic Society, and many others.

Inevitably, the endless public appearances, speeches, photo ops and dinners, combined with living out of a hotel room, even a luxurious one, took their toll. Photographs show a weary-looking man beneath the impeccably suited exterior, hollow cheeked, tired, a smile on his lips but not in his eyes. He wrote a letter to Nyeboe expressing his concern about having a victory so costly that it is really a defeat. The transition was exhausting.

One day in mid-November, as they stood on the roof of a skyscraper scanning "the stony desert of New York," Arnarulunguaq launched into a penetrating speech: "Ah, we used to think Nature was the greatest and most wonderful of all! Yet here we are among mountains and great gulfs and precipices, all made by the work of human hands. . . . Those tiny beings we see down there far below, hurrying this way and that. They live among these stone walls . . . stone, stone and stone—there is no game to be seen anywhere, and yet they manage to live and find their daily food. . . . I see things more than my mind can grasp; and the only way to save oneself from madness is to suppose that we have all died suddenly before we knew, and that this is part of another life."

Rasmussen had one final meeting planned in New York, one that may have made him anxious: Dagmar had crossed the Atlantic on a steamer to meet him after so many years apart. What transpired between them is private. He rarely mentions her or his children in any of his writings; even in *Across Arctic America*, he describes his visit to New York but not meeting Dagmar there;

she was equally circumspect. Before they departed for Europe together, Rasmussen commented that the past four years had been "a great and rich experience for me. I think that there are more tasks for me in the future, but they can only be poor in comparison with the Fifth Thule Expedition. The wise saying of course is that a person with initiative can achieve ever higher goals, but I am unable. My field of work has been and will continue to be north of the Arctic Circle. I cannot spread my interests as Amundsen and other explorers, for it is the Eskimos that own my heart."

Before arriving in Copenhagen, the steamer first put into Oslo, where the Greenlanders and Dagmar were met by several prominent Nordic explorers, including his old hero and inspiration Fridtjof Nansen, as well as Otto Sverdrup and Peter Freuchen, who now sported a wooden leg. Rasmussen then gave a speech at the Norwegian Geographical Society. In Copenhagen, the celebration of Rasmussen's return was jubilant, featuring many cultural and political luminaries, and included a torchlit procession and an audience with King Christian X, who presented Rasmussen, Miteq and Arnarulunguaq with medals. Rasmussen was covered in garlands while the Danish national anthem played. He was the foremost Danish national of international stature, and he already had an impressive history of courageous achievements. He was feted as a hero, having done something extraordinary in pursuing his grand vision with bravery and tenacity.

He was also in debt. The expedition's expenses, including the cost of shipping, transportation and travel, and the salaries of its members over the years, had been enormous. Most of these expenses, apart from being covered by some Danish government funding, had to be recouped from the profits of Thule Station, the sale of Rasmussen's books and the proceeds from the lecture

circuit. From Alaska, Rasmussen had written to Nyeboe, requesting more money, lamenting that he had no time to sort out the
overabundance of material that he had collected. Now he ended
his nomadic ways and settled down to a routine of working at
Hundested, his country home overlooking the sea. He began to
write, and perhaps also to reacquaint himself with his wife and
children. His oldest daughter, Hanne, was now fifteen years old,
Inge was thirteen, and Niels was five; the boy had been a toddler
when his father had left Denmark and had no memory of him.
So it was surely a changed world to which the peripatetic Rasmussen returned at the end of 1924. He was now regarded more
as a respected statesman than as a devil-be-damned adventurer
and irreverent celebrity. His adventure was called work and his
writing was now more academic, in accordance with his international stature as an ethnographer.

Rasmussen enjoyed the attention, the fame and publicity, the
seemingly endless requests for speeches and opinions. He was
granted an honorary doctorate by the University of Copenhagen,
among other distinctions, and more were to come in the following years. The Fifth Thule Expedition collected 15,000 to 20,000
ethnological and archaeological treasures that were donated to
the Danish National Museum, including items that covered the
entire spectrum of Inuit material culture: clothing, tools, amulets,
even kayaks and sleds. The collection was a colossal donation
that made Copenhagen an international center for polar and Inuit cultural research. It included comprehensive collections from
the Igloolik, Caribou, Netsilik and Copper Inuit, in addition to
collections from Mackenzie Delta and northern Alaska. Also included were extensive archaeological collections of artifacts from
sites throughout Greenland, Canada and Alaska, as well as geological, botanical and zoological collections. The expedition also
contributed to polar knowledge by mapping vast areas of coastline previously only vaguely charted.

Rasmussen now had a herculean publishing schedule ahead of him. He set to work on his most ambitious work to date: *The Report of the Fifth Thule Expedition*, a massive compilation of all the reports from the expedition published over a number of years, which would be his lasting contribution to scholarship. More prosaically and profitably, he also wrote the *Narrative of the Fifth Thule Expedition*, published in English as *Across Arctic America* in 1927. *Across Arctic America* was a popular account of his adventures since leaving Greenland in June 1921: the exploration of the Hudson Bay region of Arctic Canada and an account of this expedition's great dogsled journey through the Northwest Passage to Alaska, his dalliance in Siberia and a brief account of the trip across America and on to Europe. Once again, his own exploits take a back seat to portraying the Inuit he met, lived with, and interviewed.

The book includes a great many stories, poems and songs, and a discussion of various unusual beliefs and taboos, told haphazardly, woven into the account rather than organized, analyzed, and compared, as Rasmussen did for the comprehensive *Report*—chapters of which served as doctoral theses for Birket-Smith and Mathiassen. Birket-Smith wrote that "when we were back again, he never got tired of emphasizing the work of his collaborators while he kept his own person in the background." This genuine humility, coupled with the widespread knowledge of Rasmussen's daring escapades—the awareness that whatever he said about others, his own accomplishments were much greater—only served to magnify his reputation, bolstering his fame and esteem.

Across Arctic America lacks the youthful charm and flighty poetical musings that characterized Rasmussen's earlier works. This journey was an adventure, a celebration of life and living, but it was also his work, and he took great pains to emphasize the scientific planning, goals and accomplishments of the expedition. He knew now that his future reputation would be based not upon exuberance and poetry but on science—on verifiable facts and knowledge. It was necessary to bind his cultural interest and literary skill to something concrete to give it substance. Ethnographic science would give his work the legitimacy by which it could be accepted by institutions, both in Denmark and internationally. Rasmussen began his culturally divided life in the Inuit world, then entered the Danish world, then returned to live again as an Inuit as a young adult, and finally returned to the Danish world in his mid-forties; he would never again overwinter or live with the Inuit after the Fifth Thule Expedition. He was now drawn to the institutions and the establishment that he had shunned as a youth, that he had abandoned to live in Greenland. He had a job to do, an important job, and it was no longer just some vague or fluid objective combined with a love of travel and meeting people.

Rasmussen was very much aware of the timeliness of his journey. His collections of stories, poems, songs and legends of an oral culture on the cusp of great social and technological upheaval would now be written down for posterity, just when they were at risk of disappearing. Many of the Inuit living closest to the Hudson's Bay Company trading posts, RCMP outposts and Christian missions had already lost a great deal of their oral tradition. Rasmussen's meetings with important angakut gave him insights into and knowledge of the Inuit spiritual world just as these beliefs were being undermined and discouraged by outside influences.

It was not always easy for him to collect the stories—why would people tell intimate stories to an outsider, a stranger? Rasmussen's greatest strength was his ability to convince the Inuit that he wasn't an outsider, and thereby to gain access to their innermost beliefs and traditions. In Greenland, this became easier over the years because his reputation preceded him—he was eventually known by nearly everyone. But in North America, he was not yet known, and he often had less time to spend with each tribe in each region. To be accepted, he had to rely on his language skills, his persuasiveness, his charming personality and his skills as a hunter and dog driver. His technique was always the same: patience and cultural blending. "I determined to begin by doing nothing," he wrote, "but simply to live amongst them, be as communicative as possible myself, and wait for an opportunity when the desire to narrate should overmaster their reserve."

Oddly, his hatred and fear of math, one of the causes of his less-than-successful academic career, aided him unintentionally. His lack of numerical proficiency ensured that he could never do any of the navigating or charting work on expeditions. This had two effects: he was free to devote time to other pursuits, such as hunting, cooking, and talking with people about their activities and concerns; and he was never seen using any scientific instruments. Science was a foreign activity to the Inuit in the early twentieth century, and anyone involved in it might have been viewed with suspicion. Rasmussen would not have been as accepted if he had been directly involved in strange, incomprehensible activities instead of the familiar ones like dog driving and hunting. It was acceptable for him to be in charge of others, who were obviously foreigners doing scientific work, but it would have undermined the feeling of equality that existed between Rasmussen and his Inuit friends if they had seen him doing things they didn't understand. If the Inuit had seen him pull out a theodolite and start to measure the angle of sun, it would have affected the way they related to him, tainting him as an outsider, not to be trusted with intimate wisdom. His methods were evidently correct. Igjugarjuk, an angakoq and chief from the vicinity of west Hudson Bay, proclaimed that Rasmussen "was the first white man he had ever seen who was also an Eskimo."

For Rasmussen, the interviews and collecting were more than work. He took great pleasure in recording the stories and legends he heard and in writing about them afterward. He found the individual tales of bravery, adventure and challenge similar to the tales of the ancient Greek myths. Greenlanders and most North American Inuit were nomads who loved travel and the adventure of daily life; they had plenty of tales of unusual occurrences to relate. "When the conversation turns on their adventures, their tales run on apace. The narrator is fired by the many gestures in illustration of his story, which is now listened to in breathless silence, now accompanied by laughter and shouts of acclamation. It is no read-up knowledge that the Greenlander spins out, but it is a fragment of his own restless life that he is retelling to his comrades." Rasmussen's own storytelling prowess is undisputed; his poetic sensibilities are clearly evident in the interpretation and translation of the stories and poems he recorded.

Rasmussen's view of the Inuit was so different from that of other people at the time because he had a window into their rich inner world. He was not put off by the shabby, often rough external image. When he was inhabiting this inner world, a bubble of awe enveloped him and he saw the Inuit in a heroic mold. The reality perceived by many other observers was quite different: a barren landscape, scraps of tattered hides, old chopped and chewed-up bones lying around, dirty cold stones to sit on, huts made from snow, mangy dogs, greasy old furs as garments and people who reeked of rancid oil. To newly arrived outsiders, the impression was less than heroic, but these were facts of life in the Arctic. And conditions were likely similar for Bronze Age Greeks, crammed aboard tiny ships in less than sanitary conditions. Odysseus's epic adventures would not have seemed heroic to a casual observer, either, with the men grimy, scabrous from the salt water, and emaciated from lack of food. Much is in the perception. Rasmussen understood that beneath the veneer of daily life lies the hidden world shared by the participants.

THE TRADITIONAL INUIT poetry and stories of the North American Arctic, as in Greenland, are not carefree tales of adventure and obstacles overcome. Frequently, they are preoccupied with the darker, more disturbing themes of death, starvation, murder, evil spirits, hunger, disease, cannibalism, intertribal conflict, infanticide and suicide by elders. Female infanticide must have been common. Rasmussen had heard about it, but his direct evidence came from counting the men and women in each region, and he found that men outnumbered women by one-fourth. The shortage of women led to fights over wives and to polyandry, or husband sharing, which also led to murder. These seemingly brutal practices resulted directly from the requirements of the harsh land the people occupied. As Rasmussen was fond of saying, a life in such a raw and unforgiving environment doesn't produce squeamish hothouse plants. Rather than be condemned for transgressing southern morality, he claimed, the Inuit should be lauded for building a society in the world's outermost regions, and its most rugged conditions.

> *The autumn comes blowing;*
> *Ah, I tremble, I tremble at the harsh northern wind*
> *That strikes me piteously in its might*
> *While the waves threaten to upset my kayak.*
> *The autumn comes blowing;*
> *Ah, I tremble, I tremble lest the storm and the seas*
> *Send me down to the clammy ooze in the depths of the waters.*
> *Rarely I see the water calm,*
> *the waves cast me about;*
> *And I tremble, I tremble at the thought of the hour*
> *When the gulls shall hack at my dead body.*

Less common are the amusing, even whimsical, stories and poems, such as the tale of the little mosquito that Rasmussen heard while traveling west of King William Island.

There was once a tiny mosquito that flew out into the world. It was so small that it thought people did not notice it. But when it was hungry, it landed on the hand of a boy and while it rested it heard someone say: "U-uh, that nasty mosquito, crush it fast." But then the mosquito could suddenly speak so that the boy could hear it. "Spare my life, spare my life. I have a little grandson who will cry if I do not come home." Just think—so small and yet a grandfather!

WHAT RASMUSSEN DEMONSTRATED through his lifelong interest in Inuit folklore, mythology and poetry, and confirmed by his epic journey to visit the remotest people on the planet, is that even on the fringes of human habitation, where survival is a constant struggle and material possessions are of necessity simple and transient, art flourishes. In the Arctic, artistry took its greatest and most powerful form in the oral storytelling traditions. Easily transported, storytelling needs no materials other than imagination and memory, and it can be enjoyed and appreciated, pondered and changed, anytime and anywhere, under any conditions, alone or in a group. Rasmussen showed that artistic expression is not a luxury of complex and powerful civilizations. The rich and inner world of art and metaphor, story and imagination, are not products of a centralized political structure, population density, complex social order or other defining aspects of "civilization" but are inherent traits of humanity.

There is no specific word for "inspiration" in the Inuit language, Rasmussen wrote; instead, the phrase "to feel emotion" is used in its place. Because all people feel emotions in the course of their lives, "all human beings are poets in the Eskimo sense of the word." Most Inuit oral poems are simple songs chanted spontaneously, changing slightly with each telling, celebrating great happiness or sorrow, a successful hunt, the birth of a child, starvation, drowning and other momentous life experiences. The Inuit frequently improvised, he told a *New York Times* reporter in 1925, "making up words and melody as they go along, after the fashion of the troubadours. . . . When it helps dramatization the dancers wear masks and animal heads, some representing the evil spirits which play an important part in their philosophy, others wolves, or other familiar four-footed creatures. There is considerable beauty and rhythm and tune in Eskimo music.

"Every man and woman makes poems and songs. I doubt if there are any people who have developed, primitive as it is, the fine sense of rhythm of these people . . . I have said that they are all poets and composers, yet unconsciously much of the song and poetry of their grandfathers for hundreds of years has been stamped upon them, and by listening closely a man can be projected back a thousand or two thousand years." Rasmussen further elaborated on his theory: "The songs are born in the minds of men as bubbles rising from the depths of the sea to break on the surface."

Rasmussen also sought to clarify and promote his answer to one of the great questions about the Inuit and the purported reason for his epic journey: the "origin of the Eskimo race." His theory of their origin was similar to one propounded by the influential Danish geographer Hans Peder Steensby. As Rasmussen explained to the *New York Times* in 1926: "The Eskimos and the North American Indians were once the same people. They came over together in ancient times from Asia. What are now the Indians is a race that split off from the Eskimos. They developed in the land of trees to the South, the Eskimos in the treeless lands of the North. After centuries these Eskimos of North America migrated eastward all the way to Greenland." Rasmussen was mostly right. Researchers now know that the Arctic was peopled in several waves of migrations, with the Inuit culture probably originating in Alaska about 1,500 to 2,000 years ago and migrating across northern Alaska, Canada and finally to Greenland over a period of several centuries. However, they did not arrive with other Native Americans, as Rasmussen supposed, but on a separate wave; nor did the Inuit develop their distinctive culture somewhere in the center of Canada and later migrate to the edges, but rather moved from west to east.

In 1926, Rasmussen planned a trip to southern France and northern Spain to study the caves occupied by "the old Cro Magnons or men of the old stone age"—the creators of the famous cave art that is thought to be about 25,000 years old. He wanted to see if it was possible to link them with Inuit cultures. According to a theory then proposed by the Scottish professor Boyd Dawkins, the Inuit and the European Cro-Magnons were the same "race." Rasmussen discounted the theory but nevertheless suggested that they were "spiritually like-minded." He was intimately familiar with Inuit stone tools and compared them to the tools discovered in France and Spain; to his mind at least, they appeared fundamentally the same. His mind was always working along unusual, if not entirely scientific, lines of thought, and he was willing to debate his ideas and explore them further. Despite the inaccuracy of some of his theories, Rasmussen essentially proved that the Inuit were the most dispersed people in history, having a similar language, material and intellectual culture and similar artistic sentiments throughout their broad northern territory.

WHILE RASMUSSEN WORKED on his books and lectures, organized the collection of stories and songs, described his journeys, and fine-tuned his theories in the office of his famous house in Hundested, he dreamed of new horizons and the open expanse of snow-clad hills and icebergs bobbing in blue polar waters. Even in his forties, the youthful-looking Rasmussen retained his dreamy imagination. The traits that led him to seek freedom and adventure in Greenland dogged him in Hundested as he toiled away on his manuscripts. In the cool evenings, he strolled in the gardens and hills of the estate, with the salty breeze blowing off the water, reliving old memories—by this time, he certainly had many to draw on—perhaps again feeling himself in the Arctic, with the chill breeze coming off a glacier and hearing the barking of dogs in the distance, and with a new destination in his mind's eye.

Rasmussen's days were extraordinarily busy. He wrote for both Danish and foreign magazines and newspapers, popular and scholarly books, and scientific journals. He traveled frequently to Copenhagen to give lectures, speeches and presentations, and hosted innumerable distinguished visitors, attended meetings with business partners, publishers and colleagues. It was a social whirlwind: he had many friends and acquaintances, and there were so many demands on his time that he must have struggled to meet the competing demands of his wife and three children. It is not uncommon that great figures in history are not always remembered by their immediate families as being so great. There is no evidence that Rasmussen was abusive toward or neglectful of his children, he just wasn't around much for them. The younger ones surely could hardly have known him, and they must have had a limited relationship.

DESPITE ALL THE writing and lecturing, it didn't take Rasmussen long to be on the road again. After only a few months in Copenhagen, he returned to New York, for a week in late March 1925. He arrived with Nyeboe, who would be showing Leo Hansen's motion picture clips of the Fifth Thule Expedition in the city. In April, Rasmussen traveled north to Ottawa, where he had been hired by the Canadian government as a consultant on Arctic policy.

His controversial remarks of a few years earlier about Ellesmere Island being "no man's land," and the Canadian government's concern that he might be a spy intent on promoting Danish sovereignty in the Arctic, were apparently forgotten. Now he was an honored guest, his opinions on the welfare of the Canadian Inuit actively sought. The Danish celebrity was a sought-after consultant to Canada rather than a threat to territorial sovereignty. "It's not easy to give advice to an organization on the entire Arctic Canada, when you only have eight days to do it," he complained to Nyeboe. Nevertheless, the Canadian ethnologist Diamond Jenness remembered that when Rasmussen "visited Ottawa, by special invitation, to advise our government in its administration of the Eskimos, everyone who sat around the council table with him carried away a warm feeling of affection and esteem."*

Rasmussen returned to Denmark in May 1925 and continued his frenetic work schedule there, not journeying to Greenland at all that year. He was frequently in meetings with scientific and government colleagues, in addition to keeping to his own personal writing treadmill. Hundested was sometimes ridiculously busy with the comings and goings of flocks of visitors in addition to his own family's activities.

In the summer, when Dagmar and their children were at the country house, he rented out an additional farmhouse to escape

---

*This wasn't the last time Rasmussen visited Ottawa on business. The following year, on November 24, 1926, the *Ottawa Citizen* carried a story promoting Rasmussen's upcoming December 6 visit—a slide and motion picture lecture titled, "Three Years of Eskimo Life in Arctic Canada." The news story praised his achievements and claimed that his "exploits" would "never be surpassed."

the endless demands of family and visitors and to get some peace and quiet to complete his writing. He did not go entirely alone, though: Arnarulunguaq came along, with several other Greenlanders; and his secretary Emmy Langenberg was there, as was Tom Kristensen, his personal editorial assistant, employed by the publishing house Gyldendal and whose job it was to keep Rasmussen focused on his writing.

According to Kristensen, Rasmussen was an early riser; even when he stayed up late he began his day at 6 a.m. with a bath, a strong cup of coffee and a piece of bread. Sometimes he did his writing while pacing the wooden floor of his office and dictating to his secretaries. His literary output remained prodigious, despite his ceremonial duties, outings and trips abroad. A man of extremes, he occasionally surfaced from his all-consuming work to party and release tension. He swung like a pendulum between solitude and socializing, work and play.

In one of these bouts of play, Rasmussen met Rigmor Fritsche, a young woman from a neighboring farmstead not many years older than his daughter Hanne. Fritsche, who was in an unhappy marriage, frequently came over to visit, and when Dagmar and the children weren't around, they went walking together. They also went out to nightclubs in Copenhagen, Rasmussen claiming Fritsche was his secretary, though he already had one. Rumors began to circulate; Rasmussen was too famous for such a dalliance to go unnoticed. Dagmar heard the gossip, and although there is no record of her reaction, she surely must have been hurt, perhaps even embarrassed, though she probably had become inured to this sort of behavior over the years. It was one thing to turn a blind eye to extramarital affairs in Greenland, where different cultural mores applied and no one was around to report on it, but quite another to do so in Copenhagen, even if only for a summer. At the height of Rasmussen's fame and public acclaim in the late 1920s, a portrait of him with Dagmar and their children shows the unsmiling couple, each staring stone-faced in a different direction.

In addition to New York and Ottawa, Rasmussen visited London to give a speech at the Royal Geographical Society in November 1925, as he had been awarded the Founder's Medal the previous year. Early in 1926, the Danish edition of the narrative of the Fifth Thule Expedition, titled *From Greenland to the Pacific*, was published to great acclaim and became a best-seller. And by May 1926, Rasmussen was off to Scotland to accept an honorary doctorate from the University of St. Andrews. During this time, Rasmussen's formerly robust health showed signs of decline. He now had developed an unspecified problem with his kidneys, or gallstones. At one point his doctor forbade him to visit Paris, where he wanted to escape the pressures of fame and enjoy some freedom.

Between May and September 1926, Rasmussen returned to Greenland as a guide and cultural adviser on the Morrisey expedition, also known as the George Palmer Putnam American Museum Expedition, a general reconnaissance voyage along the coast of western Greenland led by the well-known New York publisher George Palmer Putnam. In Greenland, Rasmussen was reunited with his old traveling companion Inukitsoq, who had traveled with him and Freuchen across the Greenland Ice Cap on the First Thule Expedition, nearly fifteen years earlier. Inukitsoq told Rasmussen of his amazing airplane ride with Richard Byrd, in which they had flown from Thule in "a large hissing metal bird" over rock-strewn fjords, headlands and glaciers, covering in a few hours distances that in the past had taken many hard weeks of travel. The era of the dogsled was drawing to a close, and soon flight would revolutionize the exploration and mapping of the Arctic.

He returned for a brief stop in Denmark, then boarded a steamship and recrossed the Atlantic to New York for a lecture tour in October. The Morrisey expedition was famous in the United States, receiving dozens of newspaper updates on its progress, adventures and discoveries. Although Rasmussen was only one of many participants in the expedition, he received considerable American exposure, all of which pleased his publishers. While in New York, he joined two other Arctic luminaries from the recent expedition, Bob Bartlett and George Palmer Putnam, for a series of live radio broadcasts complete with "musical background furnished by an orchestra." G.P. Putnam's Sons became the publisher of *Across Arctic America* the following year. Rasmussen's lectures included prestigious engagements, such as with the American Geographical Society and the National Geographic Society. Isaiah Bowman, director of the American Geographical Society, announced, "In the history of Arctic exploration Rasmussen's expeditions have never been surpassed and seldom if ever equalled."

Rasmussen returned to Denmark in November to resume his literary labors and his occasionally flamboyant public life. His expenses were high, but his income, from his books and speaking engagements and his share of the profits of Thule Station, was also high. Yet it took years to pay off the debt incurred by the Fifth Thule Expedition. There were continuing disagreements with the investor Nyeboe over the disposition of the profits, misunderstandings resulting from poor record keeping and poor communication. More than Rasmussen's prolific literary output, it was the profits from Thule Station, in particular the pelts of Arctic foxes, prized as the best in the world, that made it all possible.

The one major sadness for Rasmussen in these years concerned Arnarulunguaq, who had contracted tuberculosis before arriving in Copenhagen. After all the travails and dangers of the past years, she had sickened when all believed the dangers were over. She appeared to be wasting away day by day and was finally operated on in the hospital. She and Rasmussen had been through a lot together, and he took her sickness hard. His account of their journey through the Arctic dwells on her enthusiasm and boundless energy. Although her husband had died during the expedition's early days in Greenland, she had still pressed onward for the adventure of a lifetime—across foreign seas and along strange coasts, struggling over mountain passes with all the equipment and dogs, enduring ferocious storms, to meet possibly dangerous strangers. She had beheld the staggering peculiarity of southern cities and experienced the odd customs of southern peoples.

Rasmussen recalled one occasion when Arnarulunguaq had nearly died. East of Point Barrow in early 1924, as their heavy sleds crossed new ice, Hansen and Miteq had heard behind them a horrifying crack and Rasmussen's cry of alarm. Arnarulunguaq was nowhere to be seen. She had plunged through a fissure in the ice into open water and passed out. She was in danger of being sucked under the ice by the current. Rasmussen tore off his overcoat, dove into the freezing water, and pulled her limp body to the ice edge. Yet the ice crumbled around them as he tried to climb out of the hole. They needed a way to get out of the water. "Try with the whip," Rasmussen calmly suggested. They nearly froze to death before finally being dragged out. Stripped of their icy, wet clothes, they were wrapped in sleeping bags and sheltered in a hastily constructed snow hut. Soon they were joking and drinking hot coffee together.

Arnarulunguaq was certainly the most traveled woman among her people, and it was an open secret that she was Rasmussen's lover during the journey. Rasmussen's editor and friend Tom Kristensen joked that when Rasmussen returned from the Fifth Thule Expedition and was at the height of his fame, "there were letters from lady-admirers, because Knud was very much a man who attracted women's attention . . . ask[ing] to join the next expedition in hope of fulfilling the same contribution as 'the little woman.'"

Arnarulunguaq did recover and was eventually able to return to Thule, and she remarried there. She lived in a house of imported pine that Rasmussen had acquired for her as compensation for her many years of work for the expedition.

The Fifth Thule Expedition enabled Rasmussen to achieve one of his life's great ambitions. He no longer had to explain the significance of his actions. He was internationally famous, but he also had to live with that fame. The international acclaim was no doubt gratifying, yet for Rasmussen it was also something of a gilded cage. His schedule was now so demanding that it required the assistance of two secretaries. His family was still young, and he had little of the freedom that he so cherished, that had always brought him back to Greenland and its open spaces.

In Denmark, he had no anonymity. With many eyes on him at all times, he was no longer a free man.

13

FINAL JOURNEYS

When you go home to your countrymen, you can tell them what you have just heard. Tell them that you did meet me when I was still stronger than death. You see my own eye is blinded. Minik thrust it out for me, when he desired to satisfy his hunger with my flesh. Look at my body: it is covered with deep scars; those are the marks of bear's claws. Death has been near me many times, my family are disappearing; I shall soon be the only one left. But as long as I can hold a walrus and kill a bear, I shall still be glad to live.

—Merqusaq, recorded and translated by
Knud Rasmussen, *The People of the Polar North*

IN RASMUSSEN'S TIME, the North and South Poles were the great geographical mysteries of the world. Many explorers—Roald Amundsen, Ernest Shackleton, Robert Falcon Scott, Robert Peary, Richard Byrd, Vilhjalmur Stefansson and Fridtjof Nansen, among them—offered examples of heroism in these often previously unexplored regions. They were real-life heroes, venturing into the unknown and returning with fascinating information about the fringes of the planet. These explorers became household names, and their exploits featured regularly in newspapers and magazines. People flocked to see them on the lecture circuit and, by the 1920s, listened to them via the new technology of broadcast radio. Motion pictures became popular as the decade advanced, and film brought to life the people and geography of the poles like never before.

Rasmussen was unique among this polar pantheon; his goals were cultural as well as geographical, and he was the first to reveal to outsiders the lives and customs of the little-understood people who dwelt on the edge of the habitable world. His career was based on this distinction, and his reputation grew over the years as his many publications demonstrated the breadth of his knowledge. Although the great deeds of one season are often overshadowed by those of the following season, this did not happen in Rasmussen's case.

The first volumes of his monumental *Report of the Fifth Thule Expedition* rolled off the presses in 1927, keeping Rasmussen's name in the limelight. Hardly a season went by without a new Rasmussen publication, whether a collection of poetry, myths and legends or a scientific paper. The *Report*, some of it published posthumously, would eventually run to thirty-two monographs in ten massive volumes—the most exhaustive study of Inuit oral culture, beliefs and philosophy ever undertaken. It is more scholarly and thorough than the popular books that related the tale of his and his companions' adventures.

The many volumes included titles such as *Intellectual Culture of the Iglulik Eskimos; Observations on the Intellectual Culture of the Caribou Eskimos; Iglulik and Caribou Eskimo Texts; The Netsilik Eskimos: Social Life and Spiritual Culture;* and *Intellectual Culture of the Copper Eskimos.* The monographs included notes on vocabularies, each particular angakoq's regional dialect, lists of all the place names and peoples visited, and comments on regional variations in social conventions and material culture. Birket-Smith called the work "a profound study of intellectual life among the various tribal groups of the Central Eskimos, a description so penetrating that nothing like it exists from any other Eskimos and on the whole from very few aboriginal peoples. Rasmussen accounts for all the taboos, the training of angakut, magic formulae and amulets, and describes the various divinities, especially the Mother of the Sea Beasts, the Moon Man, and the strange Spirit of the Weather, which is a being half impersonal, half a kind of supreme power." Extraordinarily comprehensive, the *Report* is a priceless contribution to world culture that would have been impossible to compile even a few years later. Rasmussen's popular books, in order to reach a larger audience, blended material from the *Report* with the story of his own adventures. *Across Arctic America* was published in North America to favorable reviews in publications such as the *New York Times*, where Vilhjalmur Stefansson pronounced it "a notable achievement in the literature of Arctic exploration."

RASMUSSEN MADE SUMMER trips to Greenland in 1927, 1928, and 1929, and traveled all the way north to Thule. Although his trips were no longer noteworthy for their adventure or geographical discoveries, his star continued its trajectory. He remained a cultural luminary on both sides of the Atlantic, his opinions and advice were sought by many, and his scientific recognition vied with his popular appeal. He was called to expound on Arctic matters whenever they were in the news. When Amundsen and Lincoln Ellsworth hadn't returned from their famous Arctic flight from Spitsbergen to the North Pole in June 1925, for example, Rasmussen was consulted for his expert opinion. He thought that it would just be a matter of time before they safely returned. "Amundsen has shown," he stated to a reporter for the *New York Times*, "that the time has come for the using of flying machines for Arctic exploration." He publicly disagreed with

Stefansson's theory of blond-haired, blue-eyed natives in Arctic Canada having descended from wayward Norse Vikings in the Northwest Passage.

Because he was the acknowledged world expert on the Inuit, Rasmussen's influence transcended art and literature. His opinion was sought on practical matters as well. Canadian Arctic policy was influenced by his opinions, and he was asked to comment on Danish colonial policy as compared with Canadian and American approaches. After all Rasmussen had seen, it was the American approach in Alaska that he thought was the way of the future. He was an outspoken critic of the Danish policy of isolating the Inuit from outside influences, other than those of their arrogant and paternalistic colonial managers. He claimed that many of the Greenlanders lived in a form of "primitive squalor" compared with the Alaskan Inuit, who had made great strides in integrating themselves into the changing society and economy, albeit at the loss of some of their traditional beliefs and traditions. It was the byzantine workings of the entrenched Danish colonial bureaucracy, price controls and restricted access to world influences, he wrote, that kept "our Eskimos down." The loss of traditional culture in Alaska was a loss that saddened him, but it was a loss he believed to be necessary for their survival. No people could ever hope to live isolated from the rest of the world in an era of rapidly changing technology, travel and communication.

Rasmussen's international prominence and devotion to the Inuit, his articles and lectures on their culture and life, began giving them a voice. It was the voice of a unified culture that spanned three countries rather than merely being a scattered collection of isolated primitives dominated by outside political and economic interests. Rasmussen's concern was always for the welfare of the Inuit, and for this he was a hero. Birket-Smith recalled that "in Greenland people flocked to the place, when his arrival was announced in the village, old men and women came stumbling to

press the hand of 'dear little Knud,' the young girls sent him lov-
ing glances, the children crowded around him—it was the arrival
of a victor. He was a chief among them."

But Rasmussen acknowledged that the changes were not always
for the better. There were now dueling legal systems and competing methods of dispute resolution, one age-old and the other
new and imported. Which custom should be followed, which law
should be obeyed? The old ways had given way in a single generation to dependence on the manufactured goods provided by
Thule Station in Greenland and by the Hudson's Bay Company
in Canada, and there was no going back: these items made life
easier and safer. Nevertheless, the introduction of trade goods had
unintended consequences. Firearms, for example, allowed hunters to obtain food more easily and perhaps relieved famine, but
they could also wreak havoc on animal populations. "In the old
days," Rasmussen wrote, concerning Inuit and the caribou, "their
settlements were located along the caribou migration routes. Men
hunted with bows and arrows, which required extreme patience,
waiting for an animal to (maybe) wander within range. Later, they
got guns, which could kill from a greater distance, making it much
easier to fill the freezer. In response, the caribou abandoned their
old routes, and went elsewhere. The hunters starved, and their settlements became Arctic ruins. While one group starved, another
group several miles away might be feasting on abundant meat."

Tuberculosis had become common in southern Greenland,
and Rasmussen feared it would spread like the Spanish flu. He
saw that a hospital with a doctor was needed for the northern
region of Greenland. It was constructed in 1928 and offered free
medicine for all, paid for by Thule Station. In 1929, he arranged
for the construction of a school, and the hiring of a teacher, for
the northern region as well. Rasmussen also wanted to assess the
possibility of importing reindeer to replace the diminishing caribou populations, and he devoted his charisma and influence to

establishing the Council of Hunters in northern Greenland. He called the hunters of various tribes together, said that he had spoken with the old people about the problems they faced, and proposed enacting some laws for the entire region. The Inuit agreed, forming a council of elected individuals to enforce the laws. The Council of Hunters would manage local issues such as sanitation and animal conservation, and would enforce other basic laws such as those setting appropriate punishments for crimes committed during clashes between clan members—Rasmussen would be the ultimate authority. The resulting Thule Law was proclaimed on June 7, 1929, Rasmussen's fiftieth birthday, the same year he was nominated for, but didn't win, a Nobel Prize in literature.

The Thule Law was officially recognized by the Danish government in 1931 when it took over the administration of the Thule District of northern Greenland and Rasmussen was recognized as the Danish government's representative in northern Greenland. The northerners accepted Danish colonization because Rasmussen, the respected authority, backed it. In Copenhagen, there was a large celebration attended by many of his former adventuring comrades such as Freuchen and Moltke, as well as the Danish cultural and political literati.

AS RASMUSSEN BECAME older, his enthusiasm for activities that formerly brought him joy waned. Freuchen recalled times from their youth, during the First Thule Expedition in 1912, when they routinely danced into the night even after long days on the trail, when the night "rang with our shouts and laughter." On one occasion, the older manager of a trading post had expressed his amusement but declined to participate. Rasmussen had wondered aloud: "Peter, do you think we shall ever be so old that we will not dance whenever we have the chance?" Many years later, however, he and

Freuchen were amazed at the enthusiasm of the young people for dancing. They found it "inconceivable" that they, too, once had the energy and inclination for such frivolity.

Even Greenland was no longer the escape it had once been for Rasmussen. Thule was not the same place: Freuchen was not there; and Navarana was dead, as were many of Rasmussen's other friends. He was too old for the adventures he had once launched from Greenland and he could never return in spirit, though on occasion he was there briefly in person. His adventures were now limited to predictable and safe summer jaunts. And his relationship with Freuchen, once his close comrade in danger and in life on the edge of the world, had drifted, partly over minor disagreements about money for Freuchen's services and his removal from Thule Station. Freuchen had become a journalist and was on his way to becoming a famous novelist, scriptwriter and memoirist in the United States; he and his new wife, Magdalene, were visitors at Hundested, but he and Rasmussen were no longer inseparable.

In Copenhagen, Rasmussen became restless and uneasy. The responsibility of living up to his heroic image grew tiresome. He regularly smoked cigars now, not bothering to hide his habit or limit it to Arctic adventures or fieldwork, as he had in the past. He was often described as smoking while he wrote and smoking during the endless social gatherings at Hundested, and photographs of the time show a cigar in his hand even when he was lounging on a bench with Dagmar. He was also drinking more. Although he was always a bon vivant, ready for a party in Greenland or a celebration in Copenhagen, his "celebrations" now seemed routine, and reports of his excessive drinking suggest it may have been the sign of a deeper melancholy. Despite his age, he would sometimes show up late at the popular Copenhagen nightclub Adlon, so inebriated that his long-suffering secretary Emmy Langenberg was tasked with keeping an eye on him and with trying to sober him up. Sometimes he would enthrall onlookers with his energetic and wild dancing, clearing the dance floor and monopolizing it for a frenetic spectacle.

RASMUSSEN CONTINUED TO have a weakness for women. Certainly his attitude toward women was influenced by Greenlandic tradition, in which sexual relationships were more fluid and less formal than those in early twentieth-century Europe or America; but he also felt he could get away with it. His fame and naturally outgoing social demeanor placed him in situations that made affairs possible, and he took advantage of the opportunity. Rasmussen felt that the boundaries and constraints of society that applied to others didn't apply to him in the same way, and he was right. For much of his life he led two lives, one in Greenland and the Arctic and the other in Denmark, and sometimes he found it hard to keep each set of customs straight.

Rasmussen was not always happy during these years. He yearned for freedom, yet it was his discipline that made his prodigious accomplishments possible, that both consumed his time and bestowed celebrity. Dagmar remained the foil to her husband's flamboyant energy. She was quiet and reserved, an accomplished pianist who entertained the many guests who were constantly in Rasmussen's entourage at Hundested. But Rasmussen's relationship with Dagmar was undoubtedly strained, despite her patient acceptance of his dalliances. She complained that she hardly ever saw him. He was away from home more often than not, for years at a time, and happily left her to manage a household and raise their children alone. When he was in Denmark he was often in great demand socially and seemed always to be working on his writing or his next great plan.

In the summer of 1929, Rasmussen brought Hanne with him to Greenland, along with Peter Freuchen, who was godfather to all of Rasmussen's children. His eldest daughter was almost twenty years old. He took great pride in showing her the country, the scene of so many of his adventures, a place she had only ever heard her father describe and reminisce about. It was a triumphant tour of the coastal communities from his birthplace of Jakobshavn (Ilulissat) to Thule. A kind and sweet young woman who took after her mother temperamentally, Hanne was welcomed with great warmth along the entire coast, and Rasmussen shone with pride as he introduced her to people he had known for decades.

On the return voyage to Denmark, he met the American artists Rockwell and Frances Kent. Rockwell was an artist and writer, world traveler, and charming philanderer. Rasmussen felt an instant affinity for Rockwell and invited him and Frances to stay at Hundested for several months, where Rockwell took over a small attic room for his painting. Sometime in the fall of 1929, Rockwell and Dagmar had an affair. She had fallen in love, and later wrote to him at his New York farm, "Asgaard," in the Adirondack Mountains, pondering whether she should join him there. Oddly, the affair, which Rasmussen knew about, improved his and Dagmar's relationship, and she later reported that he was kind and solicitous toward her when she needed support. Gaining confidence in herself, she and Hanne visited the United States in the summer of 1930 and stayed all summer at Asgaard; Hanne remained until the spring of 1931. Dagmar exchanged letters with Rockwell and Frances for several years, although the affair had ended.

In the spring of 1930, Rasmussen did not make his annual trip to Greenland. Instead, he traveled to Oslo to deliver the eulogy at Nansen's funeral, then went on a holiday to Switzerland and Italy. There he suffered a serious bout of flu and finally rested, avoiding reading, writing and socializing. The break energized him and inspired him to dream of a new expedition, more ambitious than anything he had done in years. In keeping with tradition, he called it the Sixth Thule Expedition.

AT THE AGE of fifty-one, after years of relatively sedentary existence, Rasmussen found that his sense of adventure was awakened
once again. Now he foresaw a sailing expedition to the remotest
regions of coastal East Greenland, to visit communities that had
seldom been seen by outsiders. East Greenland was often hemmed
in by pack ice and storms. Twenty-seven years earlier, at the end of
the Danish Literary Expedition, Rasmussen had looked northeast
from Cape Farewell and imagined that someday he might journey
to that fjord-riddled, storm-bound coast. The coast both north
and south of Angmagssalik, although partly explored by several
other previous expeditions as early as the eighteenth century, had
never been visited by an expedition dedicated to collecting geographical, meteorological, literary or cultural information. In the
summer of 1919, Rasmussen had made the voyage to Angmagssalik to interview the residents and collect their stories, which
became the foundation of his book *Myths and Legends from East
Greenland*. With more time, the cultural and literary harvest would
be much greater. To cover the seven hundred miles of coastline,
the expedition would have to sail about 2,500 miles.

Rasmussen spent the winter of 1930–1931 arranging the financing, selecting expedition members and planning his route. This
expedition's goal was to chart the coast, collect flora and fauna,
measure temperatures and magnetism, and search for ruins. Rasmussen, meanwhile, would meet and interview people to gather
evidence of "the ancient intellectual culture." The Sixth Thule Expedition consisted of nine individuals traveling in cramped quar-
ters on a small boat. Rasmussen asked Dagmar if he could name
his boat after her, "in the hope that it will be able to carry me safely
and return home to you. You have always been my great shielding
genius. This time, I must rely on others . . . so I have on this trip
so many, many times more use for your great love and protection."

This was the first expedition in which Rasmussen's expertise in dogsledding and hunting would not help him. In fact, dog-sleds were almost passé, with the recent development of motorized sleds. This journey would be mostly by boat, and he would be merely a passenger—a directing passenger, certainly, but he would not command respect for his superior knowledge and skills in sailing. The voyage would be difficult and challenging for the captain and the sailors, not for the scientists. Rasmussen's personal skills, usually the bedrock of his expeditions, would be of little use in getting there.

Perhaps the most interesting member of the expedition was one of the Greenlanders, Christian Poulsen, a guide who had grown up in East Greenland and was familiar with the many fjords and strong currents in the region. Rasmussen had interviewed him years before in Angmagssalik. Poulsen's original name was Autdaruta; he had given up this name when he moved west and was baptized.

Poulsen was also a murderer. Now about sixty years old, many years earlier he had killed his wife and eaten her raw heart to prevent her spirit from haunting him. He laughed at the story now, and Rasmussen, never one to judge morality, apparently laughed with him; Poulsen was an excellent storyteller, with his facial expressions, voices and gesticulating arms. He claimed that he had never murdered anyone for pleasure, but only in the best interests of the community. He was also an excellent and good-natured guide. After the expedition, Rasmussen gave him some timbers to build a new home in Nuuk. Poulsen was inordinately pleased, announcing, "I'll have to find me a wife, but it must be a young, beefy wife, so I can be happy with her and she can enjoy the house and the next man when I'm dead."

The expedition had about ten weeks—the months of July, August and early September—before the ferocious northeast storms would make sailing dangerous. The expedition's ship, *Dagmar*, sailed into Nuuk in June and, after a brief stopover, headed south and east. The shore was "wild and colossal," Rasmussen wrote, "an inaccessible cliff coast with numbers of fjords, in which the shining white inland ice tongues out and spreads quantities of icebergs out over the fairway. And in between the fjords sky-scraping promontories, glacier-shorn, wind worn."

As they sailed past a bare island named Griffenfeldt, Poulsen related an old story that entranced Rasmussen. In ages past, white men used to live in the region, and they were on friendly terms with the Inuit. Among them "lived a man who was very fond of his wife, and the white men challenged him to prove his love by walking across a rope stretched between the two pinnacles," two mountains that loomed over the island. "He accepted the challenge. He was strong and loved his wife, and it was an easy feat to him. But when he had got halfway across the white men suddenly began to swing the rope; the man held on, but the line cut so deep into his arms and legs that at last his muscles gave way, and he fell into the sea. Afterwards one of the white men married his wife, and from them descend all the pale-eyed and fair-haired men on the East Coast." Rasmussen recorded several similarly unusual stories on the journey.

On this voyage, the first to visit East Greenland by sailing from West Greenland instead of from Iceland, Rasmussen met dozens of residents and enjoyed glorious weather. Farther along the coast they went, stopping in well-known regions such as the Dronning Maria Valley, where the salmon river was legendary; it wound its way through the fertile, "bloom-carpeted and bush-grown valley in among calving glaciers and savage alpine crags." Each step in the lush valley squashed "black, lustrous crowberries . . . the soles of our kamiks becoming red with the flowing juice." Poulsen told how the valley was a place for various tribes to gather in the summer to fish and cool themselves in the broad, shallow river. In the evenings the men on the expedition lounged around campfires roasting fish. On August 30, the *Dagmar* reached Angmagssalik and dropped off presents and supplies. Rasmussen spent several days visiting, including a day with his old friend Mathiassen, who was doing archaeological excavations in the area, before heading south again to avoid the storms.

By mid-September the sailing season had advanced, and the *Dagmar* was nearly crushed by pack ice in a storm that destroyed its rudder and knocked out the engine. The ship was nearly swamped in battling the "foaming backwash of the waves," while drifting without a rudder in a sea littered with icebergs. Near-hurricane-force winds blew the ship 125 miles off course, into the open waters of the Denmark Strait, requiring five days of sailing to return to the calmer waters along the coast. It wasn't until October 2, after two weeks of storms, that they rounded Cape Farewell and returned to West Greenland.

The most interesting aspect of the voyage was not its dangerous passage, but Rasmussen's observations of the unusual cultural practices he encountered. East Greenlanders were prone to "more lively fantasy than one finds elsewhere, except perhaps in Alaska." They believed that they were not the only beings who inhabited the isolated patches of fertile land along the fjords. The "other kinds" of beings, however, were seen only by angakut. There were *Ignerssuit,* or beach spirits, benevolent spirits who happened to have no noses. And *Timersit,* enormous giants who dwelt far inland on the ice cap. *Inerajuvaitsiat* were mountain dwarves who could expand to great size when they wanted; *Isserqat* lived underground and could tickle people to death just for amusement. *Tarrajassuit* were shadow people, invisible but deadly to the touch. The most feared creatures were *Erqitdlit,* bloodthirsty ice-dwellers who had human bodies with the heads of dogs and could massacre entire villages on a whim. Each of these spirit beings was featured not only in the legends of the region, but also, and to a lesser extent, throughout the polar world.

The food of the region was also one of Rasmussen's favorite topics. There was *porusit*, a whole sealskin tied like a bag and filled with blubber, berries and other herbs, lightly fermented for about six months, until it "melted on one's gums." Another regional delicacy was *qajulat*—seal blood boiled until stiff and then mixed with slightly rancid seal oil—"Gorgeous! One could taste it all day, and it was long before one was hungry again." An especially delectable dish, reserved for feasts, was bearded seal caught in the early summer and cached away whole without any cleaning or butchering, its rotting body swelling with gas all summer until it was "properly appetising . . . one would almost fight for the meat nearest the blubber, for there it was particularly tender and juicy."

Overall, Rasmussen's impression of the East Greenlanders was as positive as his impression of Inuit wherever he had traveled. "Life on the East Coast is undoubtedly the hardest struggle for existence any human being has to endure, and it is true, judged from the Danish standards. But to the frugal and hardy Eskimos it was an Eldorado . . . All those who have lived up there, and built a house in some sheltered cove, have never allowed their spirit to be broken by its severity; rather they were enthralled by its grand beauty." This was a magical world, the world of the Inuit, a land of extremes and contrasts, where life and death were never far apart. It was so different from European-American life, in which one could get bogged down in life's mundane problems. One song Rasmussen recorded during the voyage seemed to him to capture everything about the land that could be put into words.

I came down
Where the ocean lies before the shore
And looked out over
The small lands in the north
Lying blue under the clear sky,
And I thought:

Someday, when I am tired, And lie down to rest,
Someday, when I die, All this that I see

Will be the same to others,

And the air will arch blue
And quiver in the heat
In just the same way
To those who live when I am gone
But I became faint

At all this beauty

THIS LATEST EXPEDITION demonstrated that Greenland's east coast, for generations so choked with ice as to make navigation dangerous if not foolhardy, was now navigable from early July to mid-September. Rasmussen immediately began planning an even more audacious expedition for the following summer. He spent the winter of 1931–1932 in preparing proposals, choosing expedition members and calculating the logistics of the scheme. The Seventh Thule Expedition was to be larger and more complicated than anything Rasmussen had ever undertaken. "Where once a few isolated umiaks battled their way along that deserted coast through breakers and ice," now the coast would be open to an armada of Rasmussen's design. He would command sixty-two expedition members, twenty-five of them Greenlanders in kayaks. There would be seven motorboats of varying sizes, including the large expedition ship *Stauning* (diplomatically named after the prime minister, who happened to be Rasmussen's friend), and an airplane.

"This coast is so extraordinarily wild and so indented that there are more than fifty large and small inlets and sounds," Rasmussen recorded, and the expedition's objective was to explore them all. From the very start, the planned multiyear exercise, dubbed "the expedition of many journeys," was split into a number of groups, each with independent leaders and objectives. Rasmussen would be the grand coordinator, maintaining communication with the many boats and the airplane from his position aboard the *Stauning*. He departed from Copenhagen in late May for southern Greenland to interview and select Greenlanders to accompany him east.

He also had something new to do. He had been hired as the Greenland adviser for German filmmaker Arnold Fanck's motion picture *S.O.S. Iceberg*. Starring Leni Riefenstahl and primarily filmed in West Greenland, the film would be a large project. Rasmussen was hired to organize Inuit kayakers and extras. The film crew soon descended on isolated communities in the Uummannaq district, including Ilulissat, briefly shattering the peace with machinery and many cast and crew members, before departing as quickly as it had arrived. Rasmussen worked with the filmmakers for about ten days, then used his earnings to help finance the Seventh Thule Expedition.

The rest of that expedition had massed in Nuuk. In June, Rasmussen was joined there by some familiar companions, including Mathiassen and Peder Pedersen. Over the next three months, the expedition's many boats wound up the serpentine fjords and along the broken, erratic coast from Cape Farewell to Angmagssalik. Although the expedition was not like the tightly knit group of a sled journey, in which individual actions and leadership determined not only success but survival, Rasmussen apparently remained the charming and charismatic leader, urging the many teams on to great efforts, constantly assessing their abilities and inclinations. Hundreds of aerial photographs were taken during thousands of miles of flying, to be used later to perfect maps being drawn up by the Geodetic Institute in Copenhagen. Other teams of scientists studied the region's geology and meteorology and took sonar measurements of ocean depths, and of course Rasmussen collected ethnographic material.

The entire expedition went off without any difficulties or complaints; there were no accidents, disasters or insurmountable problems, no food shortages or sunken ships. Rasmussen's unerring sense of human nature kept the dozens of people and intermingling teams happy and productive, focused on the task. Christian Poulsen came along again, as Rasmussen's companion. Rasmussen missed the immediate connection to the land that he got from dogsledding, so to escape the technology and the Danish scientists, he and Poulsen would often take a boat ashore and head inland with backpacks to hunt and explore, to smoke giant cigars, laugh at private jokes, and celebrate their freedom.

Rasmussen organized coffee parties in every settlement they came upon, with drumming, dancing, singing and storytelling to pass the long summer evenings. He feasted on East Greenlandic delicacies; once they learned of his love for their type of food, hunters brought him special treats they had been preparing for months—green, rotten, tender meats and blubber sacs. He likely partook of these spicy local foods more often than he should have; on the return journey, he was overtaken with severe stomach cramps and had to be hospitalized in West Greenland. The nurse thought it was food poisoning, as in previous years Rasmussen had endured several bouts of illness that had hospitalized him. His years of hard living and a staggering workload had begun to take their toll. But after he returned to Denmark on November 5, he brushed off his illness and continued to eat, drink, and smoke as he had always done. One photo from the time shows Rasmussen in casual clothes, lounging on a wicker deck chair and smoking a cigar. Dagmar sits beside him, her head turned in his direction, looking prim in a black dress and holding a teacup and saucer in both hands. Rasmussen's cheeks look slightly gaunt and he appears weary.

Rasmussen's reunion with his family was brief, however, and
he was soon off to the Permanent Court of International Justice
at The Hague. He was part of a twenty-person Danish delegation, consisting mostly of lawyers, politicians and officials with the
foreign commission. For several years, Denmark and Norway had
been locked in a territorial dispute over the sovereignty of East
Greenland. The legal arguments were rooted in history dating
back to the Norse colonization of Greenland a thousand years earlier and were further complicated by the historical merging of the
Danish and Norwegian royal families in the Middle Ages, as well
as several recent territorial agreements between the two nations. In
July 1932, a band of Norwegian hunters had raised the Norwegian
flag at Myggbutta, an uninhabited but frequently visited summer
hunting ground for Inuit hunters in the far north. It was rich in
game and, as the *New York Times* put it, "probably in minerals."

Norwegian newspapers decried the Danish presence in a land
they believed belonged to Norway. Rasmussen was asked to speak
on behalf of Greenlanders, to offer a perspective on the conflict
that might more accurately reflect the interests of the indigenous peoples who lived there rather than the governments of the
two European nations claiming colonial suzerainty. The conflict
deeply troubled Rasmussen, who always had a great respect for
Norway and its explorers and statesmen, such as Fridtjof Nansen.
One of his own ancestors had come from Norway and settled in
Greenland. Rasmussen didn't speak long, but he was appreciated
as one "whose incorruptibility was universally recognized, whose
mind could not be poisoned by hate," as Freuchen put it. Rasmussen said: "I consider myself entitled to defend Greenlanders
not only because of blood ties that bind me to them, but also
because of the fact that I have ever since my childhood been in
continuous connection with them. We speak the same language
as hunters and scientists, we have the same interests, and I therefore am considered in all conditions as one of their own. I would

not with any justification occupy the position I have if I failed them on an occasion like this—if I failed to defend my childhood friends, all my old expedition mates." He spoke as a citizen of the land, and his opinion helped sway the court in Denmark's favor.

IN DECEMBER 1932 and the early months of 1933, Rasmussen set to work on yet another ambitious plan, this one inspired by his work on the Hollywood film *S.O.S. Iceberg* the previous spring. He now wanted to make his own feature film, to be shot entirely in East Greenland and featuring a Greenlandic cast in a traditional Greenlandic story. *The Wedding of Palo*, as the film was eventually titled, was in some ways a refutation of the opinions of Robert Flaherty, the director of *Nanook of the North*. Flaherty had claimed that "films are well-suited to portraying the lives of primitive people whose lives are simply lived and who feel strongly, but whose activities are external and dramatic rather than internal and complicated. I don't think you could make a good film of the love affairs of an Eskimo." *The Wedding of Palo* was a love story.

Rasmussen no doubt intended the film to be more than merely a fictional story set in Greenland; he envisioned a folklore-inspired tale, almost a documentary disguised as fiction. The film should, in his words, "be at all costs, true to life" but also have commercial appeal to attract financing. The *New York Times* reported that he would be trying to "portray the strange life of the Greenlanders by means of sound pictures."

Rasmussen always had good commercial instincts for his books, and he had big hopes for this new medium as well. In fact, he had already planned two more related films, one to be set in Thule and the other in West Greenland. Together, these three films would provide a window into the Greenland Inuit world's three regions and their various levels of contact with European culture. In *The Wedding of Palo*, Rasmussen wanted to portray the culture of the Greenland Inuit as it was before contact with Europeans and to show that these indigenous people experienced the same emotions and desires as people everywhere—they too felt love, jealousy, desire for revenge. He envisioned a film that was a celebration of their life and traditions, wrapped in a fictional tale of love, betrayal and heroism.

Mere months remained to set it all in place—to raise funds, negotiate contracts, write the script, hire the crew, decide on and purchase the equipment and arrange for its transport to Greenland. But the film was just one component of Rasmussen's grand plan for the season. He also wanted to continue with the scientific work of the year before, which required interviewing and hiring for the scientific positions; to work on his translation of Inuit poems, stories and other folklore; and to oversee the ongoing work of the Fifth Thule Expedition. He was drowning in paperwork.

There was a brief holiday in Italy, in February; but otherwise, Rasmussen worked steadily until the early June sailing. In Greenland, while the scientific parties continued their work along the coast, he traveled to Angmagssalik and began selecting the actors for his film. To get a large crowd together, he organized a giant coffee party and invited anyone in the vicinity who could make it. Rasmussen presided over drumming, dancing and singing competitions as well as kayaking displays and shooting contests. He wasn't necessarily interested in the winners of these contests, but in those who had distinctive facial characteristics and emotive gesticulations, important qualities in an era of film with limited dialogue, as the actors would be given creative license in bringing the story to life. The plot of *The Wedding of Palo* was simple: two young men are rivals for the same woman, named Navarana after Freuchen's deceased wife. The men oppose each other in a traditional singing duel; insults lead to a stabbing and an abduction, a flight by kayak, followed by the inevitable rescue. It was an amalgam of stories and legends that Rasmussen had heard from people along the coast.

Rasmussen helped director Friedrich Dalsheim scout locations to ensure that his vision was realized and that the scenes and actions were true depictions of life. He also translated between the Greenlandic actors and the Danish film crew for each scene and choreographed the kayak chase scene. Hundreds of small problems and details required his attention; he put in long hours under the midnight sun, under stressful conditions. Throughout the summer, he was periodically sick with various colds and undetermined illnesses that occasionally kept him bedridden. This was unusual for a man whose iron constitution had always seen him through staggering levels of exertion and hardship with rarely a complaint. He remained in good spirits, though.

While in Greenland working on the film, he kept up his Greenlandic diet of mostly raw meat and indulged his love of Greenlandic cuisine's mature and aged delicacies. In August, the aviators Charles Lindbergh and his wife, Anne Morrow Lindbergh, stopped in Angmagssalik on their 30,000-mile world tour to scout potential commercial airline routes. Their craft was a single-propeller Lockheed Sirius float plane recently christened *Tingmissartoq*, "one who flies like a big bird," by an Inuk boy in Nuuk. They landed in the calm waters of the bay, and Rasmussen, delighted with their company, presented them with a large walrus tusk as a memento of their visit and "gave an Arctic dinner for the notable guests, consisting of all kinds of special Greenland fare."

Rasmussen's illness probably began as stomach upset from too much rotted or fermented meat, but it soon took on other aspects. He began to have fevers and headaches and was often overcome with weakness and dizziness. He would be ill for a few days, then rally and seem to be on the mend. But the fever would return. Signe Vest, the only nurse on the coast of East Greenland, was in wireless telegraph contact with the nearest physician, Laurent Christensen, who was six hundred miles away in Nuuk, and in early October Christensen ordered Rasmussen to the hospital in Nuuk. After several days at sea, the ship *Kivioq* arrived in Nuuk and Rasmussen staggered to the doctor's house. It soon became evident that the illness had evolved into virulent flu with pneumonia.

Such was the seriousness of his illness and the extent of Rasmussen's fame that the *Hans Egede*, the only regularly scheduled ship plying the route between Copenhagen and Greenland, made a special detour to Nuuk to collect Rasmussen and take him to Copenhagen. Bedridden and delirious throughout the two-week voyage, he was given a blood transfusion. On his arrival in Copenhagen, the cheers of the crowd waiting at the dock revived him. He rolled from his stretcher and shuffled down the gangplank on unsteady legs, clinging to the handrail while waving weakly to his fans. Flashing his boyish grin, he was helped into a waiting ambulance and rushed off to the hospital.

After several weeks of fever and delirium, his "wonderful constitution" seemed to be defeating the illness, which was diagnosed as a rare form of botulism from contaminated meat, complicated by influenza and pneumonia. From his hospital bed, Rasmussen sent out Christmas greetings expressing his wish to return to Greenland. He was, after all, only fifty-four years old. "I believe I shall recover soon and be back at work," his physician reported him as saying. Two days later, on December 21, 1933, he was dead.

EPILOGUE

TIMELESS STORIES

Only the Air Spirits know
What I shall find beyond the mountains
Yet I urge my sledge team on
Drive on and on
On and on!

—Author unknown; song overheard by
Knud Rasmussen near the Bellows,
Hudson Bay, in 1923; from *Across Arctic America*

THE NATIONAL OUTPOURING of grief in Denmark was quick and strong, and tributes soon came in from around the world. Danish prime minister Thorvald Stauning proclaimed Knud Rasmussen "one of the best men Denmark ever bred" and arranged a state funeral for him. The *New York Times* and the London *Times* published detailed obituaries highlighting the adventurer's expeditions and contributions to science and literature.

Peter Freuchen wrote of his friend: "Knud Rasmussen is dead. His casket is surrounded by sorrow, sorrow from all parts of the world. But sorrow was never felt about his deeds, which were clean and unspotted." Fellow explorer Kaj Birket-Smith wrote in the *Danish Journal of Geography*, "The Greenlander and the Dane were merged in Knud Rasmussen, that great, gifted man. There was no warmer or more sensitive heart, and no one could be so carried away by things, always ready to help by word or deed. No one could create joy around him as he could." The French explorer and anthropologist Jean Malaurie called him the "father of Eskimology," and certainly the greatest polar ethnographer of the century, and probably of all time.

Colleagues were quick to describe their shock and to praise Rasmussen's professional and personal attributes. Canadian ethnologist Diamond Jenness wrote that "Dr. Rasmussen understood and interpreted, as no one else was able to do, the inner spirit of the Eskimos, the reasons that underlay their customs, their conceptions of life and death and the world that lies beyond . . . As for the Eskimos, it may truly be said that he gave his life to their cause." The Danish philologist William Thalbitzer wrote in *American Anthropologist* that Rasmussen's "research was so far congenial with scientific research that his results may be considered as scientific while at the same time sensitive and imaginative. At his most untimely death Greenland and Eskimo research has suffered a painful loss."

In the intervening years since his death, Rasmussen's reputation as an ethnographer has not diminished or been superseded. The author and anthropologist Elizabeth Cruwys wrote in 2003 that "over half a century later, his writings are still regarded as some of the finest sources of ethnographic information in the Arctic." The academic journal *Inuit Studies* devoted an entire volume in 1988 to Rasmussen as an ethnographer, with contributions from over a dozen scholars, including a discussion of some of Rasmussen's as yet unpublished works. Some scholars working in the same discipline have found that "some transcriptions were wrong, his sampling was weak, his numbers do not always add up," as anthropologists Inge Kleivan and Ernest S. Burch Jr. write in the introduction to the volume. Nevertheless, they conclude that Rasmussen "ranks first among the hundreds of people who have written about Inuit life. In recent years others have carried out more scientifically sophisticated research, but no one has even approached the scope of Rasmussen's accomplishments with regard to basic ethnographic data on more Inuit groups . . . or is likely to do in the future. Furthermore, writing in a pleasing, almost poetic, style that appealed to the layman as much as the specialist, Rasmussen did more than anyone else to bring the essence of Inuit life before the general public."

Rasmussen's work is the foundation upon which further knowledge of Inuit culture has been built—even though some of his theories have been rejected and his concept of the interrelatedness of the different branches of the Inuit language has been revised. But it is important to recall that Rasmussen did his work in an era when merely getting to the locations to do the fieldwork was an epic struggle, in a time without accurate maps, reliable transportation or communication technology. He is the giant upon whose shoulders other scholars of the Inuit have stood to gain their vista.

Rasmussen's contributions to Arctic ethnography and literature are unique in that his subjects were not only sources of data, but his friends. His goal was not merely the collection and interpretation of this data to advance a scientific career: he was a wanderer and a poet, keen to immerse himself in the polar world and its peoples, to understand them and seek out something grander than data, something that hinted at the mystery of their lives and at the mystery of life in general. To Rasmussen, the world was a magical place, not in the sense of spells and powers, but in the sense of the unexplained. His contribution to science was to collect the various oral expressions of Inuit life in order to celebrate the unique philosophy they represented; to organize and interpret the unscientific. No one else has combined such incredible geographical explorations with such literary power and philosophical depth.

Posthumous publications of his work continued for many years, including articles, poems, songs and legends of East Greenland, as well as the more scientific publications of the Fifth Thule Expedition. There are literally hundreds of publications by Rasmussen, in many languages. His film, *The Wedding of Palo*, was a great success when it was released posthumously on both sides of the Atlantic. In Denmark, it played to full houses and received rave reviews, including a filmed introduction by the prime minister. Although the dialogue was in Greenlandic and Danish, subtitles printed at the bottom gave the gist of the story. It likewise was praised in the *New York Times*: "It must be regarded as one of the most accurate, absorbing and truly dramatic native pictures we have seen . . . Besides possessing unusual theatrical appeal, it embodies those elusive and indefinable qualities which go to make up a work of art."

Rasmussen's personal story of struggle, adventure, friendship and discovery has not remained as well known as his academic reputation. Despite its epic scope, a brilliantly chronicled blend of action, leadership, science and literary talent, his story has faded from general knowledge. In the years following his death, several biographies were published in Danish, including collections of personal reminiscences by his friends and colleagues, and essays about his work. Peter Freuchen wrote a full and colorful memoir of their time together, including stories from Rasmussen's childhood, which he dedicated to Rasmussen's children. But Rasmussen's personal story is little known outside of Denmark. Apart from specialists in the Arctic, Inuit ethnography and Arctic exploration, few know what an adventurous life Rasmussen led and what an intriguing individual he was.

The Inuit are a philosophical and thoughtful people, as Rasmussen himself was. Although he didn't literally believe in magic, perhaps he was searching for answers in the wisdom of the angakut to assuage his own insecurities and fears. His yearning drew him to Inuit legends and poetry and their themes of the power of life and death. Happiness, for Rasmussen, as for most people, came sporadically despite his bonhomie. He kept darkness at bay through activity and performance. In politics he remained neutral, always writing and speaking as if he were above mundane, day-to-day matters. He was absorbed in myth and legend, things he considered of higher artistic concern than daily political squabbling. It was his good fortune to achieve fame early, in the 1920s, the wealthy era before the Great Depression and the rise of fascism in Europe that led to World War II, in a time when stories and poetry from remote regions of the globe were welcomed.

Without doubt, his explorations are legendary, and his collections and translations of Inuit philosophy, legends and poetry a groundbreaking literary and cultural feat, but perhaps Knud Rasmussen's underlying greatness lay in his warmth—his genuine passion for life and his deep respect for all those whose world he shared. His longtime friend Peter Freuchen summed it up best: "Naturally he made mistakes, but few people have ever judged others so fairly, and I have never known a man who could forget others' faults so quickly and completely and find compensating good points . . . Knud Rasmussen, throughout his whole life, left the people he visited richer than when he came to them."

A NOTE ON SOURCES

What is a person's life?

There is, of course, the chronology of events that can be marked on a time line, such as birth, marriage, children, career accomplishments and personal successes and failures.

There are also the effects upon people of the decisions of others—decisions over which they had no control, such as how and where they were raised and went to school. There are the vagaries of fate, such as illnesses, accidents and injuries, as well as good fortune. Then there are the decisions they made, whether in reacting to events or in acting to further their dreams and plans. How a person responds to a failure or a successful event is as important and interesting as the event itself in answering the biographer's key question.

But there is more to consider. There are the ways in which people influence those they were close to, and how they were perceived by others. How people are remembered by others at various points in their life is often different—and sometimes very different—from how they perceive themselves. Lives are also lived within a historical context: the challenges people face, and the decisions they make, are related to the economic opportunities and cultural mores of their era. In creating a biographical portrait, the available sources and the weight the biographer gives them are also important. There are the subject's own reminiscences, correspondence with friends and colleagues, newspaper accounts and the memoirs of others. Some of this subject matter is internal, as with the thoughts and ideas revealed in diaries and letters, whereas some is descriptive and external, such as that found in formal publications. Both are revealing, especially when there is a disconnect between the two.

Sometimes, personal diaries or letters are regarded by historians and biographers as providing greater insight into an individual's personality or motives than, for example, another's recollection or a contemporary newspaper account, but this is not necessarily the case. Naturally, something written for public consumption, such as a travelogue or book, has an intended audience and is tailored to it, and reveals how the author wishes to appear. But so equally does a "private" diary have an intended audience—people often write in diaries to vent anger with someone in mind or to work through personal dilemmas. A journal reflects a person's thoughts at one moment in time, not overall impressions or opinions over a longer period. A moment of anger revealed in a journal, a flash of temper not indicative of someone's general attitude, may give a distorted view of a personality. A famous person's "private" journal may be written with the knowledge that it may one day be public, and the author may deliberately offer justifications and rationalizations for actions and behavior under the guise of privacy. And what if a private diary contradicts an individual's public account of the same events? Or contradicts others' reminiscences of the same events? There is no source material that can be taken as the absolute truth when it comes to questions of motivation and character.

In *White Eskimo*, I am as concerned with who Knud Rasmussen was to the world as I am with what the world was to Rasmussen. In Rasmussen's case, this story includes a detailed look at his literary, cultural and professional accomplishments—his records and interpretations of the Inuit myths, songs, poems and legends that he spent his life collecting and translating. To omit these details would be similar to discussing the life of a painter without considering the artist's motivation and inspiration. This broad and inclusive approach may seem self-evident, but it has not been shared by Rasmussen's Danish biographers.

There has never been a full English-language biography of Rasmussen; the closest to this was Peter Freuchen's memoir of his time spent adventuring with him. I turned to Danish sources to gain a complete picture of Rasmussen's life (more on this later) and was shocked to discover that the Danish biographies are very much concerned with Rasmussen as a Danish public figure and national hero. Oddly, they fall short in presenting the Greenlandic-Inuit world that Rasmussen belonged to, and which he interpreted for the world; in these other biographies, the cultural and intellectual worlds of the Inuit seem almost an externality, the source of Rasmussen's fame but not worthy of consideration in their own right. In other words, the priority in these biographies was to detail Rasmussen's relationships within the literary and cultural circles of early twentieth-century Denmark at the expense of exploring the intellectual and cultural world of Greenland and the Arctic.

White Eskimo, by contrast, revolves around Rasmussen's Greenlandic-Inuit world more than his Danish world, because that was, and is, the source of Rasmussen's professional acclaim as well as his personal cultural background. Importantly, it was, and remains, the realm of Rasmussen's great contribution to global culture and knowledge. My priority was not to describe the nuances of how he influenced Danish intellectual and academic life—the many people he knew and the many ceremonies he attended—only to note that he was a cultural luminary in Denmark, because being a national hero "somewhere" influenced his actions.

White Eskimo is not an academic study, not a detailed analysis of Rasmussen's ethnographic work and contribution to science. Rather, it is a narrative and intuitive look at those elements of Rasmussen's life and accomplishments that have a global resonance. If a picture is worth a thousand words, then sometimes a story is worth a thousand statistics in forming the idea of who a person was.

White Eskimo is my second book (*The Last Viking: The Life of Roald Amundsen* was the first) to profile the story of a somewhat-overlooked historical personality. Writers research and write, naturally, in their native language. Roald Amundsen is a popular hero in Norway just as Knud Rasmussen is in Denmark, and they routinely have biographies written about them in their home countries every few years. Yet they are hardly celebrated in North America. This is not a reflection of the caliber of their adventures, discoveries and contributions to science and literature. Rasmussen and Amundsen stand up by comparison to any of the polar greats, from Peary and Cook to Franklin and Rae. They are overlooked not because their accomplishments are second tier but because they didn't primarily speak or write in English.

The history of polar exploration, for example, is disproportionately seen through the eyes of British Royal Navy commanders. Rasmussen's adventures do not fit within the standard story of Arctic exploration, so we know little about him or his work. This, in itself, raises questions about what we know of the past: our understanding of events and people is often determined by the vagaries of documentary evidence and principal language.

During his lifetime, however, Rasmussen was famous, and many of his books and articles were translated into and published in English. He even wrote in English occasionally. But his reputation and status suffered in the intervening decades because the lack of English-language source material on his life prevented English-language writers from retelling his amazing story for succeeding generations. In recent years this task has become a little easier. With the increasing interest in the full pantheon of polar explorers has come the translation into English of many old books, memoirs, articles and collections of correspondence. But for Rasmussen there was still not enough upon which to base a full-length biography. My research indicated that there were many Danish sources—collections of personal letters, travel diaries, reminiscences of friends and biographies. It became clear that I would need to access these if I were to tell Rasmussen's story for an English-speaking audience, and I unfortunately don't speak or read Danish. But the increasing availability of material in a digital format gave me an idea: I could use digital translation software—now readily available at a reasonable cost—to access the Danish material. If I could use my computer to translate Danish sources into rough English, I could proceed.

That this proved to be a considerable amount of work is an understatement. The software I selected, Babylon, is capable of rendering Danish to English one page at a time so long as the material is in digital format. Not every language will convert to English clearly, I suspect, but Danish to English works reasonably well.

The one major problem was that not every source was available as an e-book or in other digital format. I had to obtain Danish books and convert them into a digital format before I could translate them. I began by scanning books page by page into individual JPEGs, but I soon realized that unless I could find a quicker method, I would be at the task for many months just to digitize the books. My wife, Nicky, told me that she could use a large photocopier that could scan multiple pages, and rather than print copies, she could send them to my computer as PDF files. I decided I would carefully cut the pages out of books so the machine could take them double-sided, one chapter at a time, through the multiple document feed, and in short order I would have entire books sent to my computer in a series of PDF files. Because the books would be destroyed in the process, I had to purchase them rather than use library copies.

Unfortunately, I then discovered that Danish is not one of the world's major languages, at least not according to software companies. There are many programs that will convert a PDF into a text file, which is the format needed for translation software. But at the time there was only one that would recognize Danish—the most expensive one, naturally. It is called ReadIris Pro, and it worked flawlessly. After many weeks I had converted hundreds of pages of Danish text on paper into Danish PDF files, converted the Danish PDFs into Danish electronic text documents, at which point the translation software translated them into English two pages at a time and I could print them. It was a time-consuming process, but it achieved the desired result—access to sources written in a foreign language.

During the time I was working on *White Eskimo*, the quality of translation available for free from Google Translate improved dramatically and overtook the quality of translation from the software I had purchased; oddly, sometimes one program would provide a much clearer translation than the other, and the same passage on different days might translate slightly differently. The English text resulting from this procedure is no literary masterpiece—it is peppered with illogical sentence structure and untranslatable Danish words with no English equivalent. But it was clear enough to understand. I could polish the choppy prose later by consulting a native Danish and English speaker for the pieces I wanted to quote. Nevertheless, it was a slow process. I had the good fortune to enlist the assistance of Dr. Peter Schledermann, a Danish-Canadian Arctic archaeologist who provided me with skillful Danish-to-English translations for numerous quoted passages in *White Eskimo*.

It is my hope that this method of obtaining and reading source material in languages other than English will open up new vistas for historians and biographers, and give us new stories.

A few key sources were invaluable in writing *White Eskimo*:

Bogen om Knud (Book of Knud), is a series of personal reminiscences about Rasmussen written just after he died by ten of the people who knew him best, including Harald Moltke, Peter Freuchen, Erik Rindom, Kaj Birket-Smith and Tom Kristensen. (The book has no named editor, so I have listed it under "Various authors" in the Selected Bibliography.) The book presents vignettes and scenes from times and places throughout Rasmussen's life. These reminiscences do not give the official portrait of the national hero and legend but portray Rasmussen intimately as he was remembered by his friends.

As a window into Rasmussen's pre-fame days (as a youth in Copenhagen, his years as a student and his time in Lapland) I relied upon *Den unge Knud Rasmussen: Belyst gennem breve og andre kilder, 1893–1902 (The Young Knud Rasmussen: Illuminated Through Letters and Other Sources),* edited by Knud Michelsen. This is a collection of all of Rasmussen's various extant correspondence from that period of his life, consisting of dozens of annotated letters to and from friends and family, about girls, his longing for Greenland and his dreams, among other topics.

For a man who wrote so much and has had so much written about him, contemporaneously and posthumously, Rasmussen has left very little in the way of personal correspondence—apparently his family destroyed the letters between him and Dagmar after he died. Although Rasmussen never wrote his autobiography, he sprinkled his numerous writings with many autobiographical references and details. Many people were deeply affected by Rasmussen and his singular personality, so a careful reading of these sources reveals Rasmussen's individuality. A rounded portrait of his life in Denmark, and indeed his general personality, can be gleaned from his public behavior and from references and descriptions by the people who knew him.

I was particularly aided in some of these more obscure sources by a recent Danish book, *Manden bag helten (The Man Behind the Hero),* by Niels Barfoed, which is available as an e-book. *Manden bag helten* is not a biography in the traditional sense, but rather a series of essays about Rasmussen and his interactions with key people in his life, including Ludvig Mylius-Erichsen, Dagmar Andersen, Rockwell Kent, Herluf Møller, Hans Sørensen, Erik Rindom, Emil Nolde and Marius Nyeboe. Of particular interest are the lesser-known people Barfoed references, especially the young women Euphemia, Anna Olivia, Ellen Hallas, Vilhelmine Clausen and Rigmor Fritsche. Barfoed provides additional detail on Rasmussen's relationships with these women through his discovery of many previously unknown letters, in archives in Denmark and in personal collections of the descendants of the people he profiles. This book was invaluable to me because it provided specific detail for events that were only alluded to or discussed generally by other writers. Nearly everyone who knew Rasmussen mentioned that he was "a ladies' man," but Barfoed lent substance to this by locating the letters of several of the women with whom Rasmussen had relationships. These details are new even to Danish biographers.

The correspondence between Knud and Dagmar Rasmussen and Rockwell and Frances Kent is available for viewing in its entirety at the

Smithsonian Institution's Archives of American Art, the Rockwell Kent papers, online at http://www.aaa.si.edu/collections/rockwell-kent-papers -9557. The letters have been beautifully scanned and can be easily read online. It is interesting to see that Rasmussen was quite fluent in English, though with the occasional odd turn of phrase and similar imperfections. Another useful work is Constance Martin's *Rockwell Kent's Distant Shores: The Story of an Exhibition.*

The Danish Royal Library in Copenhagen has digitized all of Rasmussen's journals, most of which are the raw materials that became the foundation for his books. They are handwritten and in Danish and are difficult to read—I tried but was unable to make any sense of them, so I stuck to various translations provided by the Danish authors Kirsten Hastrup and Niels Barfoed.

Newspaper articles are a good source of information for gauging the zeitgeist and public perception—they reveal how a person was described by the press at the time and how he or she acted on the public stage. Early twentieth-century newspaper stories are very different from typical newspaper articles today, probably because there were no other competing media, other than in-person public lectures. The articles are heavy on anecdote and description, the type of material that would be considered "fluff" today. Nevertheless, they are an invaluable tool for conveying how people spoke when being quoted, how they dressed, the food they ordered in restaurants, and so on. Contemporary articles add spice and flavor to an individual's story and highlight the social environment they lived in, rather than providing any concrete details about their expeditions or life. Rasmussen was nowhere near the public figure that Roald Amundsen was in the United States, but he did feature in newspaper accounts in periodic bursts following his expeditions, particularly in the wake of the Fifth Thule Expedition, when he made numerous public presentations in Washington, DC, and New York City.

Although there are numerous accounts of expeditions with Rasmussen that were written by, among others, Kaj Birket-Smith and Therkel Mathiassen, the key English-language source for Rasmussen's adventures, as well as for details of his childhood, is Peter Freuchen. Freuchen spent more time with Rasmussen than anyone else, often under stressful and uncertain conditions. He wrote several memoirs about his own life in the Arctic, specifically about his time with Rasmussen. *I Sailed with Rasmussen* and *Arctic Adventure* are the most thorough and interesting.

Freuchen was an amusing and entertaining writer, with a flair for salty yarns, off-color anecdotes and scenes of Rasmussen when he is at his most human, without any pretension or concern for his reputation. Freuchen wrote his books after the death of his friend, so he could say what he wanted without fear of offending Rasmussen's late-life preoccupation with respectability.

Nearly everything Rasmussen wrote is enriching in some way. Much of his writing has been translated into English and other languages. Two exceptions are his first book, *Lapland,* and his narrative account of the First Thule Expedition, *Min rejsedagbog (My Travel Diary).* In writing *White Eskimo,* I relied both on the narrative accounts Rasmussen wrote of his journeys and on the more scientific *Reports* of the expeditions. Although these sources cover the same events, the *Reports* have more details and dates, lists of equipment, details of financing, temperature records, climatic conditions and other information that the narrative accounts lack; but the narrative accounts have more of the stories and of Rasmussen's philosophizing. A general reader interested in exploring further should start with *The People of the Polar North*, Rasmussen's narrative of the Danish Literary Expedition, and *Across Arctic America*, the narrative of the Fifth Thule Expedition. There are also many editions of Rasmussen's collected Inuit poems and legends.

Readers interested in a more academic consideration of Rasmussen and his work should begin with the 1988 edition of the journal *Inuit Studies*, which was entirely devoted to Rasmussen and includes articles by experts covering a wide range of topics relating to Rasmussen's scientific work. Unfortunately, this journal isn't available online. For a general and genial tour of thousands of years of Arctic archaeology, consult *Voices in Stone* by Peter Schledermann.

There are also online resources related to Rasmussen. These are mostly in Danish, such as the website of the Knud Rasmussen House Museum at Hundested, http://www.indmus.dk/knudrh.asp. There are also some interesting Rasmussen-related videos on YouTube. See https://www.youtube.com/watch?v=7YDhCBgUG2s for film footage of the Fifth Thule Expedition taken by Leo Hansen. It is cheering to see Rasmussen smiling and waving at the camera, and there are scenes of the dogs pulling sleds around the Bellows at Hudson Bay. There are also some scenes from *The Wedding of Palo* at https://www.youtube.com/watch?v=UdW-HBUcfUE and these are also available on DVD in English. YouTube also features several excerpts of Norman Cohn and Zacharias Kunuk's 2006 film, *The Journals of Knud Rasmussen*, which fictionalizes events during part of the Fifth Thule Expedition. Although neither Rasmussen nor Freuchen are the main characters (in fact, Freuchen is shown as a short, stout drinker barely competent in Inuktitut, instead of a tall teetotaler, fully fluent in the language and culture), but the depiction of the landscape and people is magical.

To explore more online, visit YouTube and type in "Knud Rasmussen," "Peter Freuchen," "Thule," "Angmagssalik" and other terms. New material is frequently added, whereas other items seem to disappear.

SELECTED BIBLIOGRAPHY

Amdrup, Georg Carl, and Martin Vahl. *Greenland: The Colonization of Greenland and Its History Until 1929*. London: C.A. Reitzel, 1929.

Barfoed, Niels. *Manden bag helten* [The man behind the hero]. Copenhagen: Gyldendal, 2011.

Birket-Smith, Kaj. "Knud Rasmussen." *Journal de la Société des Américanistes* 25 (1933).

———. "Knud Rasmussen as an Eskimologist." *Geografisk Tidsskrift* 37 (1934).

Bravo, Michael, and Sverker Sorlin. *Narrating the Arctic: A Cultural History of Nordic Scientific Practices*. New York: Science History Publications, 2002.

Burch Jr., Ernest S. "The End of the Trail: The Work of the Fifth Thule Expedition in Alaska." *Inuit Studies* 12 (1988).

Carpenter, Edmund. "Arctic Witnesses." In *Fifty Years of Arctic Research*, edited by R. Gilberg and H.C. Gullov. Copenhagen: National Museum of Denmark, 1997.

Cruwys, E. "Profile: Knud Rasmussen." *Polar Record* 26, no. 156 (1990).

Ehrlich, Gretel. *This Cold Heaven: Seven Seasons in Greenland*. New York: Pantheon, 2001.

Fengir, Niels. *Knud Rasmussen: Greenland's Aladdin*. Copenhagen: Woldike, 1979.

Field, Edward. *Eskimo Songs and Stories, collected by Knud Rasmussen on the Fifth Thule Expedition*. New York: Delacorte Press, 1973.

Fortescue, Michael. "Thule and Back: A Critical Appraisal of Knud Rasmussen's Contribution to Eskimo Language Studies." *Inuit Studies* 12 (1988).

Frederiksen, Kurt L. *Knud Rasmussen: Kongen af Thule* [Knud Rasmussen: King of Thule]. Copenhagen: Borgen, 2009.

———. *Peter Freuchen: Den store Peter* [Peter Freuchen: The great Peter]. Copenhagen: SOHN, 2010.

Freuchen, Peter. *Arctic Adventure: My Life in the Frozen North.* New York: Farrar and Rinehart, 1935.

———. *I Sailed with Rasmussen: Freuchen's Own Story of the Great Explorer.* Translated by Arnold Andersen. New York: Julian Messner, 1958.

———. *Peter Freuchen's Adventures in the Arctic.* Edited by Dagmar Freuchen. New York: Julian Messner, 1960.

———. *Peter Freuchen's Book of the Eskimos.* Edited and with a preface by Dagmar Freuchen. Cleveland: World Publishing, 1961.

———. *Vagrant Viking: My Life and Adventures.* Translated by Johan Hambro. New York: Julian Messner, 1953.

Gilberg, Rolf. "Inughuit, Knud Rasmussen and Thule." *Inuit Studies* 12 (1988).

———. "Profile: Knud Rasmussen, 1879–1933." *Polar Record* 22, no. 137 (1984).

Grant, Erik. *Good and Bad Eskimos.* Center for Cultural Research, University of Aarhus, February 1999, available online athttp://www.hum.au.dk/ckulturf/pages/publications/eg/goodandbad.htm.

Hastrup, Kirsten. "Ultima Thule: Anthropology and the Call of the Unknown." *Journal of the Royal Anthropological Institute* 13 (2007).

———. *Vinterens hjerte: Knud Rasmussen og hans tid* [The winter heart: Knud Rasmussen and his time]. Copenhagen: Gad Publishers, 2010.

Hutchinson, Isobel Wylie. *On Greenland's Closed Shore: The Fairyland of the Arctic.* London: William Blackwood and Sons, 1930.

Jenness, Diamond. "Knud Rasmussen." *Geografisk Tidsskrift* 37 (1934).

———. *The Life of the Copper Eskimos: Report of the Canadian Arctic Expedition, 1913–18.* Ottawa: F.A. Ackland, 1922.

Jorgensen, Captain Gabel. "Dr. Knud Rasmussen's Contribution to the Exploration of the South-East Coast of Greenland, 1931–1933." *Geographical Journal* 86, no. 1 (1935).

Kleivan, Inge, et al. "Selected Works by Knud Rasmussen." *Inuit Studies* 12, nos. 1–2 (1988).

Kleivan, Inge, and Ernest S. Burch Jr. "Introduction." *Inuit Studies* 12 (1988).

Malaurie, Jean. *The Last Kings of Thule: With the Polar Eskimos, As They Face Their Destiny.* Translated by Adrienne Foulke. New York: E.P. Dutton, 1982.

Markham, Clements R. *The Lands of Silence: A History of Arctic and Antarctic Exploration.* Cambridge: Cambridge University Press, 1921.

Martin, Constance. "Rockwell Kent's Distant Shores: The Story of an Exhibition." *Arctic* 55, no. 1 (2000).

Mathiassen, Therkel. "Knud Rasmussen's Sledge Expeditions and the Founding of the Thule Trading Station." *Geografisk Tidsskrift* 37 (1934).

————. *Report on the Expedition.* Copenhagen: Gyldendalske Boghandel, Nordisk Forlag, 1945.

McGrath, Robin. "Reassessing Traditional Inuit Poetry." In *Native Writers and Canadian Writing,* ed. W.H. New. Vancouver: University of British Columbia Press, 1990.

North, Dick. *Arctic Exodus: The Last Great Trail Drive.* Toronto: Macmillan, 1991.

Nyeboe, M. Ib. "Fifth Thule Expedition from Greenland to the Pacific." *Geographical Journal* 27 (1924).

Rasmussen, Knud. *Across Arctic America: Narrative of the Fifth Thule Expedition.* Introduction by Terrence Cole. Fairbanks: University of Alaska Press, 1999, reprint of a 1927 original.

————. *The Alaskan Eskimos: As Described in the Posthumous Notes of Knud Rasmussen.* Copenhagen: Gyldendal, 1952.

————. "The Arctic Station at Thule, North Star Bay." *Meddelelser om Grønland* 51 (1915).

————. *Den unge Knud Rasmussen: Belyst gennem breve og andre kilder, 1893–1902* [The young Knud Rasmussen: Illuminated through letters and other sources]. Edited by Knud Michelsen. Copenhagen: Forlaget Falcon, 2011.

————. *Eskimo Folk Tales.* Edited and translated by W. Worster. Copenhagen: Gyldendal, 1921.

————. *Eskimo Poems from Canada and Greenland.* Translated by Tom Lowenstein. Pittsburgh: University of Pittsburgh Press, 1973.

————. "Eskimos and Stone-Age Peoples: A Suggestion of an International Investigation." *Geografisk Tidsskrift* 32 (1929).

————. *Greenland by the Polar Sea: The Story of the Thule Expedition from Melville Bay to Cape Morris Jessup.* Translated by Asta and Rowland Kenney. London: William Heinemann, 1921.

————. *A Journey to the Arctic: The Travels of Knud Rasmussen.* Cambridge, MA: The Educational Development Center, 1967.

———. *Knud Rasmussen's Posthumous Notes on East Greenland Legends and Myths*. Edited by H. Ostermann. Copenhagen: C.A. Reitzels Forlag, 1939.

———. *Knud Rasmussen's Posthumous Notes on the Life and Doings of the East Greenlanders in Olden Times*. Edited by H. Ostermann. New York: AMS Press, 1976.

———. *Lapland*. Copenhagen: Gyldendal, 1907.

———. *Min rejsedagbog: Første Thule ekspedition 1912* [My travel diary, first Thule expedition]. Copenhagen: Gyldendal, 2005, commemorative edition.

———. *The People of the Polar North: A Record*. Translated by G. Herring. London: K. Paul, Trench, Trubner, 1908.

———. "Report of the First Thule Expedition, 1912." *Meddelelser om Grønland* 51 (1915).

———. "Report of the Second Thule Expedition for the Exploration of Greenland from Melville Bay to De Long Fjord, 1916–1918." *Meddelelser om Grønland* 65 (1927).

———. *Report of the Fifth Thule Expedition, 1921–1924*. 10 vols. Copenhagen: Gyldendal, Nordisk Forlag, 1945.

———. "South-East Greenland: The Seventh Thule Expedition, from Cape Farewell to Umivik." *Geografisk Tidsskrift* 36 (1932).

———. "South-East Greenland: The Sixth Thule Expedition, from Cape Farewell to Angmagssalik." *Geografisk Tidsskrift* 35 (1932).

Remie, Cornelius H.W. "Flying Like a Butterfly: Knud Rasmussen Among the Netsilingmiut." *Inuit Studies* 12 (1988).

Riis Carstensen, Andreas Christian. *Two Summers in Greenland. An Artist's Adventures Among Ice and Islands, in Fiords and Mountains*. London: British Library, Historical Print Editions, 2011 reprint of an 1890 original.

Schledermann, Peter. "The Muskox Patrol: High Arctic Sovereignty Revisited." *Arctic* 56, no. 1 (March 2003).

———. *Voices in Stone: A Personal Journey into the Arctic Past*. Calgary, Alberta, Canada: The Arctic Institute of North America, 1996.

Søby, Regitze. "Some of the Works of Knud Rasmussen As Yet Unpublished." *Inuit Studies* 12 (1988).

Sonne, Birgitte. "In Love with Eskimo Imagination and Intelligence." *Inuit Studies* 12 (1988).

Speake, Jennifer, ed. *Literature of Travel and Exploration: An Encyclopedia*. New York: Fitzroy Dearborn, 2003.

Spencer, Michael. "The Sixth and Seventh Thule Expeditions of Knud Rasmussen." *Geographical Journal* 83, no. 2 (1934).

Thalbitzer, William. "Knud Rasmussen: In Memoriam." *American Anthropologist* 36 (1934).

Treude, Erhard. "The Work of Knud Rasmussen in the Canadian Arctic as Described by RCMP Inspector Stuart Wood." *Inuit Studies* 28 (2004).

Various authors, no listed editor. *Bogen om Knud: Skrevet af hans venner* [Book of Knud: Written by his friends]. Copenhagen: Westermann, 1943 reprint.

Vaughan, Richard. *Northwest Greenland: A History*. Orono: University of Maine Press, 1991.

Wright, Shelley. *Our Ice Is Vanishing—Sikuvut Nunguliqtuq: A History of Inuit, Newcomers, and Climate Change*. Montreal and Kingston: McGill-Queen's University Press, 2014.

ACKNOWLEDGMENTS

In writing *White Eskimo*, I had the good fortune to work again with John Eerkes-Medrano and Merloyd Lawrence, the two talented editors who did such a fine job editing and positioning my previous book, *The Last Viking: The Life of Roald Amundsen*. I have worked with John on five books now. *White Eskimo* was an incredibly challenging and complex project, and their wisdom and insight helped me to shape the manuscript and find and clarify some new ideas. Sadly, John passed away as this book was going to print. I'll miss his quiet enthusiasm and meaningful suggestions.

Others on the team who helped bring this book into the world include designer Jonathan Sainsbury, copy editor Michele Wynn, publicist Lissa Warren, mapmaker Scott Manktelow, Amber Morris, Anna Comfort O'Keeffe, Scott McIntyre, and Howard White. Peter Schledermann was incredibly generous with his time and expertise, and as a native Danish-speaking Arctic archaeologist familiar with Rasmussen, he had a lot to offer.

The Arctic Institute of North America once again proved to be invaluable as a source of many original-edition books on Knud Rasmussen, in English and Danish. Thanks also to the Alberta Foundation for the Arts. As always, my wife, Nicky Brink, deserves credit for countless conversations, suggestions, and for reviewing the entire manuscript before I ever showed it to anyone else. I'm glad she never gets tired of her role.

PHOTO CREDITS

The photographs in this book's inserts originally appeared in the following books by Knud Rasmussen and Peter Freuchen or are courtesy of the respective institutions:

Arctic Adventure, 7, 8, 9, 11, line drawings throughout
Arktisk Institut, 2, 26, 27
Bogen om Knud, 3
Den Store Slaederejse, 21, 24,
Greenland by the Polar Sea, 10, 14, 17
Knud Rasmussen's Posthumous Notes on East Greenland Legends and Myths, 28
Library of Congress LC-F8-33032, 25
The People of the Polar North, 4, 5, 6
Report of the Fifth Thule Expedition, 19, 20, 22, three maps of the great sled journey
Report of the Second Thule Expedition, 13, 15, 16
Saga Knuds Rasmussens, 1, 12

INDEX

ABOUT THE AUTHOR

Stephen R. Bown is the author of several critically acclaimed, award-winning books on the history of exploration, science, and ideas. These include *Scurvy: How a Surgeon, a Mariner and a Gentleman Solved the Greatest Medical Mystery of the Age of Sail; Madness, Betrayal and the Lash: The Epic Voyage of Captain George Vancouver;* and *The Last Viking: The Life of Roald Amundsen,* the driven and brilliant adventurer who was a contemporary of Knud Rasmussen. Bown lives with his wife and two children near Banff, Canada.

Author website: *www.stephenrbown.net*
Author Facebook page: *www.facebook.com/srbown*